W9-CEI-419

DISCARD

The Alliance Way

The Alliance Way

The Making of a Bully-Free School

TINA M. OWEN-MOORE

Harvard Education Press
Cambridge, Massachusetts

Copyright © 2019 by the President and Fellows of Harvard College

All rights reserved. No part of this publication may be reproduced or transmitted in any form or by any means, electronic or mechanical, including photocopy, recording, or any information storage and retrieval systems, without permission in writing from the publisher.

Paperback ISBN 978-1-68253-287-4
Library Edition ISBN 978-1-68253-288-1

Library of Congress Cataloging-in-Publication Data is on file.

Published by Harvard Education Press,
an imprint of the Harvard Education Publishing Group

Harvard Education Press
8 Story Street
Cambridge, MA 02138

Cover Design: Endpaper Studio
Cover Image: Mural at Alliance School, southern facade entry, by Ras `Ammar Nsoroma;
Photo by Jill Engel-Miller

The typefaces used in this book are Adobe Garamond Pro and Frutiger.

*This book is dedicated to all those
who have faced the perils of bullying —
those who have lived great lives despite
the odds and those we have lost.
The Alliance School was a dream for you.
The Alliance Way is my prayer for others.*

Contents

The Alliance Six Agreements

1. Schoolwork comes first.
2. Keep a positive reputation. We must represent ourselves well.
3. Leave it better than you found it (clean up after yourself).
4. Respect everyone's differences because we're all equal.
5. Be committed to each other and Alliance by respectfully offering encouragement and listening to each other.
6. Be here on time, every day for every class.

Preface

Almost everyone has a story about a time when they were bullied and didn't want to go to school. For me, it was seventh grade, when I made the mistake of wearing some of my grandmother's old bell-bottom pants to school. They seemed cute and fashionable at the time, and the fit was fabulous. Unfortunately, my peers did not find them as stylish as I had imagined them to be, and by the end of one school day, I couldn't walk down the hallway without students, many of whom I had never even spoken to, chiming, "ding-dong, ding-dong" when I walked by. The chiming did not stop, even long after I had stopped wearing the pants, and I remember begging my parents to either let me stay home or buy me new clothes so the harassment would stop. It was unbearable. This was one moment when the fact that my father was in the military and we were required to move every few years probably saved my life. At the end of that school year we moved, and my bullying nightmare was over.

Most young people are not so lucky. When bullying happens, they are stuck in their community schools; when they are lucky, the adults intervene, and when they are not, it can turn into a life or death matter. In a 2010 article for the *Independent*, Matt Dickinson shared the results of a study in Britain which found that at least half of suicides among young people were related to bullying.[1] This is only one small portion of the alarming statistics about bullying. Studies done by the US Secret Service and the Department of Education revealed that in two-thirds of school shootings, where the shooter survived, he or she named bullying as playing a role in motivating the attack.[2] And students who experience bullying are more likely to drop out of high school.[3] The problem of bullying felt personally urgent when I was a child, and as I watch the news and listen to the current stories of young people who have experienced bullying, the problem feels even more urgent today.

In 2004, in Milwaukee, we were given the chance to imagine what school could look like if things were different—*if bullying wasn't the norm*. I was a young teacher when a representative from TALC New Vision, the organization that was managing the Gates Foundation grants to start small schools in Milwaukee, came to one of our staff meetings and said, "If anyone has ever thought of starting a school, now is your chance. We are accepting proposals to start schools in Milwaukee." The opportunity was astounding to me. I had been a teacher at a large, central-city high school for five years, and while I loved teaching, I wished *school* could be different.

In my teacher preparation program, I had imagined that school was different. I had fallen in love with A.S. Neill's description of Summerhill School, digested with enthusiasm John Dewey's *Democracy and Education*, and wished Howard Gardner had been around when I was in high school so that the idea of multiple intelligences could have been part of my learning experience. Yet, to my dismay, when I entered the classroom, school didn't look much different than it had when I was in high school—the desks were the same, the books were the same, the rules were the same, and the lessons were the same.

The other thing that hadn't changed was the relationships in school. Adults were still in charge, some students still bullied others without consequence, and students were still separated by race, ability, income, and social group. There was no denying this, yet many well-meaning adults also didn't seem to believe any other way was possible. I believed this current reality wasn't serving students. It was unjust, and it was causing harm. I had felt the devastation in my own schooling experience, where no adults had ever intervened; I had seen the impact on my students who checked out of school after repeated incidents of bullying; and I could see the bigger picture in the news stories about students who had committed suicide or turned to extreme violence after being bullied.

I had a strong sense of pride in the school I was teaching at and a great love for my students, but I felt compelled to take a stand for students who were being ostracized, bullied, and ignored in the traditional school setting. I had been the adviser for the school's Gay Straight Alliance (GSA), and the stories I heard from students, gay and straight, about their experiences in school were devastating. One boy had been beaten in the stairway because people perceived him to be gay. He wasn't, but it didn't matter to his attackers. Another student was called a witch daily because she dressed Goth and had several piercings. A couple of girls were suspended and outed to their parents for holding hands in the hallway. My students were telling me about these things, and it seemed like every time I turned on the news, there was another story of a school shooting or of a student who had been bullied committing suicide. This was a public health issue, and something had to be done. While there had been some efforts to teach "tolerance" in schools, and some successful lawsuits against districts that had not addressed bullying, in many places, school was still very much about survival for some of the most vulnerable students, and it felt like a moral imperative that students should have the chance to feel safe in school.

I knew all of this, and I felt, at my core, that school should and could look different for all students. I had heard about the Harvey Milk High School in New York, a school that had been started to meet the needs of LGBTQ students there, and I had read about so many great schools, education philosophies, and practices in my teacher education program. I wanted those things for my students. I wanted them to have the chance to grow and learn in a place that was safe, accepting, and reflective of their experience. The chance to start a school that could be a model of acceptance for all felt like more of a calling than an opportunity, and it didn't take me long to find others who felt the same way. With this mission in mind, I gathered teachers and students together, and we started to write. I went to the students first. I gave all my students blank brochures and asked them to make a brochure for the perfect school. Then I went to the teachers who had joined the planning team, and I asked them to do the same. I took the ideas from both students and teachers, combined them with the things I had learned and believed, and started to craft a proposal. Once the initial draft was complete, I shared it with the teachers and students and made sure it represented the best of what we knew and believed. We added some things, invited community members and parents to share their thoughts, and put the final touches on our proposal. Finally, we had a proposal for a school: The Alliance School.

This is what we imagined:

- All students would be welcome. The students came up with a motto: "Be yourself. Get a great education." And the tagline they created described us as "The Alliance School—a place where it's okay to be black, white, gay, straight, Christian, gothic, Buddhist, disabled, or just plain unique."
- It would be a school based on freedom, where students were treated with dignity and were engaged in learning rather than coerced into education.
- It would be a bully-free school, designed with preventive and restorative practices to prevent and address harm.
- It would have the things students (and adults) need for survival— food, safety, shelter, love, belonging, respect, family, art, creativity, and play.
- It would be a fully inclusive space, where students would learn alongside their disabled, nondisabled, and gifted peers.
- There would be as much learning outside of school as inside of school.
- There would be art, music, dancing, fun, and adventure.
- The teaching wouldn't be relegated only to the adults. If a student had expertise to share, he or she could teach, as well.
- Teachers would be called by their first names, because after all, we're all equal.
- Along those same lines, the school would be a democratic, teacher- and student-led school, where we would all vote on policies or practices that affected the school as a whole.
- It would be a year-round school, with four intersessions, so students would never have to spend too much time away from adults who care.

- We would have a college-like, flexible schedule where students would be able to choose classes that fit their schedules, educational objectives, and personal interests.
- Our philosophy would start from the Buddhist quote that says, "If you can see yourself in others, whom can you harm." With this quote in mind, our teaching and learning would serve the double purpose of spreading knowledge and bringing people together through cooperative learning, service learning, project-based learning, inquiry-based learning, and play.
- And, in a small gesture of who we were and what we believed, we would buy every student a gift before school let out in December, because no young person should ever have to go through the holidays without knowing that he or she is known and loved.

We submitted our proposal in January of 2004, and in April, our proposal was approved. For the next year, our planning team researched and visited some great schools, such as Urban Academy in New York, Eagle Rock School in Colorado, and yes, Summerhill School in the United Kingdom. We learned best practices, developed curriculum, searched for a building, raised money for materials and supplies, enrolled students, hired teachers, signed charter contracts, learned protocols, created schedules, attended conferences, designed a logo, held open-house events, and ordered lockers, library books and so much more.

On August 1, 2005, our school opened its doors, with me serving as the lead teacher for a community of students, teachers, and families, all of whom believed in the Alliance mission—to be a safe, student-centered, and academically challenging environment to meet the needs of *all* students.

Since that date, the Alliance School has been educating students in our truly unique way, and the results speak for themselves. Students who were the most likely to drop out of school have been graduating each year and going on to work or college. Students who once may have considered suicide are alive and starting families of their own. I have been invited to so many birthday parties, baby showers, and weddings over the years, and every one brings me great joy because it is a sign that life has gone on. If the student ories are not compelling enough, the data tells its own story. When we started the school, our schoolwide attendance rate was 66 percent, and in ten years, it grew to 90 percent. In 2016, we beat the Milwaukee School District on high school attendance rates, measures of GPA, percentage of students taking AP tests, and ACT composite scores, and we did this all while serving the same population of students we started with. More than 30 percent of our students are students with identified disabilities, approximately 25 percent of our students have been homeless or in foster care while attending Alliance, and about 50 percent of our students identify as lesbian, gay, bisexual, transgender, queer, or questioning (LGBTQ).

Over the years, we have shown that creating a safe and accepting place, where all students are treated with dignity and the opportunity to be children, is one important reform that makes a difference. The academic outcomes have been outstanding, and the human outcomes of this work have been extraordinary. If there was ever a high school in the United States that produced happy, confident, caring citizens, Alliance is it. At one point, my daughter, who graduated from Alliance, said to me, "Alliance students are going to be the doctors and teachers and social workers and counselors of the world, because at Alliance you don't just learn how to learn; you learn how to care."

Alliance has accomplished a great deal. We didn't know it when we were planning our school, but we were the first school in the nation started with the mission of addressing bullying and teaching others to do the same, and we were one of very few schools with an explicit mission of being an LGBTQ-friendly school. These two things captured the hearts and minds of many people, young and adult, who wished they could have attended a school like Alliance, and over the years I have heard from many who wanted to visit or learn more about Alliance. Hopefully, this book will become an inspiration for them and for anyone who is committed to carrying on this tradition of making the experience of school better for all students.

I am proud of the place that Alliance has become. We didn't do anything at Alliance to force young people into learning or kindness. We just gave them a chance to learn together, share their stories, and get to know each other well. What a simple experiment, and what a powerful result.

I truly believe that when young people are given a chance to show their goodness in this world, they step into that expectation, and when students are treated as if they need to be controlled, they step into that expectation, as well. As schools and communities, we need to open our doors to young people with the expectation and the promise of hope and love. It is not enough to expect reading, writing, and arithmetic in our schools. We must expect so much more.

In the past couple of years, I have been blessed with the opportunity to step away and to continue my learning by enrolling in the Ed.L.D. program at Harvard University's Graduate School of Education. The program has inspired me in many ways, but most importantly, it has inspired me to capture the practices and beliefs that made the Alliance School work. Alongside my studies, and with the encouragement and support of many amazing educators, I have written this book, which I hope can be a resource for others.

The Alliance Way is written as a philosophical guidebook for all of the educators, school leaders, and others who care about ensuring a safe and inclusive learning environment for young people. It is not a program for individuals to implement. It is an example of how schools can be and what it takes to get there—a road map of sorts, with plenty of places where school communities can add their own twists and turns to make the journey and destination the best they can possibly be. The book suggests a collaborative, improvement science approach to change, where school communities use the principles and practices of the Alliance School and consider how these can be implemented in their own communities. These principles and practices are captured in the stories of our community, many of which I have collected over the years knowing they would someday be powerful stories to share, and some that I have recollected through memories as I identified the core principles that have driven our success. Our everyday practice has always been about putting students at the center, so the stories of our students and our community are at the center. In most cases, I have used real names, but some names have been changed to protect the privacy of former students and staff. In this book, you will learn about many of the students who helped to make Alliance the place that it has been, including: Tocarra, the transgender Alliance heroine who helped to create our vision, yet passed away in our first year; Chris, the first student I met when the doors opened at Alliance; and Shauna, the student who inspired us to have a mission and vision that included *all* students. You will read stories of tears and triumphs, stories about voting, and protesters, and holiday parties, and reporters, and service trips. Through these stories, you will begin to see a picture of what school can be like when it makes a goal of being a safe, welcoming, and academically challenging place to meet the needs of all students. If you are searching for ways to address problems of school violence, bullying, LGBTQ acceptance, or twenty-first century democratic learning, you will find some hope in our stories, because sometimes the best practices can be found in stories.

Introduction

BULLYING IS MORE THAN the actions that exist between a few individuals. It is the accumulated consequences of all of these actions—the mental health and physical outcomes, the violence created, the devastated families and communities, the economic impact, the trust lost, and the failed relationships that result.

There are many reasons for schools to take bullying seriously. Bullying has an impact on students, staff, and community. It has short-term and long-term effects, economic and relational consequences, and it directly interferes with the academic outcomes of any school community. It must be addressed for a school community to be successful.

Yet, addressing bullying is not an easy challenge. Bullying is about relationships, or more importantly, the absence of relationships, and the quality of relationships in a school is a consequence of the school's culture. Bullying rarely happens without the necessary ingredients to support it, and it rarely stops without the necessary ingredients to prevent it. This book focuses on those preventive ingredients, sharing the practices that we have found to be key to creating a culture that welcomes everyone and prevents bullying.[1]

WHAT IS BULLYING?

It is important to start this book by addressing the question of what bullying is. As someone who started a school with a mission to address bullying and to teach others to do the same, it seems counterintuitive for me to say this, but I don't like the word *bullying*. On the website stopbullying.gov,[2] bullying is defined as "unwanted, aggressive behavior among school aged children that involves a real or perceived power imbalance. The behavior is repeated, or has the potential to be repeated, over time." This definition suggests a pattern that could have been prevented or interrupted, yet the definition implies that children alone are the victims and perpetrators of bullying.

This definition, as well as others, stands in contrast to what I believe about bullying. It suggests a binary of victims and perpetrators, and it ignores the systems that create and reinforce these behaviors. As a result of this tendency to look at the binary alone, young people are often punished in ways that force them to pay a high price for participating in the very culture that created the behaviors it rewarded. And the school goes on, without consequence, despite the fact that it has allowed a culture that celebrates bullying to develop, when it could have been prevented.

Bullying is the result of a culture that supports and allows bullying. Some bullying experts, such as Dorothy Espelage, have pushed beyond the binary, applying Urie Bronfenbrenner's Ecological Systems theory to describe the nested systems in which students reside and to identify how these systems influence bullying behaviors. In an article for *Theory Into Practice*, Espelage describes the microsystems, mesosystems, exosystems, macrosystems, and chronosystems that make up a child's experience of the world and impact his or her likelihood of participating in or experiencing bullying.[3] This socioecological model is a more effective lens for looking at the problem of bullying in schools and creating a systems approach to preventing and addressing it. When school communities look at the problem of bullying as a systems problem, it is possible to uncover, predict, prevent, and address bullying, and in doing so, to build healthier communities where students can learn and grow.

DIFFERENTIATING BETWEEN
CONFLICT AND BULLYING

To address the system, one must first be able to differentiate between bullying and conflict. Many people confuse the two, and this can cause a lot of harm. Conflict is something that happens between two people or groups of people. There is no imbalance of power, and both are active participants in the conflict. Most issues in schools are actually issues of conflict, not bullying. In these situations it is possible to bring people together to mediate such conflict, whether through restorative justice practices or other mediation strategies.

However, when the issue is one of bullying—where individuals repeatedly exercise their power, derived from the sociocultural system, to cause harm to others—it is never appropriate to bring a bullied student to a circle or mediation with the student or students who have done the bullying. The imbalance of power can potentially allow the bully to use the structure to continue the bullying pattern. In cases where there has been a pattern of documented incidents of harm, to one individual or to many individuals, the person causing such harm must be addressed away from those who have been harmed, and the focus must be on making the harm visible and repairing the harm that was caused. This is one of the first steps in preventing the devastating effects of bullying.

MAKING THE ISSUE VISIBLE

A few years ago, I was invited to do a presentation about bullying at a local middle school in Milwaukee. It was Family Night, and they wanted to have someone come in and speak to the families and students about bullying—what it is, why it happens, and what to do about it. As a school that has invested itself deeply in this work, we know that presentations about numbers, definitions, and threats don't work. Bullying is a problem of relationship, and when dealing with problems of relationship, you have to make people *feel* what you're talking about if you want them to make any kind of change.

I worked with a group of students to plan for this presentation. We asked ourselves, "What would be the best way to get people to understand the *impact* of bullying?" We decided to open with two students sharing their own experiences of being bullied and why they chose to come to Alliance. Then we did an activity that would bring it home for the students and for the adults.

For this activity, we divided the room in half and asked the parents and adults to go to one side of the room. Then we had the students go to the other side of the room. We gave each group large sheets of paper and some directions. We told the students to work in groups of three or four students to draw pictures of what bullying was and to include a definition. The students were enthusiastic about the task. They knew what bullying was. They knew what it looked like, and they knew how to define it. They laughed and joked as they drew pictures of people being hit, beat up, and called names.

While they were working on their drawings, we asked the parents and adult family members to do a different task. We asked each of them to draw a picture of the person from elementary, middle, or high school who had made their lives so miserable that they didn't want to go to school. The adults were stunned for a minute, but it only took a couple of seconds for them to think about it, and then they started to draw. Each of them had a story to tell, and they were ready to share them. After about fifteen minutes, we asked the young people to come to the front of the room and teach the group what bullying was and what it looked like. The smaller groups took turns presenting their pictures, and they still couldn't help but laugh and joke a little bit as they presented. I imagine it was because the topic was sensitive to them, and they didn't want to acknowledge it, so they hid behind humor and ribbing. It was a little painful to watch, especially for my students who had been targets of bullying, but we knew it was going to happen before we started the activity, so we let it run its course, and then we moved on.

Once the four groups of students had presented, it was the adults' turn. We invited each of the adult family members to come up and share their pictures and stories of the people who had made school miserable for them. Every single one of them was willing to share his or her story—moms, dads, grandpas, uncles. The students sat, stunned by the stories they were hearing. I don't think they had ever imagined that these people, who were the strongest people they knew, could have possibly been so vulnerable, so hurt by anyone. You could see that their own actions and the actions they had witnessed over the years were starting to register. The most powerful point came last, though. An older, African American grandmother, who had become blind with age, was led to the front of the room by her grandson, a young man in his twenties. He held up the picture that he had helped her to draw. The sketch was a simple drawing. It was a large circle of a face with a stick body; eyes, nose, and mouth; and a ponytail. The woman said, "Penny Carson. That was her name. Penny Carson used to chase me home from school every day. If she caught me, she would grab me by my hair, pull me down to the ground, and beat me up. I might of stayed in school, if it wasn't for Penny Carson. I just couldn't go, not as long as Penny was going to be there."

She looked out to nowhere, unable to see the people in the room where she was standing, and it was almost as if she could see Penny Carson standing there in front of her. Her eyes were brimming with tears of anger, hurt, resentment, and regret, as she looked back into her memories of school.

This woman was somebody's grandmother, a woman of great respect in the community, and as she spoke, you could see every face in the room filling with sadness and a recognition of the real meaning of bullying. It was no longer just a definition. It was the pain on the face of a blind, elderly grandmother, decades later. I think that moment and that story had more impact on the actions of the young people in that room than any character lesson ever could.

The issue of bullying is a devastating one. It hides behind fears, power struggles, trauma, systemic racism, oppression, status, and culture. You can't teach people about it with textbook definitions and statistics. You can buy all of the trust balls, and kindness posters, and character curricula you want, but they won't make people less likely to harm each other. To address bullying, you have to focus on relationships.

Many attempts to address bullying start with the idea of giving young people information we think they don't know, but the truth is that most people who bully, both as adults and as young people, know that what they are doing is wrong, and they choose the behavior anyway. They choose it for a variety of reasons—it gives them status, protects them from harm, increases their wealth or opportunity, provides a release for anger, makes them visible, or makes them invisible. They choose bullying because the culture allows and rewards it, or because the community does not hold them accountable for the harm that they cause. And they choose bullying because they do not know their own power in the world. At the Alliance School, we decided to take a chance at building something better, a place where young people know their power in the world and where bullying is not the norm. We were successful, and the school remains a place where it doesn't matter who you are or what you believe in, you are welcome. The Alliance School is the nation's first school started with a mission to address bullying and teach others to do the same.

MAKING ROOM FOR THE GOOD

Putting an end to bullying is more complex than just identifying it and handing out consequences. You can do this all day long, and you will never put an end to a bullying culture, because as long as young people want to bully others, they will find ways to do so. Our strongest tool in addressing bullying is to make it so that young people don't want to bully others. People often ask, "But how do you change the hearts and minds of young people so they don't want to harm others?" I would argue that it's not a change at all—that young people come to us with this genuine sense of justice and concern for each other. The circumstances that surround them either support this genuine concern or depress it.

At Alliance, we look at bullying through the lens of preventing and addressing harm. Most people, and especially young people, do not want to harm others. It is actually very rare for someone to have tendencies toward deliberately causing pain and suffering to others. Despite this, many young people do participate in harmful activities, insults, or aggressive behaviors. When pressed about their own harmful actions, they will often minimize the harm caused, making comments such as: "Words don't hurt," "I didn't mean to hurt anybody," and "People say things like that to me, and I don't get hurt." They don't want to believe that they have caused anyone harm. Knowing this, it is easier to believe that when people do cause harm, they naturally want to reverse it. The Alliance principle of "do no harm" hangs in this balance.

At Alliance, it is an expressed belief that it is not okay to cause harm to another person, and when we do cause harm, whether intentional or not, we are responsible for repairing the harm we caused. Sometimes this comes in the form of simple awareness and an apology, other times it means sitting in a "repair-harm" circle with a peer, and at still other times it takes consequences from the community to hold someone accountable for the harm they have caused.

By addressing harm when it happens, we rarely have incidents rise to the level of bullying, because we address incidents before they become repeated or severe. With this belief, it is impossible for anyone to excuse their own harmful behavior; the question is not whether or not one intended harm, but whether or not harm happened.

DO NO HARM

Harm can happen, whether intentional or not, and teaching young people to avoid doing harm and to address harm when it happens is at the heart of our practice. This means that, as a community, we hold ourselves and each other to the promise of not doing harm, so that when harm happens, we feel an obligation to address it.

Even our rules were built around this idea. Rather than having a rule about not wearing hats or hoodies, we have a rule that says that you cannot wear something that is hurtful to another person. This can, at times, be challenging, especially when young people push the boundaries on revealing or "shocking" clothing, but we always come back to the question of harm when thinking about and deciding how to address concerns.

For example, a young woman was coming to school wearing extremely short skirts and tops that revealed her bra underneath. A group of students were upset by how revealing her clothes were. They wanted me to make her stop. When I pushed them on why, they told me they were concerned that she may get attacked or raped for dressing the way she dressed. Once again, I pushed, questioning whether anyone should be able to say they couldn't control themselves because of the way another person dressed. They started to see the problem with policing her appearance rather than policing those who would cause her harm because of her appearance.

The conversation did not stop there, though. The group did feel there was an element of harm to the community caused by her dressing in ways that went against societal norms for modesty. She was making our school "look bad." Rather than deciding to police her dress, though, this small group of two or three concerned young women decided to have a conversation with her. They wanted to try to understand why she was choosing to dress in ways that pushed against these expectations and see if they could reach out to her in another way. They asked me to help facilitate the conversation—so it would not be perceived as an attack—and I agreed to do so.

When the students sat down to meet, a powerful conversation took place. The concerned students started by acknowledging that their original concerns were part of a larger societal problem of putting the blame for sexual assault on women, and they explained that they were sorry for having participated in that kind of thinking. They then went on to explain how they were personally affected by the young woman's choice of dress. One girl shared, "If my grandma comes into this school and sees you dressed like this, there's no way she's letting me stay in this school, and I love this school." This comment really hit home for the young woman. She agreed that her own grandmother would feel the same way if she came into the school and found her dressed that way. She shared that perhaps she had been so busy testing the adults on the school motto of "Be yourself. Get a great education," that she had forgotten to look around at her peers. She also acknowledged that while she should have a right to dress how she wanted without worrying about being attacked, the world was not that evolved yet, and she honestly didn't feel safe out in the world the way she felt in our school. She had pushed boundaries within the school because she knew it was a safe place.

There are a million reasons why young people do the things that they do, but it is truly rare that their actions come from an intention to harm a community that cares about them. They are testing adults, expressing individuality, challenging societal norms, standing up for justice, and pushing boundaries—all normal behaviors for adolescents. By holding to the principle of "do no harm," we were better able to change behavior and build a community that cares. And once we had this principle, we began to frame our antibullying strategy around this idea. We didn't want to just have a culture where bullying was not the norm, we wanted to have a culture where *harm* was not the norm, and when harm happened, it was addressed. So, we built our strategy around preventing and addressing harm.

PREVENTING HARM

The Alliance philosophy uses a two-pronged approach to bullying—first preventing harm, and then addressing harm when it happens. We spend most of our energy and planning on preventing harm, and this book reflects that. We do this through our culture, curriculum, practices, celebrations, community building, decision-making, and more. Everything we do is purposefully designed with the intention of preventing harm through powerful relationships among members of the community and a culture that supports the community's values.

The Alliance philosophy rests on the idea that relationships matter—people are less likely to do harm when they know each other well. The Buddhist quote that keeps us centered on this idea is, "If you can see yourself in others, whom can you harm?" When people know each other well, they are more likely to see themselves in others, so much of what we do focuses on building those relationships. We do this in many ways, which will be highlighted in great detail throughout this book. The idea is that everything a school community does should be looked at through the lens of building relationships—"If we do it this way, will it strengthen bonds between people or build walls between people? Is there a way we can do it so people are getting to know each other better? Did we build in enough time for breaking bread?"

For us, this is especially important when it comes to building relationships across difference. Because of this, we have intentionally built a community that uses a full-inclusion model and does not have any form of tracking. There are no honors classes and regular classes. Every class is taught the way that honors classes are taught. If we offer an Advanced Placement (AP) class, the class is open to all students of all abilities. Students with disabilities are just as likely to be in AP classes as their nondisabled peers, and there is no segregation by race, class, or gender. The more diverse a classroom is, the better it is for academic growth and for building relationships. This is part of what it means to get to know each other well.

We also build in opportunities for students to share stories and experiences across difference. Students of different backgrounds, cultures, and abilities often find themselves drawn to friendships with people who look like them or believe what they believe. They can also develop assumptions about others when they don't understand their motivations, beliefs, or cultural norms. It is important to create opportunities for people to get to hear each other's stories, so they begin to understand how they are more similar to each other than they are different. We work to develop these connections across difference through our programming and our schoolwide circles. You will learn more about this in the chapter on restorative practices.

And our teachers know that they have the power to build connections between young people through their instructional practices. Teachers use stories, group activities, service learning, and more to build those connections. In our classrooms, you will rarely see students in rows, because they can learn so much more from each other in groups, and, as a staff, we are intentional about building relationships among students. The teachers build opportunities for choice and movement in the classroom, so that students are connected through the teaching and learning activities. All of these things help to build a culture where harm is not the norm, because people begin to know and care for each other as individuals and as members of a community when they are given the chance to work together.

Throughout the chapters in this book, you will see how the practices we use prevent harm by building connections, community, and a culture that celebrates the relationships between us.

ADDRESSING HARM

We also know that even in a school with a strong culture, harm will happen, intentionally and unintentionally. The second piece of our practice is to have systems in place to address harm when it happens. We spend a lot of time and energy teaching young people how to report and respond to harm when they experience it or witness it. We hold a conference at the beginning of the year where we teach our students how to respond to and report harm, how to participate in and request a repair-harm circle, how to use reporting forms, and whom to report to. We make sure students know what to do when they see harmful words or actions online, and we treat online actions just as seriously as we would treat them if they happened in the school.

And we don't just focus on teaching our students. We also spend time as a staff learning about best practices and developing our own strategies for addressing, documenting, and responding to harm. We regularly participate in trainings, discuss research, and share practices that we have found to be useful in our own classrooms. If the community of adults does not work together, there is no way to identify and respond to patterns that are developing, and this is part of the problem that allows incidents of harm to escalate in many schools, eventually becoming a problem with persistent bullying. We are also careful to create systems that protect the anonymity of reporters, making the environment safe for those who are willing to take a stand against bullying.

Finally, we engage students in the work to address harm. When the school was first started, we created a student-led discipline council that would respond when students repeatedly engaged in acts that harmed individuals or the community. This was highly successful on its own, and then we learned about restorative practices, which enabled us to take this to another level of success. We created two classes where students learn to facilitate repair-harm and community-building circles. Through these classes, they gain critical skills for life and become leaders in their school and home communities. They learn the difference between conflict and bullying and what strategies to use to address each.

By choosing to work hard at preventing harm and having strategies to address harm when it happens, we rarely have cases that rise to the level of bullying. Of course, when we do, we must address that. All of these scenarios are highlighted in this book, told through the stories of the community and the choices we make to deliberately stop bullying in its tracks. Our efforts make a real difference for a lot of young people, and the principles we have learned to live by are principles that can live anywhere.

This book is meant to help those in schools and communities to create the kind of culture we have created at Alliance—where young people feel safe and accepted for who they are and where bullying is not the norm.

HOW TO USE THIS BOOK

This book is written in chapters designed to highlight the philosophies and practices that make the Alliance School the safe and accepting community that it is. Each chapter focuses on one principle or ideology that is a key to the school's success and illustrates how it worked through the stories of our community. Rather than providing a series of steps to follow, it is written in a way that allows school leaders, individuals, or communities to read about the principles and think about how to put those principles in place in their communities. It is a book written from the perspective of a school community, yet the principles illustrated would be key to creating an effective culture in any workplace or community.

While we recognize that some people may focus on the fact that we were small and had the opportunity to build our school from scratch, we learned about these practices and philosophies from large schools, small schools, new and existing schools, organizations, businesses, and groups. We know they can be applied anywhere because we have seen their effectiveness in other places, and we know that research supports these practices. By highlighting the philosophies we used to build a welcoming school culture, those who want to create such cultures can think about how to bring them to life in their own schools and communities.

For example, the chapter on teaming illustrates how we built connections as a staff, so that staff members knew each other well and were more likely to be able to work together. We worked consciously to build a culture where staff members know each other and can assume best intentions in working together. The practices illustrated in the teaming chapter are practices that could be used anywhere to build a stronger culture, but they are not the only practices. It is highly likely that by reading the chapter, you will begin to imagine similar practices that would work in your community, workplace, or school. What will you do to make sure the people in your organization know each other well?

The chapter on acceptance, "A Place for *All* Students," illustrates what it means to build a community that accepts everyone. Through the stories of young people who had been shut out of other places, it is possible to see how a community can act differently to ensure that all individuals feel safe and accepted. Acceptance of difference and diversity is a value that is worth building in any community. For some organizations this can be a challenge, especially in communities that have been traditionally homogenous. What does it mean to demonstrate an extraordinary welcome to those who are different from us, to understand that even if we believe different things, we can still treat each other with dignity and respect? What does it look like to hold the principle of "do no harm" even when we don't understand another's beliefs, actions, or history? The acceptance chapter provides an example of what it looks like to demonstrate the kind of extraordinary welcome that pushes us past our fears and misunderstandings.

The stories in these chapters and the philosophies they represent are at the heart of creating safe and accepting communities where everyone can thrive. It is my hope that if you are reading this book, it is because you hope to build a community that celebrates these values. I hope this book will serve as a conversation starter and a guidebook. I envision communities reading the chapters together and developing strategies for implementing the practices highlighted in the chapters of the book. I imagine young people and adults thinking together about *how* to build communities where everyone can thrive. And I hope that as more people develop new and unique strategies for building stronger and more accepting communities, we can continue to share those practices, so that seeing ourselves in others becomes part of the way we all live in the world.

This book is written for anyone who cares about transforming the school experience, so that all students are given the chance to thrive, rather than just survive, at school. It is for the adult who experienced bullying in school and wishes their experience could have been different. It is for the teacher who wants to make the classroom safe and accepting for all students, and it is for the parent who wants to change the culture of a child's school. It is for the reformer who is looking for the levers of change that put dignity and equity at the forefront of policy and practice. And it is for anyone who wants to spend a day in a place where a hug welcomes you at the door, where who you are matters, and where love and learning live side by side. I hear from people every day who want to know how to create a school or develop a school culture like the one we built at Alliance. This book is for all of you and for all who want to know the secrets of what makes Alliance tick. The chapters ahead will capture the histories, the practices, the policies, the people, and the beliefs that make Alliance the hope-filled place that it is. I invite you to be part of it. Welcome to—*The Alliance Way*.

1

A Core Belief

If you can see yourself in others, whom can you harm?
THE DALAI LAMA

MY FIRST TEACHING EXPERIENCE was at a large, urban high school on the south side of Milwaukee. About 97 percent of the students at the school were Latinx, and the neighborhood around the school reminded me of El Paso, the city where I had spent my high school years. The neighborhood was a combination of all of the things I loved about my hometown (the music, food, art, and generosity) and all of the things that had been challenging (the gangs, crime, and machismo culture).

On my first day, two young men were sitting in the front of the classroom. I am pretty certain that my supervising teacher had put them there so she could keep an eye on them. I was standing in the front of the classroom, just in front of their desk, while she was introducing me as "a new teacher who would be helping out in the classroom for the next few weeks." I could hear the two boys joking with each other in Spanish and nodding to me, so I listened for what they were saying.

"She wants you," the boy with the shorter hair said, pointing to me with his chin and poking his friend with his elbow. "The teacher wants you."

The two boys laughed, thinking the joke was just between the two of them and that there was no way this naïve-looking, white woman standing in front of them was going to understand what they were saying. Unfortunately for them, one can't live five years in El Paso without picking up a significant amount of Spanish, so when I heard what they were saying, I leaned in, fingers on their desk, and said, quietly but so the rest of the class could hear me, "Entiendo Español" (I understand Spanish). The two boys sank into their chairs with embarrassment, smiling sheepishly, while the other students around them laughed.

This was my entry into the classroom "family." The students appreciated my limited knowledge of Spanish, as well as my calm sense of humor, and I settled in quickly and became more and more excited about becoming a teacher.

My cooperating teacher helped me to do this. She was an older, African American woman with a great big laugh and a theatrical presence. I was there to observe two of her English classes, two days a week. It was early in my education program, so I was just supposed to be observing, but she knew the students wouldn't tolerate having someone just sitting in the back of the room watching them, so she started to engage me in the class activities right away. The students were working on memorizing a poem while I was there, and I can still remember it word for word, because I was working alongside them. The poem was "The Bridge Builder," by Will Allen Dromgoole, and the students would recite it every day at the start of class.

An old man going a lone highway,
Came, at the evening cold and gray . . .[1]

At first, I didn't understand why she was having them memorize this poem. I was still hearing the voices of my education instructors telling us that rote memorization was a thing of the past, and students had to learn critical thinking, not just memorization. So I watched, as each day she reviewed this poem with them and tested them for memorization.

One thing I could see was the students loved the poem, as well as the challenge of memorizing it. It connected to something in them. Rather than dismissing the exercise as unimportant, I started to think about how I could take this poem that they loved and bring it beyond just memorization. I started to bring in other stories, songs, and project ideas that had to do with bridges to share them with the teacher. She really loved the things I brought, especially as we tried them out and watched as the students opened up and engaged in the lessons. After a couple of weeks, she patted me on the arm and declared that I should start teaching already and asked if I wanted to teach two classes each week. I was nervous, but to be honest, I was thrilled. I couldn't wait to start teaching.

I loved it more than I could have imagined. I loved coming up with ideas, trying to find ways to make the lessons relevant and engaging, and challenging students to think critically and create work that would have an impact on the world. From the moment I started contemplating teaching as a career, I always had this theory that students shouldn't do "throwaway work." If they were going to write, they should publish. If they were going to dance, they should perform. If they were going to present information, they should present it to the people who needed most to learn it. The students had too much untapped power that could be used to make a difference in the world, and it would be a shame to let it all go to waste on worksheets and chapter questions. I also loved finding what the students were great at and helping them learn to use these talents as their outlets for communication.

For example, I remember I once had to teach a story from the school's recommended textbook. The title was "Metonymy, or The Husband's Revenge," by Rachel de Queiroz. Metonymy is a figure of speech where one calls something by one of its characteristics or something that it is closely associated with, like calling the Queen "the crown," or calling a car "wheels." I decided to do an activity that asked the students to use graffiti to create an example of metonymy. I thought I was going to have a group of very excited students, but instead they just sat there looking at me with stunned looks on their faces when I told them what the assignment was.

I tried to explain it a little better, but one of the boys stopped me. "We know what you said, Ms. But we can't do that."

Most of the boys called me "Miss" with a long *z* sound, as if they were saying Mizzz, and if they really wanted to be funny, they called me "Mizzz Teacher Lady."

"Why not?" I asked.

"Cuz it's taggin', Mizzz Teacher Lady. We can't do that. We get suspended for taggin' in school."

The other students nodded their heads, looking from one to the next, as if to confirm with each person that what he had said was the truth, kind of like a high school "Amen" going through the classroom. I wasn't quite sure if they were seriously worried that they would get suspended for doing this lesson or if they were just joking with me, trying to find any angle possible to get out of doing any work, but I wasn't about to turn back now. I had even done my own graffiti example as a model for them, and that had been a lot of work. In middle school, I had been quite good at drawing bubble letters, so much so that other students would ask me to draw their names for them. I drew on those immature and rarely used skills for this lesson. On a blank sheet of paper, I had drawn the word *wheels* in bubble letters to represent a car, my own simple example of metonymy. The letters were in the shape of a vehicle and at the bottom were tires. It wasn't a bad example, yet I knew it was nothing compared to what they could do. I took out my model, showed it to the students, and said, "Well, not today you won't. Today, you'll be graded for your tagging, so it better be good."

The students took a look at my example and started to laugh. With a mix of amusement and perhaps a hint of appreciation, they gave a quick nod to the competition and took me up on the challenge. "I got something better than that," one of the students boasted.

"Look, she thinks she's cool, with her bubble letters and shit," another student quipped, smiling at me with appreciation for my art, while ribbing me lightly for it. "We can show her how this is done."

Once a couple of students were in for the challenge, the others were ready to follow.

"Prove it," I said, with a wink and a smile, and the game was on. The students all started to imagine what words they could use for their graffitied examples, and soon they were all at work.

Of course, in every class I've ever taught, there were a couple of students who flourished under the old "answer the questions at the end of the chapter" style of teaching, and these students would beg and plead for more traditional assignments. "Can't I just write an essay? Do I have to? I can't draw!" They would pout to no end about having to be creative in English class, but I would push them by quoting the research about creativity, brain development, and the connection between making art and ACT scores.[2] Usually these students were the type who cared about their grades, so they would fuss and whine for a bit, and then they would do whatever it took to earn the grade, and I think, secretly, they were thrilled that I saw the power in them. I would tell them, "No throwaway work. You are too powerful for that." They wanted someone to notice this in them, and they wanted to be challenged to use it. And the best part was that once they started to use their power and their talents this way, they rarely wanted to go back to the old ways. Once they saw what they were capable of, they rarely wanted to settle for less.

This was just the beginning, though. I was lucky to have my cooperating teacher that year. She loved the project-based learning, and her excitement combined with the students' excitement made me know that I had found the right career. It was also great to have her backup when things were tough. She had a strong presence, and there was no nonsense going on in that classroom with her around. I was just learning how to create solid lesson plans, but I still had a lot to learn about developing a classroom culture.

On my last day at the school, the students threw me a surprise party. I was so happy and so thankful for all that I had learned with them. It had been a great year, but the following year would be my first real test. This time, I would have several classes, every day of the week, and this time, I would be on my own.

FINDING A CORE BELIEF

As I began my first year of teaching, I didn't stop with the project-based learning. The belief that students have too much power for throwaway work followed me into my official practice. I had students hosting poetry cafes, creating papier-mâché body parts for *The Tell-Tale Heart*, pretending to be Holden Caulfield's therapist, writing their memoirs, and more. I was having a great time of it, even if it was a challenge to be a first-year teacher, but I still wasn't sure how to create an environment where students respected each other the way I hoped they would. I also knew that making the classroom engaging was not enough. I wanted my students to know their stories were safe with me, and beyond this, I wanted them to know their stories were safe with each other. This was because of my own classroom experience, which profoundly shaped my beliefs about the kind of teacher I wanted to become, and when the time came, the kind of school I wanted to create.

When I was in ninth grade, my English teacher gave us an assignment to write about our families. "Who are your people? How will you celebrate Christmas? What are your family traditions?" she asked. I could tell she was expecting glowing pictures of our family lives, but that wasn't the portrait of my family. My family was a mess. I had just recently spoken up about being abused by my father, who had been tried and sent to the US Penitentiary at Fort Leavenworth. My mom had moved back to El Paso, Texas, with me and my three younger siblings. She had been a homemaker for seventeen years while my father was in the military, and she was suddenly on her own with no job experience, no college education, four children, and a mess of mental health issues. Life was tough.

English class had always been my favorite, though, so I thought I could find refuge in this assignment. "I want to know your stories," she assured us. And I, broken as I was and feeling so alone in the world, wanted desperately to share them with her. With her positivity and encouragement, I decided to write the truth. I was nervous, but I had always been a strong writer, and I really loved this teacher, so I thought my story would be safe with her. I wrote about my family, the abuse, my father's imprisonment, and the poverty we were suddenly facing. "There would be no Christmas in our house," I wrote. I was just thirteen years old, and I thought she would understand.

A few days later, I received my graded paper, and I was devastated. There was a big, red F at the top of the paper, and a note that said, "Don't ever write this stuff again. It's not appropriate for school." I was so embarrassed. I had never received a failing grade before, especially not in English class, and her words filled me with shame. I never went back to that class. I hid behind the school building every day, and I failed freshman English, something I never would have imagined was possible.

Many years later, it was a sort of tribute to my past that I became a ninth-grade English teacher. I knew from the start that my experience in that ninth-grade class would have a tremendous impact on the teacher I would become. My own experience led me to believe that students needed a safe place to give voice to their stories in order to move forward in their lives. With this in mind, I created a project where I would invite the students to write novels of their life stories. They would work on these novels from the beginning of the year to the end of the year, writing a chapter each marking period, and then at the end of the year we would bind them and they would have them to keep. Through this process, I got to know the students well, so I had particular insights into why they acted the way they did. I knew why the bully was bullying, and I knew that the bullied student was already carrying too much to be the target of the bully's angst. I knew these things, but I couldn't say these things to the students, because to do so would be to reveal too much of the students' personal stories. I felt like I was always asking them to just "trust me" and be good to each other.

I knew I needed to find a safe way to make their stories visible in the classroom, so, as English teachers often do, I decided to use a novel to do it. The novel we read was *Tears of a Tiger*, a story about a young man who ended up committing suicide because he was struggling with depression and had just too much to carry. His friends had not been aware of all of the things he was dealing with emotionally, so they were shocked and devastated to learn he had done this and they hadn't been able to help. The novel was hard to read because the story was so sad, but the students really loved it because they could relate to so many of the characters in the book. I felt like many of my students were similar to the main character, because they were also carrying so much trauma and hardship that their peers were not aware of. So after reading the novel, I decided to do an exercise that would help students see what their peers were carrying, without revealing their identities. I gave all of the students a handful of torn pieces of paper, and I told them to write on the individual pieces of paper all of the hard things that they were currently dealing with or had dealt with in their lives. I told them to only write what they wanted people to know, but to know that it would be anonymous and that this was an exercise in healing and connection. I gave them fifteen minutes, and the students went to work writing. They were eager, but anxious, to put these truths on paper. I had to make sure that each person had enough space to write without anyone seeing what they were writing, and several students asked to exchange pens with me so their papers wouldn't be distinguishable from the others by the color of the ink. Once they felt safe, they wrote without stopping. Some of them even asked for more scraps of paper to write on. Once they were finished, I had them all throw their papers into one large box, and then I added a whole bunch of torn pages from one of the books that had fallen apart. I mixed this all up, and then I asked each student to reach into the box and grab a couple of handfuls of paper. Then, I asked them to take the papers they had and arrange them into a collage. I gave them cardboard squares and glue so they could arrange the papers any way they liked, and I invited them to read the papers as they created their collages.

As the students arranged their papers on their desks, I could hear them gasp as they read the things people had written. Several students even called me over to their desks to look at what others had written.

"My mother was diagnosed with AIDS."

"I had a miscarriage in the summer."

"I was raped."

"My brother wants me to join a gang."

"My father was killed in a gang shooting."

"I was sexually abused by my mother's boyfriend."

And the list went on. I knew these stories were true, because I had read their life stories in their novels, met their parents, talked to the school counselors, visited their homes, and listened to them when they needed someone to talk to. When the students had finished their collages, I had them line the collages up along the chalkboard, so they could do a gallery walk and read everyone's stories. The room was heavy with silence as people read, and there were even some tears shed. As people moved around, it seemed like the room was filled with a sense of sadness for what people had gone through, but relief because people knew they weren't alone anymore. When everyone had seen all of the collages, I asked people to return to their seats, and then I spoke to the class, trying not to let myself cry. I told them, "Thank you for being so brave today. Your lives are more similar to the character in the book than you may know." I pointed at the collages. "These things that you wrote. I know these things about you, because you have shared them with me, and I am so grateful. But I am also struggling, because when I see you hurting each other it tears me up inside, because I know that you all already have too much to carry, and I don't want to lose any of you. I hope that you will remember these things as the year goes on, and be good to each other, because you never know what someone else is dealing with." I had tears in my eyes when I said it, and several students came up to give me hugs and to hug each other. Even the tougher kids in the class gave each other fist bumps or nods, and everyone seemed to get what I was saying. Then the bell rang. The class was over, and the students went on to their next classes. I didn't know, at that time, if the lesson had made a difference, but I did know that for that moment, at least, the class had been powerfully connected by our shared experiences.

As time went on, I learned that the lesson had been more powerful than I could have imagined. Our class was definitely changed. It wasn't just a class anymore. Somehow it had become a community of people who cared deeply for each other, and this changed the way people treated each other, and the way they allowed themselves to interact with each other. The name-calling and ribbing were almost nonexistent, and the class suddenly wanted to do things to help others. If one student started to give another student a hard time, other students in the class would interrupt, saying, "Hey, be cool. You don't know what he's going through." I couldn't get over the impact of this lesson. It was so powerful, and yet so simple.

The lesson changed me as a teacher, as well. I suddenly knew it was my responsibility to build community in the classroom, to get kids to know each other better, because without it we would never get beyond the superficiality of novel lessons and temporary behavioral interventions. I started planning more group work, made the lessons more personal, and used team-building activities to get students to know each other well. One year, I even put students in groups based on their horoscopes and told them they would get along because they were astrologically paired to do so. I don't know if it was the stars or a self-fulfilling prophecy effect, but that was the best year ever.

When I focused on connections, healing, and belonging, through stories and activities to build relationships across difference, the culture changed, and the classroom became a sanctuary and a joyful place to learn. I remembered I had studied Abraham Maslow in college, learning about his "hierarchy of needs," and this all made so much sense. If a student's basic needs for safety, security, and belonging aren't met, how can he or she focus on the higher needs of intellectual pursuits? I suddenly realized this was a key to preventing bullying and an important factor in producing academic gains, as well. I knew that if I was going to get kids to a place where they truly cared about academic rigor, I first had to create an environment that was physically, intellectually, and emotionally safe.

I made creating this environment part of my teaching mission, and when I decided to start a school that would focus on reducing bullying, I knew sharing stories and creating community would be the foundation of our school.

One day in a bookstore, on the front of a simple white card, I saw a quote by the Dalai Lama that said, "If you can see yourself in others, whom can you harm?" It struck me as the key to what I had seen in the classroom, and I decided to build our school philosophy and practice around this idea. If we were going to create a place where harm was not the norm, we had to create a place where people came to know each other well. We would do this by focusing on relationships in everything we did.

RELATIONSHIPS MATTER

As I looked to the research, I found plenty to support the idea that positive relationships between teachers and students and positive relationships among students have a strong impact when it comes to reducing bullying.

In an article for the *Journal of Youth and Adolescence*, researchers found that students who reported better relationships with their teachers demonstrated fewer problem behaviors at the time of the study and up to four years later.[3] In another study, a social skills group intervention was used to help young people form positive peer relationships across difference. The intervention resulted in reduced aggression and bullying behaviors among students who participated.[4]

These types of interventions can become part of a school's regular practice, using group work, connecting activities, and identity work to help young people get to know each other well. And there is no better way to build relationships among students, and relationships between students and teachers, than to have people sit with each other, work together, and share their stories. Yet this information is rarely taught in teacher preparation programs. Teachers must be trained in how to create a culture where building relationships and sharing stories are norms in the classroom, starting with the simple stories of life and moving to the more personal when the class is ready for it. It is no longer enough to teach students in rows and through independent work. The world is demanding more from our young people, and even more important, if we are going to address bullying, we must start here. We must teach young people how to be in community with each other.

THE ALLIANCE SCHOOL

This relationship building is especially important at the Alliance School, a small but uniquely diverse school in the city of Milwaukee, Wisconsin. The city itself is a complicated place. It is just ninety miles from the city of Chicago and shares some of the characteristics of the larger city. It's a beautiful place to live, situated on the shores of Lake Michigan, with a thriving arts culture and strong Midwestern values. Breweries abound, and there are many great restaurants and universities in the city. These are some of the city's strengths. The city is also one of the most segregated cities in the US, and it has been named in numerous articles as one of the worst places in the country for black families.[5] The poverty in the city is persistent, and violence is a constant threat in many of the neighborhoods.

The Alliance School is located on the edge of one of these neighborhoods. Just outside of the 53206 zip code—which claims the unfortunate title of the most incarcerated zip code in the world—the school sits, immersed in all of the good and bad that the city has to offer.[6] Students come to the school from all parts of the city and from the suburbs surrounding the city, all seeking refuge in the school's mission.

This creates a uniquely diverse student body. Traditionally, the school has been about 40 percent African American students, 25 percent Caucasian students, 25 percent Latinx students, 5 percent Asian American students, and 1 percent Native American students. There are students who come from extreme poverty and those who come from generous wealth. About one-third of the students have been identified as students with disabilities, and many of our students are homeless or in foster care. About 50 percent of the students identify as LGBTQ, about 90 percent qualify for free or reduced-price lunch, and most of the students reside in the central city.

We could not have created a more diverse student body if we tried, which has always meant that the need for building connections across difference has been more important than ever. There are students at our school who might never have talked to each other if it wasn't for the Alliance School.

When we first started the school, we had a schoolwide community meeting at which this became aboundingly clear. I was speaking to the whole student body, and I looked out and saw that all of the black students were sitting on one side of the room and all of the white students were sitting on the other side of the room. I could not contain my shock. I said to the students, "Oh my goodness. I can't believe this is happening!" And I invited them to look around the room. The students saw it immediately, too, and they weren't accepting it. They got up and moved themselves around the room, making sure they were mixed by gender, race, sexual orientation, and peer groups. I was proud of them in that moment, because I could see they wanted to be better and were willing to do what it would take to build bridges across difference. It didn't stop there. We made it part of our practice to always be looking around the room and asking ourselves if we were seeing any self-segregation or segregation based on policy or practice, and when we did see it, we worked together to address it, because we knew how important it was to realizing our mission.

With a population this diverse, it has never been an easy endeavor to build strong relationships. We had to do a lot to build trust and to convince students of the incredible value of the great diversity in our building. This was especially hard when it came to building bridges between LGBTQ students and students who did not identify as LGBTQ. But we had a core belief that guided us—*If you can see yourself in others, whom can you harm?*—and by committing ourselves to the work of helping students to see themselves in others, we were able to realize our mission. This core belief framed everything we did, and it continues to be at the core of the school's thinking as the community plans into the future. From the beginning, we wanted to build strong relationships and develop a culture where students supported each other and where bullying was not the norm, so every day we planned with this in mind. There are many ways we did this, from the number of students we enrolled, to the ways we planned to teach, to the intentional use of stories in the classroom. Here are some of the ways we built and strengthened relationships at the Alliance School.

Choosing Small

Our first act was deciding to be a small school—a place where, like the famous TV show *Cheers,* "everybody knows your name." For us, this meant starting at one hundred students and never growing beyond four hundred. We know that not every school can be as small as this one, but there are many ways to be small. Schools can build communities within communities, where students and teachers get to know each other like family. We did this at the large high school where I taught before starting Alliance. The school was divided into academies, and I taught in the Freshman Academy. There were about four hundred students in the Academy, and those four hundred students were divided into four families of one hundred students apiece. Each family had a core group of teachers, one from each subject area, who worked together to support the family of students. I was the English teacher on one of these teams, and I met weekly with the other teachers to develop shared curriculum plans, plan field trips together, identify students who were struggling, contact parents together, and to benchmark our work against standards. It was a powerful way of working together, and the relationships in our freshman family were strong.

Other schools do something similar when they use the house system, which divides a larger school or university into houses, each with their own faculty, traditions, and cultures. Harvard and Yale Universities use house systems like this for their residence halls, and many high schools do this as well. The house system provides schools with a way of building small communities inside of larger communities, which is one of the keys to developing strong relationships.

In addition to keeping the school community itself small, we worked to keep all class sizes under thirty. Gym classes and some popular electives may occasionally have gone above this limit, but it was only with teacher permission and a firm commitment from the student to be an asset to the class. As budgets have become tighter over the years, this has become harder and harder, but we have always done our best to keep our classes as small as we possibly can.

Teaching to Build Connection

Another thing we did to build relationships was to adopt teaching practices that build opportunities for students to connect with each other and develop empathy for others. We used collaborative learning, restorative practices, advisories, service learning, and the arts to bring students together. If you walk into our classrooms, you will rarely see fluorescent lighting or individual desks in rows. Instead, you will see that many rooms have couches, movable desks, comfortable lighting, and students working in groups or pairs. It is a place where even the classroom environment invites students to connect with each other and with their teachers.

Just as we arrange our classroom environment for group work, we also are deliberate about how we assign students to groups. We group students so that they will get to know each other well. Over the years, I have used many strategies for forming such groupings. Sometimes, I used four-corner activities to move students into groups. For these activities, I would place topics in all four corners of the room and ask people to move to their favorite ice cream, movie, music genre, season, or some other featured topic. It was amazing how honest students were about their favorites, despite saying they wanted to sit with friends they knew. I also grouped students based on strengths for specific tasks or grouped them to focus on particular shared learning goals. The key was to be deliberate about the intention of the grouping and to let students know that it wasn't about separating them from their friends. It was about helping them develop new and vital friendships. Once in groups, I would often ask the students to start their work by answering a question about themselves or by sharing a story that was connected to the project or the work. In the horoscope groups, I had them read their horoscopes and make name tents with pictures on them that represented their unique qualities. I would often have the groups make something together that would represent who they were as a team.

These were just a few of the many classroom strategies used to build strong relationships, and I would often model these strategies in our staff meetings. All of the teachers at Alliance have their own unique ways of building connections in the classroom, but some of our teaching practices have been built on shared beliefs. For example, all of our teachers have been trained in service learning techniques, so that students work together to learn the subject area skills through work for and with the community, and we hold a shared theory of no throwaway work. This means that we are always trying to engage our students in real work that has an impact. Over the years, we have worked with different community organizations to make this possible. For example, for a few years we were able to work with a local agency to run a food pantry out of the school. The students were able to sign up for the work experience class, where they would package, deliver, and manage all of the operations for the food pantry. The students delivered over one hundred bags of food every week to seniors who lived in the low-income senior housing units across the street from the school. This helped them to develop relationships with each other and to develop relationships with the neighbors in the community. It was not unusual to see our students talking to the seniors at the bus stops, and we always invited these neighbors to our school events and activities, as well.

Another project we did in collaboration with the community was an arts project with Sasha Sicurella, founder of the I AM: International Foundation.[7] Sasha worked with the students to create self-portraits that would capture who they were as individuals. She uses these self-portraits to build connections with young people around the world, helping them to see themselves in others through the portraiture. At the end of the project, the students' self-portraits were displayed, larger than life, at a local art gallery, and students, families, and community members came out to see the work. It was an incredible display of artistic possibility, and a powerful way to get students to see their own beauty and the beauty of others through portraiture.

Using Games to Build Connections

Games are another great way to build connections in the classroom. Some games give students a chance to work together toward a goal, others get them to share information about themselves, and others allow them to demonstrate a hidden skill or talent. I was never a very athletic student in school, and when I was very young, I was quite shy and quiet. But when it came to challenges, I was a great teammate, and could often gain extra points for my partner or team. One of my favorite games at Alliance, one we would often use in restorative practice circles, is called The World Rocks. The game requires students to sit in a circle. One student names an identity feature, saying something like, "The world rocks if you're wearing black," or, "The world rocks if you have siblings." The students who have that in common stand up and switch seats, and the person in the center finds a seat. The one person left without a seat takes the place in the center and calls out the next statement. This activity gives students a chance to learn about each other while laughing and having fun together. We follow every game by asking students to reflect on what they noticed about themselves or others while playing the game.

Programming

We are also very conscious about our programming, using it as a tool to build connections. Our ninth-grade students are in cohorts, which helps us to keep class sizes especially small (not more than twenty-five students in a class), and all of the freshmen take the same courses. During this first year of high school, upperclassmen apply to serve as mentor students and classroom assistants, and we engage the freshmen in regular team-building activities throughout the year. The students visit the ropes course at least once during the year, and they participate in several college visits together throughout the year. In the other grades, we are intentional about having multigrade classes so that older students can support younger students in their learning. We do not track students into leveled classrooms, instead allowing students to choose classes based on interest and academic need, and all students with disabilities are fully included in regular education courses.

We chose not to track students based on ability because sorting and tracking are often havens for racial bias and discriminatory practices. Students are often selected based on teachers' perceptions of their abilities, and this often leads to a separation of students based on race. Besides these tendencies toward racial bias, the research on sorting has shown little evidence of benefit for any students. John Hattie completed a meta-analysis of numerous research studies and concluded that there was little or no evidence to support tracking and found that there were serious equity concerns about the use of tracking.[8] Sorting students does not help to eradicate bullying, either. The practice separates students, perpetuating negative stereotypes and building walls between students. We choose to integrate our classes as a means to build connections and relationships between students. There is much to learn in these diverse groups, and working with others is a skill that is important for the workplace and for life.

The need for this skill in life has never been clearer than in my time at Harvard.[9] There is hardly a class where we don't work in groups to complete projects for clients. In one of my classes, we are deliberately placed into teams of five with as much diversity as possible because there is much evidence to show that diverse teams are the most productive teams. The professors look at our backgrounds and experiences, our MBTI profiles, our StrengthsFinder makeups, our ethnicities, genders, and so forth, and put us into groups to complete strategic projects together. We are encouraged to learn about our team members and to share our differences, so that we can see each other's differences as strengths. This has been one of the most powerful learning experiences for me, and it is one that can be deliberately created in high schools, as well. Students must learn to see each other's differences as strengths and to find connections with each other beyond the superficial connections that usually bring people together, and as adults within the school, we have the chance to help them develop these skills.

Advisories

Advisories are another way we encourage connections among students. Since the opening of the school, we have always had a commitment to maintaining advisory classes for our students. Advisories give students a place to bond with each other, to ask the hard questions in a safe place where long-term relationships have been developed, to plan for the future, and to focus on building community. Over the years, our advisories have changed, because each year we learn a little bit more about the needs of our students. When we first opened the school, advisory classes were multiage classes with teachers who looped with their students, keeping the same advisory class and adding new students to it each year as other students graduated. This was effective, because it provided an opportunity for older students to mentor new students in a forum that was developed for just that kind of thing, but as the year went on, we found that we were struggling to meet the needs of the seniors, who needed additional support and mentoring through the college application process. We discussed it with the students and decided to switch to grade-level advisories. We have been doing this for the past several years now and have found that, since the students stay with their advisers and classmates all four years, the grade-level advisories support bonding while allowing us to take care of some of the technical tasks of high school life. We have additional opportunities for students to develop connections across grade levels, such as through mentoring and multigrade classes in the upper grades.

There are many ways and reasons to have advisory classes, but if a school is serious about building relationships, the advisory class can be a powerful tool for making it happen, especially as schools start to think about how to change teaching practices to meet these needs.

Restorative Practices

Another common practice at the Alliance School is the use of restorative practices to build community, solve problems, and repair harm. Every Alliance teacher is trained in the use of restorative practices, and there are also two classes where students are trained to lead restorative circles. (You will learn more about these practices in chapter 9.) These practices are often referred to as "restorative justice" in education communities, but we use the phrase "restorative practices" to describe how we use the circle for more than just discipline at the school. We use the practices in a preventive and community-building fashion. When students sit in the circle, pass a talking piece around the circle, and share their stories with each other, strong bonds are built, and this becomes one of the best means for preventing and addressing bullying. The use of restorative practices has been one of the most impactful tools we have ever adopted as a community, and I encourage all schools and communities to consider learning more about how to adopt these practices for themselves.

BRINGING IT ALL TOGETHER

Stories are important, and they can be shared through restorative practices, through games, and through many other means. They bridge divides, build communities, and bring joy. At Alliance, stories have always been the secret weapon in our antibullying crusade. Students share through their writing, in community presentations, in schoolwide circles, and through the arts. Alliance is a community that cares, because it is a community connected by our shared experiences, our histories, our hopes, and our stories. If any school is going to begin the journey toward creating a safe and accepting school for all students, it must start by creating opportunities for people to get to know each other well.

When school communities work deliberately to build relationships across difference, the result is incredible. In my years at the Alliance School, it was a beautiful gift to see that students were able to thrive, rather than just survive, in school. Our school community was undoubtedly a happier and healthier place because of the work we did to make it so. For me, this all started as a simple classroom exercise that changed the dynamic of my classroom and grew into a schoolwide practice with a noticeable impact. When people walk into the school, they can feel the difference. The students are welcoming toward guests and toward each other. There are no separations or uneasy pauses between students, and you will often see students who are very different from each other sitting side by side or helping each other in the halls. There is powerful learning going on throughout the school, with families being essential members of the school community. There are no metal detectors, security guards, or school administrators to handle discipline. Instead, the community of teachers and students work together to make it the safe and accepting community we want it to be.

It is a core belief that makes this possible, a belief that when students can see themselves in others, they are less likely to cause harm. This belief has proven itself to be true time and time again, at Alliance and in every space I have been lucky enough to be part of. It is time we make this core belief a common belief in every school and community. Our students will be the ones to thank us.

2

Fifty Percent Teaming

*A strong team can take any crazy vision
and turn it into a reality.*
JOHN CARMACK

IN THE LAST FEW DAYS of school of the year I was leaving to go to Harvard, our restorative practices teacher, Heather, planned a farewell staff circle. I didn't know it was going to be such a circle. I just knew it was our staff circle day. I came into her classroom that Tuesday morning, coffee in hand and rushing from a quick hallway conversation with one of the staff members, and joined the circle, as I usually would. This circle was different today, though. Heather had invited each staff member to participate in a ceremony of gratitude by purchasing and bringing a charm that represented a story between the staff member and me. She opened the circle by inviting us to all stand and say the *In Lak'Ech*, a Mayan saying which had become tradition in our school:

"You are my other me. If I do harm to you, I do harm to myself. If I love and respect you, I love and respect myself."

We all sat, and she began the circle, saying, "Today is a very special day, because today we recognize you, Tina. We recognize you for having the vision to create Alliance, for bringing that vision to life, and for creating this place we all call home. We have a gift that we would like to give you today, this charm bracelet, and we have each brought something to add to it. Each person has brought a charm that represents our time together or a story that we share, and in our circle today we'd like you to add them to your bracelet."

I was stunned. I had never seen anything like this before, and I didn't know what to say. I looked around the circle with tears in my eyes—tears of gratitude for these people who had become another family to me, tears of sadness to be losing my place here, tears of fear that maybe I had made the wrong decision. As I looked around, I noticed that others had tears, as well. "How will I ever leave this place?" I thought. And another thought came to my mind so strongly I felt it rise up in my chest: "I have never and will never experience love the way I have experienced it here."

The teachers and staff began to share their stories, and after each story, they passed the charm around the circle for everyone to see, and when it came to me, I clumsily tried to add it to the charm bracelet. The truth was, my hands were shaking so much the teacher next to me had to help me with every single one. Some of the stories were funny, and we laughed together, and some of them were moving. I couldn't stop the tears from flowing. I was a blubbery mess by the end of the circle, and so was everyone else. I still can't believe they did that for me, but the charm bracelet is, and will always be, one of my prized possessions. I wear it on special occasions to remind me of what is possible.

THE ALLIANCE TEAM

It is possible and important to build a team that can create the culture you want for your school. If relationships among students are at the heart of a school's culture, staff relationships are just as important. At Alliance, we spent a lot of time and energy building our relationships as a staff, and because of this, we were a tight-knit group. This showed up in so many ways, whether it was covering classes for each other, celebrating weddings and important events, participating in staff retreats together, sharing meals at potlucks, babysitting for each other, taking care of each other through the hard times of life, and the list goes on.

If our core belief for students was built around getting people to know each other well, so they were more likely to support each other and less likely to do harm, then it made sense that this would also be our core belief for staff, as the expectations of the environment are the same. As a school leader, I always imagined I should be spending 50 percent of our meeting times "teaming"—or team building—and 50 percent getting the work done.[1] This may seem like a lot of teaming, and there were times when the work simply had to be put at the forefront, but the time spent on teaming saved enormous amounts of time in reduced conflict, easier communications, and shared responsibility.

Staff conflicts and destructive behaviors can quickly sideline an effort to support students, make curriculum changes, or share best practices. It is just as important to build connections among staff members as it is to build connections among students, or the same conflict-ridden, bullying culture that can develop between students can develop between adults. As a young teacher, I knew I had to consciously build my classroom team. I thought hard about the desk arrangement, the groups, the activities, and the traditions. A school is just a larger classroom, with the same need for thoughtful grouping, physical arrangement, activities, and traditions. For a school to function well, there have to be things that make the staff feel like a team, rather than a group of individuals at work. There are many ways to do this, but sharing stories is where I like to begin.

SHARING STORIES

I believe connecting is essential to relationship building. If you don't know a person's story, you will fill in the blanks with your own assumptions, which can be dangerous and disruptive to team effectiveness. We are quick to attribute blame, but slow to realize that our own actions rarely come from a place of bad intentions. We have differences, hardships, personal styles, values, and core beliefs, all of which drive us to act in different ways, but we are rarely intentionally hurtful. Connections help us to fill in the blanks with love, something that, when we learn to do it, we can teach our children to do so, as well.

For me, every staff meeting must start with some sort of connecting. People have to know each other well to work together well, so it's important to create the time and opportunity for people to see beyond their differences and build connections. A check-in gives everybody a chance to enter the room and be heard, wherever they are at, physically and emotionally.

If you attend an Alliance staff meeting, you will find that we spend a lot of time on check-ins. A check-in usually consists of two pieces: "How are you doing?" and a second question meant to build connections, gauge perspectives, or process feelings. I have found these connecting questions to be some of the best ways to build community, and while the staff may roll their eyes at the question some weeks, if anyone tried to take it away, everyone would balk.

Most days, we start with a simple question, often connected to events in the world, pop culture, or an amusing thought, and other days the question is more introspective and meant to build deeper layers of community and trust. Staff members are invited to share what they feel comfortable sharing, and there is never any pressure to answer a question that one is not ready to answer. It is always acceptable to pass.

A connecting question can be crafted to elicit a long answer or a short answer, based on the amount of time available, the goals of the task at hand, and how much time the group has previously spent connecting. And sometimes the simple question becomes a more powerful question. For one staff meeting at Alliance, I started the day with a question about socks: "Tell a story about socks." This question, seemingly simple, revealed a lot about people and their experiences. Parents shared stories of trying to keep pairs of socks together for their children. An athlete shared a story about the importance of having the right socks. One teacher shared the experience of not having socks growing up, and one teacher shared the story of how her mother bought her themed socks for every holiday from the time she was little until the present day. Everyone had a story about socks, and the stories became stories that lived between us. On holidays, we would joke about our themed socks, and parents would share tips for how to keep matching socks together.

In larger schools or groups, it may be tempting to skip such a check-in altogether and get on to business. But giving people a chance to be seen and heard in the space is not just important, it's essential in establishing the dynamic for how work will get done. To make sure this happens, no matter how large the group is, I always try to engage people in connecting by inviting people to break into smaller circles to check in, or by using questions that invite a one- to three-word answer. Recently, I facilitated a meeting for a group of people from a school district, and since the group was large and time was tight, I decided to use a quick version of the sock question. I invited participants to share: your name, your role in the district, and what kind of socks you like to wear. The question helped to bring everyone into the space, built connections between people who liked the same kinds of socks, and created a sense of community among us through laughter. If we hadn't connected first, we would have just been a group of strangers assigned to work together on a problem, and how can people trust each other if they are never given a chance to share their lives with each other?

There is a lot of power in such simple stories, and today, in the world of social media and high-stakes everything, it is more important than ever for us to build the workplace structures which support the human interactions we need to work effectively together. In the world of perfectly crafted status updates, long days, and increased responsibility, we rarely get a chance to share the stories from our lives that make us human within our communities. The importance of this is clear in how eager people are to participate, even when they are strangers to our community. Guests clearly enjoy being part of the storytelling when they visit our staff meetings. Whether it is a staff member from the central office, or someone from the media writing about our school, we always invite them to participate in the community by sharing their stories. This practice doubles the impact of our connections by helping our staff to see our guests in a deeply human way and allowing them to see us in a deeply human way, as well.

CONNECTING IT TO THE ISSUES

Of course, there are times when the issues at hand call for a deeper conversation. We have found we can use our connections time at the beginning of staff meetings to engage us in a topic that we are dealing with in the school. For example, if we are talking about what makes for memorable learning experiences, I might ask the staff to share an example of a memorable learning experience. Then we can look at the examples and find out what kinds of things they have in common, so we can think consciously about how to create these types of experiences for our students.

Another question might remind teachers of how it feels to be in the students' shoes. I might ask, "Share a story about a time when you tried really hard on something and failed." This question invites the staff member to consider what he or she needed to be successful in that circumstance and makes him or her less likely to blame the students for failure. We can do this to talk about discipline policies, as well. We could easily start a discussion about rule breaking by asking educators to share a story about a time they broke a rule at school, why they broke it, and what the consequences were. Connecting people to their own stories, and the stories of their peers, gives them a chance to remember what it was like to be a student and to think consciously about the effectiveness and impact of the policies they are considering creating.

FINDING THE TIME FOR TEAMING

I can imagine that many people will ask, "How can I find the time for this kind of teaming? The requirements of our work in the world of education are ever increasing, and the demands for achievement are ever pressing. For every moment we spend teaming, isn't that just one more moment taken away from our end goals?" But I would argue that every moment spent on teaming pays off in multiplied dividends, such as increased staff attendance, a decrease in calls for substitutes, less time spent investing in sanctions and incentives, reduced staff conflict, and so on. In my ten years of leadership at Alliance, staff turnover was almost nonexistent, with many staff members having perfect attendance every year, and staff members rarely missed staff meetings. The time we spent on teaming made the Alliance School a place where staff members wanted to be. It's not about finding time to team, it's about making teaming an important part of everything you do.

I have focused this chapter up to this point on building connections during staff meetings, but there are many ways to create connections among adults beyond the traditional staff meeting time. In the next sections, I highlight some of the ways we did this at Alliance, and I encourage you to think of ways that you might be able to do this in your own context.

FRIENDLY COMPETITION AND PLAY

A little bit of play among adults goes a long way toward building a connected and committed staff. When starting the Alliance School, the book *Fish! A Remarkable Way to Boost Morale and Improve Results* by Stephen C. Lundin, Harry Paul, and John Christensen inspired me.[2] The book highlighted four ideas that were central to building a positive workplace culture:

- choosing one's attitude
- playing at work
- making someone's day
- being present

We didn't deliberately plan to do these things in everything we did, but everyone on our planning team had read the book, and the ideas conveyed in the book helped to shape our culture—especially the idea of playing at work.

Because of this philosophy, we often found ways to engage in activities that may have seemed silly to the outsider looking in, yet these were the very things that built a shared history or "story of us" that staff members could connect to. Sometimes we did this by playing light getting-to-know-you games at meetings, and other times it was by planning staff social activities outside of school time. At staff parties, we exchanged serious and white-elephant gifts, we played harmless pranks on each other, and we participated in staff–student competitions. There was not one person in charge of making sure we had fun. Sometimes these were my ideas, and sometimes they came from the staff, and other times, the students initiated the activities. One thing was clear, though, a commitment to fun was part of our staff culture.

The perfect example of this was on Twin Day of the students' spirit week, when a group of us decided that our whole staff should show up as "twins." We got together and planned to go to a local overstock store and buy matching sweaters for all the staff members. All the teachers agreed to do it, if the self-appointed planning committee could find the sweaters. Of course, we found them, and the next day we all showed up in matching striped blue sweaters that looked like a cross between the sweater that Steve wore in *Blue's Clues* and Freddy Krueger's sweater in *Nightmare on Elm Street*. It was hilarious. The math teachers tried, unsuccessfully, to account for the multiplying by telling us what kinds of twins we were—octuplets means "eight," but how do you say "eighteen"? We all took pictures together, and the students got a kick out of the fact that all the teachers had managed to dress alike.

We were full of quirky activities like this one. They bonded us together in unique ways, because they required us to work together, despite challenging circumstances, to accomplish some task that had a visible outcome. They also provided a sense of relief from the pressures and a sense of camaraderie through the hardship. As the years went on, I don't know if everyone always knew why we did the things we did, but I do know that everyone looked forward to those quirky days.

TAKING CARE OF THE HUMAN NEEDS OF STAFF

A truly connected community takes care of each other through the hard times as well as through the good times. A year before I started Alliance, I went to visit my mother in Texas. She had been very ill with a rare form of cancer which was taking her from us quickly. Sadly, while I was in Texas, she passed away. It was one of the hardest moments of my life. I was the oldest child of four, so I took a couple of weeks off work to take care of her funeral arrangements and to take care of my younger siblings. However, in the midst of taking care of everyone and everything, I didn't have much time to think about what I might need.

A couple of weeks later, I returned to the large school where I was teaching, and my students bombarded me with questions as soon as I walked in the door.

"Where were you?" "How dare you leave us?" "Why weren't you here?" No one had told them my mother had passed.

When I told them what had happened, they felt horrible for their initial questions, and then they were upset that no one had told them. Rather than scold me, they made me sympathy cards, and told me they wished they could have been there for me. Their words of support, and the support from my colleagues who knew about my loss, carried me through that period more than anything else.

We are all human beings with losses, struggles, and joys that need to be shared so we can support each other. As school leaders, we must make the workplace as caring and humane for our educators as we expect our educators to make it for their students. We teach our educators to be informed about the effects of trauma on young people, yet we forget that our educators experience trauma as well, and it is our duty to care for them, and for all of us to care for each other.

As our school leader, I was constantly listening, trying to hear the strain in the work, the frustrations, and the joys, in order to strike the balance between getting the work done and meeting the socioemotional needs of the staff. I modeled how check-ins could be an opportunity to share the good stuff and the hard stuff, and I reminded the staff that this was the forum we had created so that we could take care of each other from week to week. I made sure my door was open, and I spent a lot of time visiting and asking people how they were doing.

There were times during the year when this was more important than others. Just like students, the holidays often stress adults, especially when those holidays are reminders of lost family members, hard times, or loneliness to come. As the students begin to argue, fight, and fall apart at these times, the adults can start to unravel, too. So it is essential to plan for these times with forethought and care. A sympathy card passed around and signed by everyone can mean a lot, and a phone call to check on someone during the holidays can mean everything to the person on the receiving end. Stress-filled times might be a good time to invite staff to share appreciations for each other in a staff meeting, or to share a story about a time when a colleague did something that supported them in a time of need.

Birthdays can be stressful times for some adults, but they can also provide an opportunity to show that you care. One year, one of our regional superintendents gave all her school leaders a form to fill out with their favorite snacks, magazines, music, and other simple things. Then, on our birthdays, she delivered a small gift bag filled with our favorite things. This was especially meaningful to me, as I had lost my parents and grandparents and wouldn't be getting many gifts that year. It couldn't have cost more than five to ten dollars for each gift bag, but I appreciated that little gift so much. It meant that she had taken the time to ask what I would like and to make sure that I was remembered on my birthday.

I took this idea and did it for our staff, as well, and they enjoyed it as much as I did. Sometimes we forget that adults need the same things that young people do. We could do a lot just by remembering each other through hard times and good times.

USING BUSINESS TOOLS TO INCREASE TEAM EFFECTIVENESS

So far, I have been speaking about many of the soft skills for building community, yet there are many business tools that have been designed with the explicit purpose of getting people to know each other's strengths, preferences, and styles so that they are better able to work together. As the lead teacher, I often coordinated the professional development activities for our staff, so I was constantly on the lookout for tools that would help us learn how to collaborate better. We learned about our Myers-Briggs Type Indicators (MBTI) together, found out what colors our personalities were, and discovered our spirit animals together. These activities created an opportunity for fun and bonding, yet they were also an intentional effort to help us to better understand each other so we could work better together.

One of the things we did together was the StrengthsFinder assessment.[3] I learned about this assessment in my master's degree program at Alverno College. We were required to take the test online and consider how we might use the tool to inform our thinking and our work. After taking the test myself, I decided to bring this tool to our staff, purchasing copies of the books for everyone and then charting everyone's results so we could learn about each other's strengths. The StrengthsFinder assessment helps people to find their hidden strengths or talents, the things they can do to near perfection, over and over again.

When I took the StrengthsFinder assessment, I learned that my top five strengths were Winning Over Others (WOO), Achiever, Maximizer, Learner, and Strategic. For me, this was the perfect set of strengths for the job I was doing. I needed to be able to convince people to believe in the Alliance mission (WOO); I needed to accomplish extraordinary results (Achiever); I needed to align people with their strengths and get them to work to their best abilities (Maximizer); I needed to constantly learn (Learner); and I needed to be strategic in my thinking to maneuver in the complicated political space that surrounds public education (Strategic). I liked this picture of myself, though I was a bit shy about it. It seemed bold and unforgiving, almost calculating, as if my actions were done with a self-interested goal in mind. But when I began to think about the goal I had in mind—to make school safe and accepting for all students—I realized there was no reason I ever should have felt shy about my strengths. These were the strengths that had helped move us to where we were: a well-recognized, award-winning, and accomplished school, with an incredibly valuable mission.

The StrengthsFinder assessment was a great tool for helping me to learn about myself and how my strengths had been assets for our school, so I was excited to bring the opportunity to take the assessment to our team. One of the premises of the book is that people are happier at work when they get to do work that is aligned with their strengths.[4] So I imagined that if we could find out what these strengths were, we would be better able to align people with them, which could only lead to a happier, more efficient workplace. This turned out to be true, but what I couldn't have imagined was how powerful the assessment would be in helping us to see each other through an asset-based lens. My experience with Tammy was a perfect example of this.

Tammy

Tammy had only been part of our team for a year, but she was making her presence known in our staff meetings. It seemed like every time we were on the verge of deciding, Tammy would sabotage the outcome by bringing up some concern for what might happen that made it impossible for us to proceed. She could not agree to move forward with any decision without a great deal of discussion, considering every dangerous possibility, and playing the devil's advocate. It was maddening, and I was beginning to think it was just a power struggle playing out. Of course, this was me filling in the blanks with my own assumptions. She wanted things to go her way, and if they didn't, nothing else could pass. This was especially infuriating because we were operating on a consensus basis, and it felt like it always took twice as long to get to a place where she, and therefore everyone, felt comfortable enough to move forward.

It was at this time that I invited the staff to take the StrengthsFinder assessment so that we could learn more about our strengths and talents. Each person took the test and printed out their results. I collected the results and made copies so everyone could learn about everyone else on the team, and so we could talk about how we might be able to better use our strengths as a team. When I read Tammy's results, I learned that one of her top strengths was Deliberative. This is how the StrengthsFinder results describe this talent:

> **Deliberative.** The genius of your Deliberative talent is found in the quality of your decisions, choices, values, and the directions you decide to pursue. Your deliberative genius involves thinking and the fact that you will take multiple things into consideration every time you make a decision or a plan. The genius of your Deliberative talent allows you to look at an issue from multiple sides. You will "play the devil's advocate" as you think through alternatives, values, and propositions, and you will look at multiple sides as you are learning. You will slow down the process whenever you are learning, planning, or deciding. But this does not mean you are "slow minded." Quite the opposite. This is part of your genius and results in very high-quality decisions and a depth of understanding.[5]

What I had seen as sabotage was a talent that was likely saving us from self-sabotage. Her questions and deep considerations, while frustrating in the context of a staff meeting, were helping us to think through our decisions more thoughtfully. Rather than trying to silence these questions, I decided to give her the chance to put her talent to use. I asked her to help me plan the staff meetings, to do some of this thinking ahead of time, and to take things off the table that might be too dangerous or unproductive. In this role, she was an extraordinary thought partner and ally, and I am certain our decisions were better because of her deliberative thinking.

Knowing Tammy's strength changed my relationship with her, and it changed her relationship with the team. We had been a group of people who dreaded her pushback, and we became a team of people who valued her insights.

This is where tools such as the StrengthsFinder assessment can be extraordinarily valuable for helping a school staff develop as a team. Tests like these can go a long way toward helping people to understand each other on teams. Of course, people must be willing to approach them with a mindset of learning and openness to the possibility that people can and will change. But when people can do this, they can provide valuable insights. The validity of these tests is only found in our truth in taking them. If we take them with an open mind, and a sincere intention to learn about ourselves, there is a lot we can gain from them. They are like mirrors that we can use to see ourselves and others more clearly.

RESTORATIVE PRACTICES

At Alliance, all teachers and staff members are trained in restorative practices. This gives us tools to use in the classroom, and at the same time, gives us the opportunity to build strong relationships among staff members. All our circle trainings start with an exercise that engages participants in sharing their values and the stories of the people who inspired those values. Through this exercise, people begin to see the motivations behind their peers' actions.

We stepped into learning about restorative practices because the practices have shown great promise for reducing bullying, resolving conflict, and building a positive school culture.[6] But over time, we learned to use the tools of restorative practices to develop the deepest of connections between us as a staff. Once a month, we devoted one full staff meeting to a staff circle. Each circle took about two hours and consisted of four questions that started as connecting questions and developed into more complex questions. For these circles, we passed around a talking piece, a central tenet of restorative practices, and each staff member would have the opportunity to speak when he or she received the talking piece. A set of questions may be something like this:

> Share a story about a time when you were truly happy in school.
> Share a story about a time when you were unhappy in school.
> What do you wish your teachers would have known about you at that time?
> How can you use this knowledge to support your students today?

These types of questions made it possible for us to see each other better, to understand each other's motivations, and to support each other in doing the work. They weren't always easy, and it took a lot of trust to be able to share this kind of vulnerability with each other, but it was this vulnerability that opened the space for each of us to support each other and our students in profound ways.

STAFF RETREATS

Another way we built connections was through our staff retreats. At least once every other year, our staff committed to participating in a staff retreat together (an agenda for one of these retreats is included in appendix B). These retreats were approved in advance and were paid for with professional development funds or grant dollars. The retreats were usually three- to four-day events that took place at a lodge or cabin where we could all share space, learn, plan, cook, and play together. The cabin could sleep fourteen to eighteen people, which was large enough for our whole staff in the first couple of years. As our staff grew, we had to reserve side-by-side cabins to host everyone. This wasn't a problem, though, because we still had enough space for the whole staff to meet and plan in one space, and at night people would go to their chosen cabin—the quiet cabin or the late-night cabin—to sleep.

As a staff that was deeply committed to our status as union teachers, there was no way we could force people to participate in these retreats, but we didn't have to. With a solid plan to do valuable work, a promise to be paid for the hours we'd be working, and the expectation of some time to have fun together when the work was done, the retreat had a way of bringing everyone to the table. If someone couldn't make it, we always knew we had enough of a majority to be making healthy decisions for the whole team, and if there was ever a question that someone who wasn't there might want to weigh in on something, we could always pick up the phone and give that person a call.

The plan for the retreat was much like the plan for our meetings—50 percent teaming and 50 percent getting the work done. We often had our retreat in midwinter, at a cabin at a waterpark resort. We would spend the day in deep reflection, planning, and accomplishing tasks, and then we would spend the evening cooking together, going to the waterpark, and closing the evening with a staff circle. These were great opportunities to work without interruption and without the pressures that come when you try to work in the school building. And the duties required to live together for several days provided another opportunity to build trust, share responsibility, and learn together. Different staff members would cook different meals together, clean the kitchen, or take care of the cabin. I had some of the best meals I've ever had at those cabin retreats, as everyone prepared their best in an effort to take care of and impress the group.

It was at these retreats that we revisited our school mission and vision, developed our norms, participated in restorative practices training, reviewed schoolwide data, developed curriculum, and collaborated to solve problems. They were uniquely powerful opportunities to get the most important work done.

While not every school can have a retreat like this one for their entire staff, there are other ways to have these kinds of experiences. People can cook together at local kitchens, attend conferences, participate in ropes course activities, visit the zoo as a staff, do community service activities, engage in experiential professional development, create art together, and so on. It's up to the school leader to make teaming a priority by providing the time, resources, and encouragement for the staff to have powerful experiences together.

A FINAL THOUGHT ON TEAMING

The staff at the Alliance School is and has always been remarkable. Most of the teachers have been there for ten years or more, and we all truly love each other. We *are* family. We didn't get there by accident. We worked hard, studied the research on team effectiveness, and took the time to get to know each other. When I decided to take the next step in my professional career and leave Alliance, it was one of the hardest decisions I ever had to make because we had built a bond that was so strong. It was that bond that made it possible for us to serve our mission and meet the needs of the young people in our care.

It's important for leaders at every level to take time to build deep and meaningful connections among staff members, both for your own well-being and for the well-being of those you are charged with caring for. As leaders, we can provide the space and opportunity for people to love and be loved through everything else that happens in life, and to build friendships that outlast television series, childhoods, and marriages. We can build strategic alliances that enable people to accomplish great things together and to transform the lives of young people. We can open ourselves to the people we work with in ways that create lasting partnerships and help us achieve the lofty goals which brought us into this profession to begin with. For me, this goal has always been to make school safe, accepting, and academically challenging for the young people who come to learn with us every day. At Alliance, it was the *team* who made it possible for us to achieve that goal.

3

A Place for *All* Students

The greatest gift that you can give to others is the
gift of unconditional love and acceptance.
BRIAN TRACY

WHEN I WAS FOURTEEN, I was a bit frightening. I wore the same torn, black jeans every day, paired with bloody-looking concert T-shirts for bands such as Slayer and Megadeth. I accessorized my black clothing with black eyeliner (way beyond the corner of my eye), black eye shadow, black lipstick, and black nail polish. In my ears, I wore upside-down crosses, and I used various sharp objects to carve "666" into my arm on a regular basis. I didn't really have a satanic bone in me, but I had learned, as a poor, messed-up, white girl in a large, primarily Latino high school, that the best way to make yourself unapproachable by bullies—or by anyone for that matter—was to make yourself just scary enough that most people would stay away. I dressed like this for almost a year and a half, until my tenth grade ROTC teacher saw through it and encouraged me to join some of the school's teams. But I never forgot what had driven me to dress this way in the first place.

When I first started teaching, I recognized these behaviors in my students for what they were—defense mechanisms to keep the world away—so I didn't let the behavior affect my perception of the students. This proved to be one of my most valuable skills as a teacher. As the motivational speaker Brian Tracy might say, this was my gift of unconditional love and acceptance. When I looked up my ratings on the website ratemyteacher.com, I noticed that one of the students had written, "[Mrs. Owen] loves all of her students, good or bad."[1]

For me, there were no bad students, only students who had been mislabeled and terribly misunderstood. It was this vision, as a teacher, that helped me to create a school where everyone is accepted, where it is "okay to be black, white, gay, straight, Christian, gothic, Buddhist, disabled, or just plain unique." Shauna was one of the students who inspired me to do so.

Shauna

Shauna didn't look like the other students in the large, mostly African American high school where I taught prior to Alliance, and that unsettled the students in her classes. She wore black clothes, black makeup, spiked jewelry and, at times, fangs. She was what some people would consider Goth, and most of the students and teachers didn't know what to think of her scary looks. I thought she was fantastic. She was creative, compassionate, and most importantly for a passionate young English teacher, she was a great writer. I could also relate to her because I, too, had been Goth in my high school years, so I could see past the black makeup and clothes. I knew that her appearance was likely about two things: expressing her individuality and keeping people at a distance so she wouldn't get hurt.

She was successful at expressing her individuality and keeping people at a distance, but her unusual appearance didn't keep her from getting hurt. Other students were constantly calling her names and throwing things at her in the halls, cafeteria, and classrooms. At some point, they started calling her a witch and doing things like riding a broom around the classroom to try to get her angry. Every time they did it, Shauna would blow up, and before she knew it, she would find herself suspended from school.

At one point, she even got so angry in one of her classes that she screamed, "I hate you people. If you don't leave me the fuck alone, I'm gonna blow up this school! I'm gonna come back here with a bomb, and I'm gonna blow up this school!"

This took place not long after the shootings at Columbine High School, where two high school students had terrorized their school community, coming in with guns and killing thirteen people, so a teacher reported the incident, and Shauna's threats were taken very seriously, as they should have been. But something else should have been done. Someone should have looked carefully into why she was making these threats and tried to intervene on her behalf, but that didn't happen. Shauna was suspended and had to face an expulsion hearing that would determine whether she would be allowed to return to the school.

By some miracle, she was allowed to return, but her attendance began to drop dramatically. She would come to school for a day and the bullying would continue, so each day of school would lead to one week of absences. She clearly cared about school, and wanted to graduate, because she kept coming back. But when she was there, she was miserable, so she failed class after class, and eventually she just stopped coming to school. It was clear that this brilliant and creative girl was on the verge of dropping out.

Shauna was not the only student who seemed to be on a path toward dropping out of school. I was the adviser for the Gay/Straight Alliance (GSA), and almost every day students would come to me and talk to me about the harassment, discrimination, or violence they were dealing with at school. Sometimes the harassment was by peers, sometimes it was by adults. They were beaten up in hallways, threatened in locker rooms, and had objects thrown at them in classrooms. The administrators rarely did anything to stop it. When I reported the incidents, they said, "If they don't want to be harassed, they should stop flaunting their sexuality. They know how people are going to act."

Not every staff member at the school acted this way. There were some amazing advocates who stood up for students when they witnessed this kind of harassment and reported the bullying when they saw it. But there were also security guards who told kids they were going to hell for being gay, and teachers who wouldn't let gay students in their classes. When I tried to talk to administrators about these things, they argued that there was nothing they could do because these teachers and staff members had a right to believe what they wanted. As a result, when the young people realized that nothing was going to be done to protect them, they stopped coming to school.

It was amid all this that I started thinking about the possibility of starting a new school. I had never imagined starting a school before, but I really believed that there were things that schools could do to reduce bullying, and I knew that if we could prove that these things worked, other schools could follow, and schools could be safer places for all students.

When I started thinking about starting this school, my first thought was that we needed to create a gay-friendly school, like the Harvey Milk High School in New York City.[2] Harvey Milk is a school that developed out of the need to support LGBTQ students who were on the verge of dropping out of school due to anti-gay harassment or bullying. The school was showing great success, with a 90 percent graduation rate and an incredible amount of support from the community. It was not without controversy, but that was outside its doors. What was happening inside was good for students, and most importantly, it was saving their lives and keeping them in school. I, on the other hand, was watching my students drop out of school, one after another, and it was devastating. I knew students deserved a better school experience, and for that to happen, we needed a place like Harvey Milk High School in Milwaukee.

However, while I was thinking about it, I also had Shauna in my thoughts. Shauna was not gay. She was just different. Harvey Milk was a great model of what can happen when young LGBTQ students are given a chance to study and learn in a safe environment, but I knew that if I was going to start a school, it had to be a school for Shauna, as well. The GSA was made up of both gay students and straight students, and Shauna was part of that club, fighting for the rights of her peers and finding a sense of community in this space. It was one of the things that kept her coming to school. The club met once a week, for a couple of hours after school, and for that little bit of time, school felt different. It felt *safe*. It only seemed natural that if we were going to start a school that would be a safe place for all students, the school would be modeled after the GSA.

In our planning process, Shauna was in our thoughts and on our planning committee. In August of 2005, when the school opened, Shauna was one of our first students. And even though she was already eighteen and able to drop out if she wanted to, she stayed in school. Two years later, Shauna graduated from the Alliance School, and I was as excited as I would have been if she was my own child. She was happy, confident, and alive.

This was the reason we started Alliance. If just one student could have a different experience of school, it was something, but if many students could have this experience every year, what a difference this would make for their lives and their communities, and for the generations to come. Shauna proved that a belief in a school for all students is the belief that makes a difference for LGBTQ students. It is also the school that makes a difference for disabled students, students of color, shy students, artistic students, and so on. When acceptance for everyone is the mission, true safety and inclusiveness is possible.

We would be tested on our definition of *all* over and over again in the years to come, but that very same word would be the glue that would bind us together, and the practice that would hold us accountable to ourselves and our students, every step of the way. Some of the most amazing success stories would be the stories of students who weren't part of the LGBTQ community, but who experienced the same bullying, discrimination, or ostracism in other schools.

Because of Shauna, I was able to see a bigger mission for the school, one that included all students. Bullying was not just something that happened to LGBTQ students, to weak students, to students with disabilities. Bullying was something that could happen to anyone, and the best way to create a safe school was to create a school where *every* student could feel welcome. Here are a few stories that exemplify the radically welcoming environment that we created.

Chris

When you create a school with a motto like ours, you know the students are going to test it. I knew this ahead of time. I just didn't realize how soon that would happen—until I walked into the building on the first day of school on August 1, 2005.

On that very first day, I decided that I would get to the school building super early in order to make sure everything was ready and to greet the students and teachers as they arrived. I got there at 6:30 in the morning, thinking I would be the first one, and that I would have plenty of time to calm my frazzled nerves before the students and staff started arriving for the 8:30 a.m. start time.

I walked through the courtyard, seagulls squawking, coffee in hand, unsure of what the day would bring, but excited by all of its promise. The building was an unlikely space for a school. It had once been a well-known brewery, as many buildings had been in Milwaukee, and later the school district had purchased it and turned it into a middle school. At the far end of the building, there was a set of rooms on the second floor that had once been used as professional development and office space for the district. With a little bit of imagination, this small space had now been transformed into an incubator space for new schools; our school was in its incubation phase, so this was our new home. There were no signs or letters to mark one's entry into the space. There was no security guard or crew of welcoming mothers to provide visitor's passes. There was only a door, on the side of a building, in a courtyard, that led to an elevator, that would take you to the second floor—where our school was born that day.

When the elevators opened on the second floor, I was surprised to see a dark and ominous figure sitting in the lobby area. My first thought was that we already had a protester, maybe someone with a bomb, because he was sitting in a chair, wearing a long, black trench coat, and clutching a Bible, head bowed in defiance. I knew there might be protesters. My heart pounded as I imagined this could be my first and last day as a school leader.

As I stepped out of the elevator, the figure slowly raised his head to look directly at me. He had dark eyeliner framing his eyes, white face paint that made his skin look paler than was natural, and a look that could send ice shivers down the back of anyone with any bit of Christian upbringing. He looked like the Devil himself, and I was terrified. I knew some protesters had become violent at Harvey Milk High School in New York. And I had no idea who this person was, or why he was looking at me as if he was about to self-detonate. I did the only thing I could imagine doing in that moment.

"Good morning," I said, in my most confident and cheerful voice, as I stepped off the elevator.

My choice to greet him rather than to run screaming seemed to appease him somewhat, and he replied in a hesitant, but appreciative, way, "Good morning."

"Are you one of our students?" I asked, remembering what I was like in high school and trying to appear unmoved by his appearance.

"Yes," he said, with a slight, twisted smile. "Yes, I am."

We both looked at each other for a moment, as if contemplating whether we were each going to accept each other's presence in this space.

"Is it okay if I read this to people?" he said, lifting the Bible so that I could see its cover.

"I don't know. What part are you going to read?" I asked, expecting to hear something about Sodom and Gomorrah or Adam and Eve. Honestly, I think he was so busy expecting me to say that he couldn't read the Bible in a public school, that he never imagined how he would respond if he was asked what he would read. He opened the Bible and read a passage from Genesis about the creation of the Earth.

I listened to the passage closely for anything that might be considered hurtful to someone, and finding nothing, I said, "Sure. That's beautiful. Read that to everyone."

He looked at me, smiled, and nodded his head. "Okay. I will," he said. Then he stood up and offered me his hand. "By the way, my name is Chris," he said.

"I'm Tina," I said. "I'm so glad you're here."

We both smiled, seeing past all the things that we might have expected from our first impressions.

"Hey, I've got a couple of things to do to get ready for everybody," I said. "How would you feel about staying here and welcoming everybody to Alliance as they come off the elevator this morning?"

Something in him lit up like a little kid at Christmas time.

"Really? I could do that?" he asked.

"Of course," I said. "You're the first one here, and I can't do it all by myself. What do you think?"

"Cool," he said. "I can do that."

That morning, Chris created a welcome poster and greeted every student and parent who stepped off the elevator into our second-floor oasis of a school. He smiled, shook each person's hand, and helped the students find their way to their first-block classes. There were some shocked looks at first, but Chris's smile was infectious, and it only took a moment for people to see that he was not a threat. And the students seemed more assured than ever by his appearance that this truly would be a place where they could be themselves and be accepted.

When I look back, it's hard to imagine how I would have made it through that morning without Chris. I never could have imagined how much work that first day would be, and I was so grateful for his positive attitude and his help. He tested our mission, and we passed the test. And we were so much better for it.

His generosity didn't stop there. Chris became like our litmus test for acceptance. He made it his responsibility to be the greeter and tour guide for the school. He often looked terrifying, with his dark makeup and imposing height, but we quickly learned that he was the sweetest person that anyone could ever imagine. He came to Alliance because he believed in the mission. He wanted our school to be a place where he could be accepted exactly as he was. And once he knew that he was part of the family, he became the best representative that the school could ever hope for. Whenever a new student came to the school, Chris was the person who wanted to give the tour, and if the student could see past all the makeup and hard-looking personality to the sweetheart just beneath, we knew the student was the right person for our school. If they freaked out at the sight of Chris, we knew they probably weren't going to take a chance and enroll. It was a strange sort of assessment, but in a school with a mission like ours, we couldn't have designed a better entrance test.

Chris finished his high school years at Alliance and never stopped being an ambassador for the school. Today, he sings in a band, has fallen in love, and shares cute cat videos on Facebook. His father calls me every now and then to thank me and all of the teachers for everything we did for his son.

Joseph and Julie

Joseph wasn't the kind of student most people would imagine attending Alliance. He was white, Christian, and from the suburbs, a young man who found his way to Alliance because he was being bullied for his religious beliefs at the school he had been attending. He was from a conservative, Christian family, and I have to admit that even I was surprised to see them in this place that was explicitly LGBTQ-friendly. But Joseph's family was there because the bullying he was experiencing was real. He had been pushed, called names, and had his cross pulled from his neck. When his family heard that there was a school with a mission of addressing bullying, they had been quick to look it up.

The first time I met them was at the Alliance Open House, and it was just a coincidence that a French television news crew was there doing a story about Alliance at the same time. The reporters, who had promised to be unobtrusive—"like flies on the wall," they said—were anything but. They didn't hesitate to approach the new family to ask them why they were considering Alliance.

"Is your son a homosexual?" the female reporter asked, while her colleague held the camera inches from Joseph's dad's face.

His dad handled it well, responding with a gentle laugh, "No, my son is not gay."

"Then why is he here?" she asked. "Isn't this the gay school?"

This was where I intervened. "Our school is not a gay school," I said. "Our school is a place for anyone who has experienced bullying or wants to be in a place where he or she can be accepted for who he or she is."

"But many of the kids here are gay," she pressed on. "Won't your son feel uncomfortable in a place with so many homosexuals?"

"Many of our students are gay, and many are not," I responded, finding myself irritated and embarrassed by the rudeness of her questioning.

"There are gay people everywhere," Joseph's dad replied. "What's he going to do, stay home to avoid people who are different from him? This school is for kids who have been bullied. If they can make sure that he doesn't get bullied like he did in his previous school, then it doesn't matter who is sitting next to him."

His candor and comfort with the brash reporters was refreshing, but I still couldn't help but wonder whether or not they would come back. The next day I was happy to see them in the office with enrollment papers.

Joseph's transition to Alliance was seamless. He was welcomed into the community without hesitation. He participated in dances, went canoeing, participated on school councils, and developed a wonderful group of friends. Things were going so well, we never could have imagined what would happen on a regular school day between classes.

One morning, Joseph was in the stairwell moving from the second to the first floor between classes. He was with a group of friends, laughing and joking around as they would often do, and he decided to slide down the bannister. Later he admitted he had been "showing off for the girls." Somehow, as he started down the bannister, he lost his balance and fell backward over the railing. He caught himself and was holding on for a moment, but he quickly lost his grip and started to tumble through the air, falling two stories, from the second-level landing to the hard basement floor. He landed face forward on his head, breaking every bone in his face and causing numerous other injuries and internal bleeding. His friends ran for help.

When I came to the landing where Joseph was lying on the ground, he was already bleeding from his nose, ears, and mouth, and was having trouble breathing. A student who was trained in CPR braced his head to keep him from choking on the blood, and I stayed with him and tried to reassure him until the paramedics could arrive. The nurse from the building next door came over and gave us directions for what to do until they arrived. Minutes later, the paramedics were there, and they rushed him off to the hospital. When he left, the nurse told me that his injuries were too severe, and she was almost certain that he would not survive the ambulance ride to the hospital. I contacted the district administration to tell them where I was going, and then I went to meet his family at the hospital.

Joseph was in a coma for almost six months, and every day he seemed to be balancing on the line between life and death. At one point all of his organs were failing. At another point, an infection ravaged his body. The doctors could offer no promise of recovery. All we could do was pray, they told us.

We did pray. Many of the staff and students visited him while he was in the hospital. Some of his friends sat with him and talked to him for hours. They brought him gifts of music and teddy bears, and helped to comfort his family, including his little sister, Julie. When he finally came out of the coma, it felt like it was a true miracle. But the struggle wasn't over yet. During his long comatose state, his muscles had forgotten how to work. He had to relearn how to use every muscle in his body. His spirit was strong, though, and he worked hard to recover his physical strength, eventually going back to school at a large school closer to home, because of the accessibility. His family's Alliance story didn't end there, though.

Despite his tragic fall, when his younger sister faced bullying at her school, the family looked to Alliance once again. Julie was just eight years old when Joseph had been hospitalized, so when she walked into Alliance for the middle school orientation, I didn't recognize her at first. I looked back and forth between her and her mother, and then it clicked. "Julie! You're here!" I said, and she smiled with nervous excitement.

After the orientation, I had a chance to talk to Julie while she waited for her dad to come and pick her up. I thought she was just coming to Alliance because her brother had loved the school, but her story was much more personal than that. She started to tell me about the year of bullying she had experienced at her previous school, and it was shocking. She had been called names, had things thrown at her, and even had Lysol poured into her food. She had eaten half of it before anyone told her it was there. She told me a student admitted to doing it under pressure from some other students, and there had not been any serious consequences for the student who had done it. The worst part was, Julie had considered that student one of her closest friends.

Her story brought me back to my days in a traditional school, and how the physical and emotional abuse always seemed to escalate when left unaddressed. I was so glad she was at Alliance, where at least I knew that she would be welcomed warmly, and if there were incidents of harm, they would not go unaddressed.

Every school would benefit from practicing radical acceptance the way Joseph and Julie's family did and the way we do at the Alliance School. While some students are statistically more likely to be the targets of bullying behaviors, there is no portrait of a bullied student. Students are bullied because they are shy, Goth, biracial, smart, disabled, pretty, Christian, atheist, gay, and the list goes on. The stories of Julie and Joseph are testaments to how this can happen to anyone, yet they are also testaments to the ways in which people can live and work together when they have a shared mission and a belief in the capacity of others. It is the school's responsibility to put a stake in the ground when it comes to acceptance for all students. This does not mean that everyone within a community has to have the same beliefs, nor does it mean that every day is easy or perfect. It simply means that no matter what we believe, and no matter what happens, we can hold ourselves and our communities to the ethic of "do no harm."

Antonio

We had enrolled many students with disabilities over the years, so I was surprised when our lead special education teacher came to talk to me about an individual education plan (IEP) that was giving her cause for concern. Antonio had been placed at Alliance for the upcoming school year, and his IEP suggested he had a tendency to cause harm.

According to the plan, it was recommended that he be in a most restrictive placement (MRP) setting, which meant his team suggested he should be receiving his education services in a classroom with just a special education teacher and a few other students with exceptional needs. It wasn't unusual for us to enroll students who had been in MRP settings before coming to Alliance, but our program was unique. Our full-inclusion model meant that all students were included in regular education classes, and they would receive the support they needed from a special education teacher in the classroom. To us, this meant less stigma (which meant less bullying), as well as higher expectations and better learning opportunities for all students. We had been very successful with this model, so it was surprising to hear this teacher, who was the first to advocate for equal access for all students, suggest that to support this student we might need to host a traditional MRP classroom within our school walls.

"You have to look at this IEP," she told me. "I'm really concerned. I don't know that we can support someone with this level of needs."

We were a small school, without administrators, security guards, or metal detectors. I looked over the IEP, and I could see why she was concerned. The plan listed numerous fights, suspensions, and expulsion hearings. There were safety plans which described in detail how the student must be escorted within the building to avoid the potential for any fights to develop in the halls. The plan described him as violent, and it was clear that the school had spent a lot of time and energy trying to keep this student away from other students. They had even made sure that he wasn't allowed to participate in the middle school graduation ceremonies with his peers. At this point, we were a school of just twelve staff members, and it seemed like it would be a real challenge for us to escort him to classes and watch his every move. We pondered over whether to do what we had never done before—create a separate MRP classroom for this student and request additional help—or to stick to our full-inclusion practice and do our best to support him with the resources we had. We decided to give him a chance in the regular classes and see what services he might need once he got started.

We had to meet with his family and change his IEP before he started, to make sure they were in agreement and to ensure his plan would reflect the program and services he would be receiving. The team chose only to share his new IEP and the necessary details of his disability with the staff, to avoid forming any preconceived expectations or concerns, and we made sure that the lead special education teacher was scheduled to be in classes with him to support him if necessary. It was a risk we knew could have consequences for teachers, peers, and the school community if it didn't go well. However, we also knew that many students who had been in MRP settings before coming to Alliance had been very successful in the small, personalized classes at Alliance. We hoped that Antonio, too, would flourish in this setting.

We were right to take such a chance on Antonio. Surprisingly, he settled into the regular education program with extraordinary ease, and rather than becoming a fighter, he soon became a leader within the school and community. He participated in everything he was invited to join. He was on the Student Leadership Team, gave tours to visitors, and became a circle keeper in the restorative practices program. At one point, there was an opportunity to help create an American Civil Liberties Union (ACLU) student alliance, and Antonio was the first to volunteer. After that, he became a student ambassador for the ACLU, serving as a nonpartisan observer at protests and advising peers about their rights. When he had been part of the community for a year, and it was time to review his IEP, I asked him about his previous IEP.

"Antonio, I have to be honest with you. Yours was the only IEP I ever saw that made me wonder if we could support the student. That old IEP doesn't seem like you at all! You are the kindest, sweetest person I have ever met! What happened?"

Antonio laughed and blushed a little. "Yeah, I was pretty bad, then, wasn't I? I got into a lot of fights. But it wasn't because I was a bad person, Tina. You know that, right? I was bullied at that school," he said. "I was bullied so bad every day, and I had to fight. That was the only thing I could do. I would just get so mad."

"You know," I teased him a little. "That was the first time I ever thought of calling Central Office and telling them we couldn't take a student, because we didn't have a security guard or anything. It said the security guard had to escort you everywhere! But you know what? I am so glad we took a chance on you, because I just adore you. I want you to know, every day, I am so glad you are here."

"I am so glad I am here, too, Tina," he said. And he gave me a hug, with tears in his eyes.

Young people interact with their environments, and Antonio was the perfect example of how a different setting could mean a different experience for one young person.

He didn't stop there, either. Antonio would go on to receive numerous community awards and recognition for his leadership and advocacy, including being honored with the *Youth Civil Libertarian of the Year Award* from the Milwaukee ACLU Chapter. As a special testament to who he was and all he did to make Alliance a better place, we honored him with the school's Tocarra Wilson Award when he graduated, a special award given every year to the student who best represented the school's ideals. That award was named for another student who was also very special to our community: Tocarra.

Tocarra

We arrived just in time to fill up the seats of the small funeral parlor that had been reserved for Tocarra's service. It was such a sad-feeling place, one that didn't expect to have so many guests for the likes of someone like Tocarra, and I couldn't help but wonder if that room had ever been as full as it was that day. The viewing was almost unbearable. The person who prepared her for the visitation must have only looked at what was between the legs to determine how to dress the body, and never once considered what gender may have been in her heart. When we walked to the front of the room, to our horror, there was Tocarra, dressed like an old man in a suit and tie, and lying in the casket looking like someone we had never met. Tocarra's best friend, Jade, was furious. "What the hell?" she said, pointing at the casket, and searching the room for who would have been responsible for it. Finding no answer in the line of students, friends, and family members waiting for their chance to view the body, she stood up tall and walked angrily to the back of the room, where a few teachers and students stood, huddled in communal fury over what they had seen, and discussing what Tocarra would have wanted instead. When it was time for the service to start, everyone shifted to their seats. My daughter and her best friend sat close to me, arms threaded through mine, tissues in hand, still shocked from the viewing and by the loss of their sweet friend, and my partner gently rubbed my back or squeezed my arm in reassurance each time a shadow of sadness drifted across my face.

Tocarra started attending Alliance the very first year we started the school. She had been one of my students at the high school where I taught before starting Alliance, and she was one of the reasons I felt so passionate about the mission of the school.

Tocarra was a transgender student who was just starting to transition when I first met her. She was lucky to have great family support, and she was very proud of who she was, but at the large high school, she was being harassed and threatened every time she wore women's clothes to school. She would often come to my room between classes just to take a "safety break" before moving on to her next class. The administrators didn't feel they could stop the students from harassing her. "If he would just stop dressing that way, he wouldn't have these problems," they said. She had just about dropped out of school by the time we started Alliance, but she hung on and transferred to the new school as soon as the paperwork could be turned in.

In a very short time, Tocarra was well-loved by the entire Alliance community. She became a mother figure for many of the younger students, and she was always making people feel welcome and accepted. She had a flair for fashion and a desire to be not just noticed, but adored. She was part of a transgender "house" community in Milwaukee and Chicago, and she regularly organized fashion shows and hair competitions. I remember one day she was checking out my winter coat (a long, light-brown princess coat, with a faux-fur trimmed hat and faux-fur trimmed cuffs), and she said to me, "Ms. Owen, when I become a woman, I want to be sexy classy, like you, not sexy slutty." It was one of the nicest compliments I'd ever received.

Late in the evening, one night in that first year, I received a call from one of the students. "Is it true?" she said. "Is Tocarra dead?" She had received a text message from someone, and she was crying when she called. I hadn't heard this from anyone, so I told her not to cry and that I would call her as soon as I found out what was happening. As the evening went on, I learned that it was true. Tocarra had suffered from heart problems in the middle of the night and had passed away. She was just eighteen years old.

I called the staff together that evening for a meeting at my house. We cried together, talked about how much we would miss Tocarra, and then made a plan for how we would talk to the students the following day. We decided we would have a community meeting first thing in the morning, and we would have a crisis team of social workers and support staff ready to talk to any student or staff member who needed to talk. I knew I was going to need their support as much as anyone.

The students were devastated when they learned about Tocarra's death, and I spent much of the morning comforting students who fell apart in my arms. It just didn't seem possible. Tocarra had been fine just days before. She had just flown to New York two weeks earlier to participate in a taping for a Jerry Springer episode, one of those "my girlfriend's really a man" episodes with lots of silly fight talk and drama to no end. Before she left for the show, she asked my opinion about it. I told her she should do what she wanted, but to remember that people already perceive the trans community in negative ways, so she should try not to reinforce the stereotypes. She wasn't one to take her role in the community lightly, so she went back and forth about whether or not she would be part of the show, but in the end, her desire to be a star, even if only for a moment, won out, and she headed to New York for her appearance on the show. I didn't really want her to go, but a couple of weeks later, as our whole school sat in the community meeting, laughing, then crying, as we watched that silly episode, where at one point one of her balloon breasts fell out of her shirt as she attempted to "fight" with her boyfriend's girlfriend, I was glad we had that memory of her.

Most of Tocarra's family lived in Chicago, so it made sense that they would plan to have her funeral there. Although it was a long way for us, many of our students and staff members wanted to attend, so we arranged for a bus. More than half of the students rode the bus that day to attend the service, including Tocarra's dearest friend at Alliance, Jade. In her blonde wig, black dress, and sunglasses, Jade looked like Marilyn Monroe as she walked into the funeral parlor holding my arm. She was also transgender, and despite the questioning looks from a few of the visitors to the service, she walked into that room with all of the pride, beauty, and anguish of a mourning widow.

Things only got harder as the sermon began. The minister did not know Tocarra. He kept calling her by a boy's name that wouldn't have been the correct name even if Tocarra had wanted to be called by her boy name, and I cringed every time he said it. He was a traditional, homophobic, Baptist minister, who preached a sermon that seemed to be condemning Tocarra to an eternity in hell, rather than raising her up for her family and friends. It was as if he was telling us, "I know what he was, and this is a warning for all of the rest of you." I was outraged for Tocarra, and at the very same time, I wanted to cover the ears of all of my students so they wouldn't have to hear the hate that was coming from his lips.

He leaned into the podium, grabbing its sides, his voice loud and angry. "We know sin when we see it, and any God-fearing child who walks on this Earth other than as God formed him is damned . . ."

I could tell that her family was feeling angry and defeated as well. Their heads were down, shoulders hunched, and they glanced at me occasionally shaking their heads.

I couldn't keep anyone from hearing him, and it was awful. Many of the students had experienced that kind of religious condemnation personally enough to know exactly what was happening, and I could feel them as they crumbled inside.

"There is no place in Heaven for the sinner who rebukes the message of the one and only Lord, Savior, Jesus Christ . . ."

The more he preached, the more upset they became, and soon the ones sitting close to me, including my daughter and her best friend, started nudging me. "Do something," they whispered. "He can't talk about her like that. He's wrong." They were right. I couldn't stand it any longer, either, so I did something I never imagined I would do—I raised my hand and asked if I could speak. The minister looked from me to Tocarra's family, who sat across the aisle, looking as if they wanted to disappear into the fabric of the carpet. I looked at Tocarra's family and said, "May I speak?"

Tocarra's mother nodded to me, uncertain but hopeful, the weight of the minister's words too much for a young mother who had already lost her child and couldn't bear the thought of losing the promise of seeing her baby in the afterlife, as well. "Please," she said, and the other members of her family nodded, as well.

I went up to the pulpit and started to talk about Tocarra as I knew her. I spoke about the young *woman* who was loving and accepting and funny, and who never gave up on anyone. I spoke about the person who had helped to build our school, with all of her great ideas and insights, and how she would never be forgotten by any of us. And most importantly, I spoke about how Tocarra had earned her place in heaven with her loving ways, her joyful spirit, her commitment to helping others. And I reassured her family and her friends that they need not worry, because we would all see her there someday. If anyone deserved a place in heaven, it was Tocarra. When I was done, I invited her family and friends to come up and speak. Her mother came first, and then her brothers, and then people lined up to share their memories. We laughed, cried, hugged each other, and sang her blessings to the universe. It was beautiful, and I'd never felt so proud of anything I'd done ever in my life. So many people lined up that eventually the minister had to stop the line and ask that people save their stories for the burial, because there were other services that had to take place in that room that day. I think he was angry, but he didn't dare try to change the story that had grown out of that room. People were emboldened now, and they weren't about to let him pin the weight of sin back on the life of the young, beautiful spirit of a woman that they had known.

That afternoon, I rode the bus back to Milwaukee in silent sadness, grateful for the chance to speak Tocarra's truth, but exhausted by the past several days of holding myself together for the students and staff. So many thoughts ran through my head as we traveled. I grieved for the loss of this young person who had become such a central figure in my life for the past couple of years. I mourned for what the world had lost in losing such a person, someone who really could change the world and make it better. I wondered about the courage that had lifted my hand in that moment when I couldn't take the minister's words any longer. And I prayed for Tocarra and for all of the fabulous transgender souls that had gone to rest in less than fabulous fashion.

That year, as we prepared for our first graduation, we knew Tocarra had to be part of it with us. We decided to create an award that we would give out in her honor every year to the person who best represented the ideals of Alliance. That first year, and every year after, we have given the Tocarra Wilson Award to the student who best represented those ideals for their entire time at Alliance. We remember Tocarra for what she brought into the world, and now, even in her afterlife, she gets to do what she did best in this life—inspire others to be their best selves.

ACCEPTING *ALL* STUDENTS

The mission of the Alliance School is to be a safe, student-centered, and academically challenging environment to meet the needs of *all* students. Everyone in the school knows that "all students" includes lesbian, gay, bisexual, and transgender students. They also know that "all students" includes straight students, students with disabilities, Christian or Muslim students, and anyone else who chooses to be part of our school community.

It is the mission that drives who we are and that brings students to the school. The mission statement is pervasive—it's on our recruitment materials and on our walls. Most importantly, thanks to the repetition and reinforcement, it's in the hearts and minds of the staff and students. Because of this, it is not unusual to see Alliance students welcoming new students— no matter what they look like or why they chose to come here—with hugs and offers to show them around. It is also common to hear students correcting other students when they say something offensive to or about another student. "We don't do that here," they say.

When new students are considering enrolling at the school, we are explicit about the mission of the school. We are sure to tell them that Alliance is a safe and accepting place for all students. We express to them that the most important thing they will need at Alliance is the ability to get along with all types of people, and we let them know that this means that they will be accepted for who they are, as well.

Any school can create a radically accepting environment like this one. It's about accepting students for who they are and holding ourselves and our students to the belief that even when we disagree, it is never okay to harm another person.

4

LGBTQ Youth and Bullying

According to the 2015 YRBS, LGB students were 140%
(12% vs. 5%) more likely to not go to school at least one
day during the 30 days prior to the survey because of safety
concerns, compared with heterosexual students.

US CENTERS FOR DISEASE CONTROL
AND PREVENTION[1]

I COULD NOT DISCUSS how we fostered an antibullying culture at the Alliance School without talking about how we created a safe and inclusive space for lesbian, gay, bisexual, transgender, and queer/questioning (LGBTQ) students. LGBTQ students, and those who are perceived to be part of the LGBTQ community, are bullied more often than their heterosexual peers because of the sexism and homophobia that exist as an undercurrent in our society. There are subtle ways, and not so subtle ways, in which this happens in schools every day.

Just as I was writing this book, I saw an example of this while visiting a highly regarded middle school. A group of three boys were standing in line in the hallway, and the boy who was second in line was repeatedly saying to the boy at the front of the line, "Ladies first! Ladies first!" The boy at the front started to try to switch places with the boy behind him, who, of course, would not move to the front of the line. Neither would the third boy. Nobody wanted to be called a lady, not even if it meant having the lead at the front of the line. This was a small example of the way sexism and homophobia play out subtly in schools every day. For these young men, nothing could be worse than being perceived as feminine, or less than manly.

For many LGBTQ students, and those who are perceived to be LGBTQ, the consequences are more serious. Jamie Nabozny was a student in Ashland, Wisconsin, in the late 80s and early 90s. As a teen, he experienced such serious bullying at school that he repeatedly left school to avoid it, and twice he attempted suicide.[2] At one point, a group of boys cornered him and his brother in a bathroom and beat them up horribly. Another time, a group of students repeatedly touched him and performed a mock rape in front of his peers. In all of the incidents, the principal refused to protect him, telling him and his parents that "boys would be boys," and that as long as he continued to be out about his sexuality, the bullying would continue. Later, while in high school, one of the same bullies urinated on him, and the high school principal did nothing except tell Jamie to go home and change his clothes. The bullying was so persistent that he eventually dropped out of school, ran away from home, and went to live with a foster family in another state. No student, no matter their appearance, sexual orientation, or belief system, should ever face this kind of intentional humiliation and harm.

That should be enough to compel all schools to protect young people. Unfortunately, in this case it was not enough, so Jamie decided to push to make sure that the Ashland schools weren't so inclined to look the other way. In 1996, he worked with Lambda Legal to sue his former school district and several of the officials. The legal team argued that his rights to Equal Protection, under the Fourteenth Amendment, had been violated. A jury agreed. They awarded him $962,000 in damages. Today, Jamie travels around speaking to youth and adults about the effects of bullying and how to stop it.[3]

This was just one of many lawsuits that organizations such as Lambda Legal took on. Yet thirty years later, and despite numerous other court findings like this one, anti-gay bullying persists in many schools. A simple search of the internet brings up stories of violent assaults, persistent harassment, and suicides of young people who didn't want to face anti-gay bullying any longer. Parents and students often report the bullying, yet many school administrators choose not to address the issues, while others don't even know how to begin to address them. This chapter is meant to fill that gap.

Part of the Alliance mission has always been to be a safe and inclusive place for LGBTQ students. As a young teacher, I saw the differential treatment and bullying of LGBTQ youth and committed myself to changing that story for young people. It shouldn't matter who you are or what you believe in. No one should ever be allowed to cause another person harm without consequence or concern, and LGBTQ students are still experiencing a great deal of harm in schools.

THE LGBTQ EXPERIENCE IN SCHOOLS

While things have improved, the experience of school for LGBTQ students is still one that is fraught with tensions and fears. According to the results of the Youth Risk Behavior Survey (conducted by the US Centers for Disease Control and Prevention), lesbian, gay, and bisexual (LGB) students still experience higher rates of verbal and physical violence in schools.[4] Thirty-four percent of self-identified LGB youth reported having been bullied at school. Forty percent of students reported that they had seriously considered suicide, and twenty-eight percent had attempted suicide in the year before the survey.[5] Debates about bathrooms and wedding cakes perpetuate news cycles and have found their way to our states' courtrooms, while LGBTQ students sit in the crossfire. While adults debate how or whether to accept that there are LGBTQ students in schools, the students themselves feel the impact.

My experiences teaching in a large high school exemplify some of the challenges that these youth face in school. Being the adviser for the school's GSA was no easy task. While the principal had expressed support for the club, she struggled to support the club's activities. Every time the students tried to accomplish something, the principal came to the group with fear and skepticism. When the group planned to participate in the Day of Silence, the principal came and said it must be stopped. When the students planned a memorial for victims of violence, the principal said it made people uncomfortable. Whatever the group decided to do, there was always a battle to be fought, so while she expressed support, the group never felt truly supported. When questions arose about what constituted discrimination, she often wavered between protecting the students and protecting her staff. This played out again and again throughout the year.

The first time I encountered this was when I learned that some staff members were telling gay students that they were going to hell. When the students went to the principal with their complaints, the principal said, "They have their beliefs, and you have yours. That's their beliefs. There's nothing I can do about that." This made the students angry, but they had learned to expect that being out meant accepting that some people would disapprove—and would not be quiet about it. They shouldered these verbal assaults, but when it came to discriminatory practices they had a harder time letting it go. One such moment happened when an assistant principal shut out students from other schools who had been attending the GSA meetings after school.

Our GSA had about fifty members, and we had been successfully meeting for several months at the school. Students from other schools in the community were attending the afterschool meetings because their schools didn't have GSAs. One day, when the students showed up at school for the meeting, one of the assistant principals, who had expressed his distaste for homosexuals and homosexuality on many occasions, turned them away. He said, "We cannot allow students from other schools to attend meetings here. It's an insurance issue."

I knew that this was not true, because there were many groups that met after school in the building, and many of those groups were made up of students and community members who did not attend the school. There was even a community recreation program that held evening classes and programs in the school. A few of the students decided to push back. They contacted central office administrators and investigated the claim that this was an insurance issue. It took two months, but they finally got an answer:

School buildings belong to the public, and any community group has a right to use the building for meetings or group activities. It was a small victory for the students, and the afterschool meetings were, once again, open to students from other schools.

By then, it was almost too late. The combination of daily abuse by peers and discrimination by adults was becoming intolerable. Many of the students who had attended the GSA meetings stopped coming to school altogether. These students were fighting battles that no young person should ever have to face in school, and most days, they were afraid to walk into the building. Because of this, their grades dropped. They went from activism to apathy as they found themselves virtually powerless to fight the fight. For some of them, participation in the GSA had been their first act of community activism, and the outright discrimination by the adults who were supposed to protect them, on top of everything else, made them feel hopeless.

We kept the group going, but, as the year went on, things started to get more and more heated between the gay students and the assistant principal who had stopped the GSA students at the door. He suspended students again and again for doing things such as holding hands in the hallway or wearing rainbows—because it "caused a disruption." The fear that students had of their parents finding out that they were gay often kept them from fighting back.

When a couple of students did decide to push back, things got serious. Two girls came to me one day holding suspension notes in their hands. They were both good students. They were on the honor roll and involved in everything from sports to student council. They had never been in trouble before, and they looked shocked to be holding the suspension slips in their hands. I took one of the slips and looked at it. It said that they were suspended for three days for "performing sexual acts in public." I was shocked when I read it, and I looked up at them with a questioning look.

"It's not true," they said. "We were just play wrestling over a cell phone, and we got suspended for it." It was hard to imagine they could have been suspended so seriously for such a small thing, but it was even harder to imagine that they would have been "performing sexual acts in public."

"Could they have done something?" I wondered.

It seemed like I was always the one standing up for LGBTQ students, and I was always careful to make sure I had all the facts before I took on a charge, so I listened carefully to everything they had to say, and then promised to investigate it further.

I wasn't sure where I was even going to start with this one. And then one of the school security guards came to see me.

"They didn't do it," he said.

I hadn't talked to this security guard much, so I was surprised that he was coming to me.

"They didn't do it," he said, again. "And there's a tape. I was video recording in the cafeteria when it happened, and I saw it. They were just playing around. One girl was trying to get the cell phone from the other girl, and they fell off the table laughing. They weren't doing anything wrong. It's on the tape. You just have to ask to see it. They shouldn't have been suspended, especially not for what he said they were being suspended for."

Armed with what he had told me, I went to the assistant principal to advocate for the girls, thinking he would be reasonable and realize his mistake. He wouldn't hear it. He told me he knew what he had seen, and he wasn't changing his mind.

"Let's look at the tape, then," I said.

The look of shock that crossed his face was unmistakable.

"What tape?" he said.

"The security guard was recording, and it's all on tape. I want to see the tape."

At this point he became angry.

"What right do you have asking me to see the tape?" he asked. "These are not your children. This is not your school. I am the administrator here. What right do you have questioning me?"

I could tell he was furious, but I was young and unafraid, especially when I felt that justice wasn't being served. His refusal to show me the tape just made me more certain that there was something there that he didn't want me to see.

"So, if I was one of their parents, you would show me the tape?" I asked.

"Of course I would," he said. "But you are not their parents. If their parents want to see the tape, they can ask me. Now, get out."

This administrator knew that the girls did not want their parents to know they were gay, and he was counting on that. After speaking to a friend at the ACLU and getting the information on how to pursue a discrimination case, I went and spoke to one of the girls who was still at school. I told her I had not been allowed to see the tape, and that I would like to talk to her parents about it. She was very nervous, because she knew the administrator would use the opportunity to tell her parents she was gay, but she was also unwilling to sit back and let the suspension be on her record as it had been written. She was a strong student and didn't want it to affect her chances of attending a good college or finding a job. I told her this was an equal rights issue, and I shared the information I had gathered from the ACLU. She agreed to go forward.

She asked me a few questions, and then I called her home. I spoke to her parents about the suspension and told them I believed she might have been unfairly suspended. I told them about my interaction with the assistant principal and how he had refused to show me the tape. I explained that he had promised to show them if they asked. These parents were very involved parents and were grateful for the call. They promised to go right to the office the next morning and request to see the tape. The next morning, they did just that, and when the assistant principal said that there was no tape, they asked to see the principal and threatened to call the ACLU.

When the principal heard what was going on, she offered a compromise. She offered to reinstate the students immediately and to remove the suspensions from their records. While the parents would have preferred to see the tape, they also did not want their daughter dragged into a public court case where her sexuality would be revealed to the public. They agreed to the compromise and left it at that.

While the situation was resolved, and I was grateful for that, there was something about the whole thing that left me feeling like we had still lost the battle. The students' academic records were saved, but the greater issue of the unfairness of the suspensions was left unaddressed, and I knew there would be more and more incidents like this to come. It felt like my students would always be fighting just to survive in the school, and they would never get to just be themselves and focus on graduating. In the coming months, as I saw the attendance rates of these two brilliant students dropping, I knew we had to do something different. School shouldn't have to be just about survival. These students should have the right to thrive, just like anyone else, and I knew it was possible.

That's when I started to write. I went home and found all the information I could about bullying, the experiences of LGBTQ students in schools, and how to create safe and inclusive environments in schools. I looked up the guidelines for the New Vision of Secondary Education grants sponsored by the Gates Foundation that a speaker at our staff meeting had spoken of, asked my students to make brochures for the perfect school, and then asked a couple of teachers if they were interested in helping to create a school with a mission of addressing bullying. When they said yes, we got to work. At this point, the proposal deadline was only forty-eight hours away, but we knew what we had to do. We took all of the information we had—from the students, from our personal experiences, and from the research—wrote our proposal, and submitted it. Then, all we could do was wait. In the meantime, we continued to teach and go on with life as usual, not hoping too much, but keeping our fingers crossed, just the same. A few months later, we received a letter. Our proposal had been selected, and we were going to start a school. We had $50,000 and a year to plan, and if we did everything right, in just a little over a year, we would open the Alliance School.

THE CHOICE TO CREATE OUR OWN SCHOOL

The choice to start a separate, explicitly gay-friendly school was not without controversy. Too many battles had been fought in history to ensure that minority groups would not have to attend segregated schools. Starting a school for students who had been bullied felt a little bit risky, even to me. But the reality was that the current schools were not able or willing to provide an equal learning experience for LGBTQ youth and bullied students within the school walls, so for these students to receive a comparable education, something radical needed to happen. We needed to create a separate school.

As we planned the school, we kept this controversy in mind. One thing we never wanted to be was a school that was just for LGBTQ students or bullied students. It was important to us that the school enroll students from all backgrounds, abilities, and beliefs. This way, we could show that it is possible to allow people to have their own beliefs while still protecting young people from harm. We also felt very strongly that we didn't want to create a separate learning environment, leaving the oppressors behind. It was important to us that one of our goals was to stop the bullying in the schools our students had come from, while creating a place of strength and support for these students to heal, grow, and learn. We made it part of our design that our students and staff would engage in teaching others about bullying, so that all schools could become safe and accepting places for all students. We also made it clear that our mission included supporting and teaching others about the LGBTQ community.

One of the first things we did when writing our proposal was to be explicit in our vision that we would be a safe place for LGBTQ students. This vision became part of everything we did as a school. LGBTQ students were listed in our brochures and in our tagline—"The Alliance School— a place where it's okay to be black, white, gay, straight, Christian, gothic, Buddhist, disabled, or just plain unique!" We created a mission that would be explicit about our desire to serve all students, and we worked with the LGBTQ community to learn what we needed to learn to make our school a gay-friendly school.

For any school to be a safe school, the mission of being a safe place for LGBTQ students must be explicit, and schools must consciously work at this. While I understand there are people who have strong religious or personal beliefs against homosexuality, from my experience, even these people can still agree that it's never okay to hurt someone because you believe something different than they do. If a school can start with an agreement to "do no harm," then it will have taken a huge leap forward in making schools safe places to learn for all students. Whether it is a transgender student, a Goth kid, or a football player, the school must take a stand to make school safe for every child. At Alliance, we take deliberate steps to make sure that the LGBTQ students feel safe and accepted at school. For us, this is a human right, which we work hard to guarantee to every student. We do this in many ways.

Educating Our Community

We start by educating our community. At the beginning of each school year, we provide professional development for all of our teachers and workshops for students on LGBTQ facts and policies. Many students, and some staff, do not know the definitions of what it means to be lesbian, gay, bisexual, or transgender. We teach people about the difference between sex and gender, and how people sometimes identify in ways that are not apparent to the people looking at them. We make it clear that people may have strong feelings about what it means to be gay, but that it is not okay to harm others for those beliefs, just like you would not harm someone for adultery or disobeying a parent, even if you felt like those were religious commandments.

We make some things very clear: We do not tolerate homophobic comments or actions. We will always call students by preferred gender pronouns and names. Families come in all shapes and sizes—and we accept them all. And students are able to use the bathrooms that align with their gender identities. We let the students know from the beginning that these things are nonnegotiable within our community, and that students will be held accountable for violating these norms.

We start by making our norms explicit, but we don't stop there. We aim to make sure that LGBTQ students know that they are loved and supported, just as they are. This isn't always easy, in a world that often pushes back so hard, but we do our best, in so many ways.

Gender-Neutral Bathrooms

The debate about bathrooms for transgender students is one that seems to plague the news cycles, yet in reality, we didn't find this to be much of an issue at our school. When students used the bathrooms that aligned to their expressed gender identities, everyone was comfortable. We didn't always know this. When we first opened our school, we thought it would be possible to make all bathrooms gender neutral and allow students to use the bathrooms of their choosing. This practice was fairly typical in businesses and universities, so we didn't anticipate any issues. Unfortunately, some straight boys would follow girls into the bathroom, and the girls complained about these boys harassing them there. They never had these issues with transgender students. As time went on, we found that it was important for us to insist that students use the bathrooms that aligned to their *expressed* gender identities. This meant that if a student identified as female, she would use the restroom for female students. If a student identified as male, he would use the restroom for male students. We also had a gender-neutral bathroom, which had a lock on the door and the expectation that students use it one at a time. This made it possible for students who were nongendered or didn't conform to a gender binary to use a restroom that did not differentiate individuals by gender identity. It turned out that many students, gender-conforming and not, preferred the gender-neutral bathroom because of the privacy gained by having a "room of one's own."

Prom King and Prom Queen

Another thing we did was to allow any student to run for prom king or prom queen without regard to perceived or expressed gender identity. Many times over the years, female students have won the vote for prom king, or transgender females have won the honor of prom queen, and the votes by their peers suggest that these honors have more to do with the character of the individuals than with any sort of popularity or gender identity. It always seemed that the people who had been the most supportive of their peers won these honors. At Alliance, it was like the prom court had somehow become a symbol of having been the "most friendly classmate" or the "least likely to bully peers." This always made us happy as a staff, especially the year when the student named prom queen was a well-loved student who had cognitive disabilities. She was so happy to have won the honor, and the whole community was thrilled for her to have the recognition.

LGBTQ Inclusive Images and Messages

Just walking through the school building reveals that Alliance is a different kind of place. Signs and images of LGBTQ inclusiveness are on the walls and in the curriculum. Many teachers have rainbow schoolhouse stickers on their classroom doors, or posters with messages of LGBTQ acceptance. One poster, titled "Every Girl Every Boy," carried a message about liberation from gender norms. It was designed by J. T. Bunnell and Irit Reinheimer and was based on a poem by Nancy R. Smith. The poster started with, "For every girl who is tired of acting weak when she is strong, there is a boy tired of appearing strong when he feels vulnerable . . ." Another poster gave students a list of adjectives they could use to replace the common use of "that's so gay." *Gay* was crossed out and replaced with a list of words, including *obnoxious, ridiculous, awful, despicable, absurd*, and *uncool*.

When students see images, hear messages, and read stories that have characters who look and act like them, they feel affirmed and respected. These kinds of symbolic acts carry a lot of weight in communicating what teachers and staff will accept. They are simple adaptations to teaching and learning, yet they say to LGBTQ students and others that it is unacceptable to cause harm to anyone, and that *anyone* includes LGBTQ and gender nonconforming students.

An Explicit Focus on the Transgender Community

The realities faced by LGBTQ students, especially in urban centers, are often grim. Kicked out of their homes by parents and foster parents, many LGBTQ youth find themselves victims of homelessness, human trafficking, and sexual victimization.

One afternoon, I was walking around during club time, and I came upon the Dance Club that was just forming that day. Many of the students had been asking for such a club, and one of the new teachers had kindly agreed to advise it. When I walked into the room, I found the teacher clearly frustrated by a scene that she had not been prepared for. Several of the students were grinding on the floor, pretending to take off their clothes, and emulating strippers on the stage. Many of these students were transgender, and the scene was particularly upsetting to me because I know how easily transgender youth are pulled into the sex trade for survival and a sense of acceptance. I stopped the music and told them we were not going to have that kind of dance club at Alliance. It's very rare that I will step into a position of authority and say "absolutely not." I have a strong belief in student voice and personal decision-making, but I could not know what I know about transgender youth and let it go on. The students were clearly upset, and no amount of talking about it was going to change that.

"I want to be a stripper when I grow up," one of them said, and several other students nodded their heads in agreement. I could tell they were not just trying to be antiauthoritarian. They truly believed this was a perfectly acceptable plan for the future and that we should support them in their decisions. This was a hard moment for me. I had been doing work in this community for too long, and I knew too much about the world they wanted to be part of. It was a world of drugs, abuse, sexual assault, and violence, and I had lost too many students to it. I certainly didn't want any of that for these kids that I loved. But I didn't have a way to communicate that in a way that wouldn't be discounting their personal experiences and realities. I had to stand my ground and then spend some time thinking over the weekend about how I could begin to address these real and pressing issues.

By Monday morning, I had more than just something to say. I had a plan. The superintendent had asked us to write a letter with our goals and our vision for the upcoming school year. I knew that I could not address achievement in the school without addressing the lack of academic focus within the transgender circle in our school, so I decided that this would be my focus for the year. I wrote the following letter to my supervisor and to the superintendent.

A Place of Hope for All Students

Dear Superintendent and Regional Superintendent,

When I was a brand-new teacher at Washington High School many years ago and didn't have money for posters and other fancy classroom decorations, I printed out funny road signs with messages that could be interpreted as academic messages and hung them around the room. I knew that my students would "read" their environment and that the messages they found there would stay with them for a lifetime, so even though I didn't have a lot of resources to work with, I knew I had to create an inviting and hopeful space for them. I also took five large pieces of white paperboard, and I did a little bit of a graffiti art. I spray-painted the words "Let this be your place of hope," and I hung those words on the wall above the bulletin board. It's been fourteen years, and students I taught way back then still remind me of those words on the wall and how much it meant to them to read that every day.

I have always believed that giving students a sense of hope is at the core of teaching and learning, especially in middle and high school. If they don't have that sense of hope, they don't have the motivation that it takes to achieve, and if they don't have the motivation to achieve, we all fail.

Once again, I am working in an environment of dwindling resources, and I am still working to bring a sense of hope to all of my students, some of whom live lives that no young person should ever have to live.

This year I intend to focus my energies on bringing that hope and building an academic community within the transgender community at our school. Approximately ten percent of our students identify as transgender, and while we have done a phenomenal job of building an environment of acceptance for them at Alliance, we have been less successful in getting our transgender students to achieve at high academic levels in the classroom. This is a group that we need to be intentional with if we are going to meet the academic goals that we have set for ourselves.

We know that the transgender community is a community that is particularly vulnerable to street crime, homelessness, sexual assault, and discrimination. The sense of hopelessness that many of these young people feel is devastating, and this has a measurable effect on individual and the school's achievement. Many of our transgender youth are absent for days at a time, as they bounce from living situation to living situation. This affects our attendance rates. Many of our transgender youth have been out of school so much that they have academic delays that make it difficult for them to be successful in the classroom, so they choose to avoid their classes. Yet they always return to school, which makes me believe that they still get a sense of hope from this place. Now we have to help them achieve.

To do this, we will start with a survey for our transgender youth to find out what their needs, barriers, interests, and hopes are. We will use this as a benchmark survey and will follow up with another one at the end of the school year to see what change has taken place.

Second, we will focus on credit attainment and grade level promotion. Right now, many of our transgender youth are far behind their grade level peers in credit attainment. So, we will focus on developing a credit recovery effort specifically aimed at this group of students.

Third, we will identify agencies in the community that can help us to do this work. There are agencies, such as FORGE and the LGBT Community Center of Milwaukee, who can provide resources and speakers for our staff and our students, so that we can better understand the needs of this target group of students.

All of these efforts, if done well, should lead to more in-class participation, credit attainment and grade level promotion for our transgender students. We will identify and track the data for these students, so that we can measure the results of our efforts.

Measurable Goal: Eighty percent of our self-identified transgender students will show an increase in credit attainment in the 2012–2013 school year, as compared to the previous school year.

You and the staff at MPS Central Services can assist by learning about the needs and struggles of this community of learners and by sharing stories of joy and success with us, as often as you can.

I have always said, that the hardest thing about the work that we do is carrying home the stories of our young people, so we need all of you to help us keep a sense of hope in this community, as well.

Sincerely,

Tina M. Owen
Lead Teacher, The Alliance School

I never heard back from the superintendent or the regional superintendent about my plan, but we continued, as a staff, to focus our efforts around meeting the needs of this community. Because of this, we exceeded our goal and noticed a marked improvement in student engagement. Forging relationships with trans-friendly workplaces and organizations helped our students to see possibilities beyond high school. Working with a local arts agency to do a collaborative project with a neighborhood organization dealing with sex trafficking victims made it possible for our young people to hear the stories of people like them who had been lulled into a world of sex, drugs, and danger. And working with local authorities to identify and deter sexual predators who had been circling our building made our school community feel just a little bit safer, at least when our students were behind the school's doors.

The realities facing the transgender community were often unthinkable, and with our minuscule budget, it was a real challenge to support the needs that often resulted from experiences outside of the school's walls. But we couldn't be a nonbullying school if we didn't make their needs a priority. This was the group that faced more threats of bullying than any student group we had known. If the school was needed by any one group, it was needed by them first.

NEVER TOO CONTROVERSIAL TO SAVE LIVES

Many good-hearted people wonder whether it is too controversial to approach the needs of the LGBTQ communities in schools. I even wondered whether or not to include a separate chapter on meeting the needs of LGBTQ students. The reality is that we cannot address the issue of bullying without addressing LGBTQ bullying, as this makes up a significant percentage of the bullying that takes place in schools.

It is not too controversial to talk about LGBTQ issues. It is essential. So many times, LGBTQ young people get the message that if they could just keep quiet about their sexuality, they wouldn't have any problems. First, this is not true, as more students are bullied for their perceived sexuality than for their true, self-identified sexuality. And second, it's not a student's job to hide parts of themselves just so others can feel comfortable. It's the other person's responsibility to examine his or her discomfort and put it in its place. Schools must hold people accountable to this. There is no excuse for causing harm to another individual, no matter how their beliefs line up or don't line up with our own. We can make schools safe for all students, and we must start by making it clear that LGBTQ students have a place of acceptance in our schools.

5

Extraordinary Care

*If you can find it in your heart to care for
somebody else, you will have succeeded.*
MAYA ANGELOU

A COMMITMENT TO EXTRAORDINARY CARE on the part of teachers
and staff is at the heart of building any caring culture. This kind of
care does not stop at the school door, nor does it stop at the end of the school
day. It is an ever-present kind of care, one that often exceeds stated job requirements or professional expectations. While many teachers in schools
around the country demonstrate this kind of care, at Alliance we have
thought deeply about how we will intentionally practice this kind of care.

When we ask students to practice living peacefully together, to believe
in an antibullying mission, we are asking them to care. Students can't become what they can't see, which means what the school models is even
more important than what the school says. Our students see what it means
to care when they look at us. This didn't happen by accident. From the beginning, our mission was centered around Abraham Maslow's hierarchy of
needs. We were creating a school that would prevent and address bullying,
and we were doing so because we believed that if students didn't feel safe,

they could not focus on academics and intellectual pursuits. This was one of the core precepts of Maslow's pyramid. As we built our school, we built this kind of extraordinary care, this commitment to supporting the whole child, into everything we did.

A FRAMEWORK FOR CARING

There is a quote that you will often hear in education circles: "If the students don't know that you care, they won't care what you know." As a young teacher, I heard this often, and it was something I saw and believed deeply. I had learned about Maslow's framework in my teacher preparation, so when I started my teaching career, it was always in my mind that part of my role as a teacher was to ensure that students had what they needed to thrive. In my early years, this meant I did way too much. I gave out Christmas presents, took in homeless students, prepared meals for my track team, made sure students had coats and gloves, helped students make doctor's appointments, and even became a foster parent. I wouldn't change any of it. But before long, despite my good intentions, I found myself exhausted and overwhelmed. At some point, I had to realize, for myself and for my own children, that there were other people who had time, love, and rooms in their homes, too. I took a chance and started to ask for help from others, and I was surprised by the outpouring of support from those around me. It was with this new knowledge that I started the Alliance School, and it was Maslow's hierarchy of needs that helped us to frame what it meant to care, and how we could all shoulder that responsibility. How I imagine Maslow's hierarchy of needs in schools can be seen in figure 5.1.

For a student to be able to pursue self-actualization, which is truly the aim of education, he or she must have a strong basis in their other needs being met. We all experience moments in our lives when one or more of the needs is not met for a time, or is not being well met, but to be open to the ideas of self-development and futuristic thinking, one must be in a space where these needs *are* being met. This puts schools in the space of having to think about these needs in order to attain the goals of education.

FIGURE 5.1 *A student view of Maslow's hierarchy of needs*

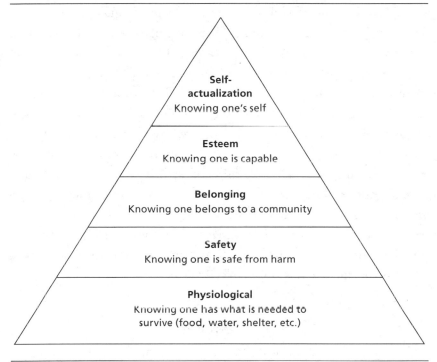

Adapted from Maslow's hierarchy of needs, in Abraham Maslow, "A Theory of Human Motivation," *Psychological Review* 50 (1943): 370–396, https://psychclassics.yorku.ca/Maslow/motivation.htm

As we planned the school, we knew this, so we worked with the community to create support systems for young people. Starting at the base of the pyramid, we asked ourselves, "What must we do to make sure these physiological needs are met?" We collaborated with youth homeless shelters and food pantries. We created a clothing and necessities "store" made up of donations from the community. We collected toiletries, socks, and feminine products, so students would have what they needed. We even installed a washer and dryer at the school, so families and students could do their wash if necessary. When it came to safety, we researched and built our model to be an exemplar of what it takes to build a safe community. We hired a full-time social worker, and created systems for reporting and addressing bullying and threats. And we worked hard to build a community that watched out for each other. The things we did to build positive relationships also became the cornerstones for belonging, and we built numerous opportunities for students to lead, create, and feel success in the community. All of this gave students a sense of esteem, and all of the pieces together opened the doors to learning and self-actualization. It wasn't enough to just teach students. We had to build the community around them, ensuring they could work and learn in a space where their needs were met, or they never would have been able to step into a learning stance. When you are in survival mode, it's hard to think of anything else.

Since this knowledge was a key concept guiding our planning and practice, it was embedded into our school mission: "The mission of The Alliance School is to be a safe, student-centered, and academically challenging environment to meet the needs of all students." It was a mission we could be proud of, and one that was personal for me.

IT'S PERSONAL

Most adults have a personal story for how they found themselves where they landed. It's no different for me. As a teenager, I faced the realities of poverty when my father went to prison. In an instant, we went from a middle-class family into deep poverty. My mother, who had been a homemaker for seventeen years, was suddenly on her own with four children between the ages of seven and thirteen. We were shipped from Guam to the continental US, and we had nothing. My mother found work at a local fast-food restaurant and at a chiropractor's office, but the two minimum-wage jobs barely provided enough to pay the rent. It was tough.

I was the oldest, and I was the one who had spoken up about my father's abuse, so I carried a lot of guilt for the weight of the poverty, and that guilt and sadness followed me to school every day. Things were so hard. We rarely, if ever, received birthday or Christmas presents over the next few years, and if my mom forgot to fill out the lunch form, which it seemed like she often did, it meant a whole year without free lunches.

Throughout those years, I would often miss school because we didn't have quarters to do laundry. No one in school ever asked how I was doing, why I was absent, or checked in on our family. As time went on, I went to school less and less, had a child at sixteen, and was on the verge of dropping out. Finally, I was recommended for night school, where I was told that if I got enough credits and took the GED test, I could earn a high school diploma. One guidance counselor in the night school program saw something in me and wouldn't let me quit. She checked on me often, made sure I had childcare arrangements, and pushed me to run for class vice president, which seemed outrageous at the time. "Just get enough credits to graduate," she would say, so I did it for her. I never imagined that years later I would become a teacher, but I give her a lot of credit for helping me to land in a position where I could go to college if I ever wanted to.

Four years after high school, I did want to go to college, and later, when I decided I wanted to be a teacher, those years in high school would have a huge impact on the teacher I would become. I remembered how hard it was to concentrate without food. I had felt the embarrassment of having your stomach growl out loud in a quiet classroom. And I knew what it was like to go through the holidays without any recognition from anyone who cared.

As a teacher, I wanted things to be different for my students. I always tried to make sure I had snacks available for anyone who was hungry and simple presents to give to my students during the holidays. It may have just been an ornament with a handwritten quote on it (because my meager teacher's salary forced me to be creative), but I made sure every student received something.

These practices followed me to Alliance, where I was able to find teachers who felt the same way, and funders who believed as much as we did that all students deserved meals if they were hungry, opportunities to participate in school activities without worrying about school fees, and gifts for the holidays. Every year, we would host fundraisers, and with those funds we would ensure that every student could have a free lunch, that there would be a part-time nurse practitioner in the school, that school fees would be covered if a student needed it, and that every student received a gift before the winter break.

The gift shopping was one of my favorite events of the year. We would list the names of all of the students, and the teachers would divide the list based on who we had relationships with or who we knew something about. Then, we would go shopping and buy a personalized, ten-dollar or less gift for every student in the school. We would wrap every gift and, on the day before the winter break, we would have a big, catered lunch, and we would give every student his or her personal, wrapped present.

I'll never forget one boy who loved basketball more than anything. He was always borrowing the school's basketball, so we bought him his own basketball to take home and keep. You could tell what it was, despite the creative wrapping job, but he wasn't about to open it. When I joked with him about opening it, he said to me, very seriously "No, Tina. I know this is going to be my only gift under the tree this year, because I'm the oldest, and my parents have to buy for the little ones. I'm going to take this home and put it under the tree." And then he hugged me and said, "Thank you, Tina," and he walked out of the building toward the buses. That was a moment when I truly knew the impact of what we were doing.

THE TEACHER'S ROLE

It is clear from the examples above that the role of a teacher is more than just instructional. It always has been. Every now and then, you will find someone who will say that it is not a teacher's job to care about students. In reality, not caring is not an option, especially in a school with a mission such as ours.

At Alliance, we hired people who understood that caring was part of their role as a teacher. We looked for signs of extraordinary care in their resumes, such as leading service trips, advising student clubs, and taking college classes with a focus on social justice or psychology. These were things that often went beyond program or teaching requirements and demonstrated a deep commitment to doing whatever it takes to support young people.

When we interviewed teachers, we asked questions that asked them to share how they would respond to a student in need, or how they might support students who need additional help (some of these questions are listed in appendix B). For example, we asked, "You're walking in the hall and a student cusses at you. What would you do?" There are two ways teachers usually responded to this question—by suggesting they would refer the student to an administrator for disciplinary consequences, or by saying that if a student was cussing at him or her, something must be wrong. For us, the latter response was a sign that this was someone who cared deeply about young people.

Once on our teaching team, our teachers made care for our students visible in their everyday actions and in many of our schoolwide traditions and practices. Our teachers were always bringing food and clothes to share, passing on furniture to young people who were moving into their first apartments, and connecting students and parents to our social worker to get resources for the families. We collected hygiene products and toiletries so that no student would ever have to go without them. If one of us traveled, we brought home the soaps and shampoos from hotels to fill our stockpile of toiletries. When we hosted school-supply drives, we requested socks and deodorant on the list of requested supplies, and, when we left for the summer intercession, we made sure that all of our students had information about who to call if they needed support. We were always trying to think of the next thing we could do to make sure our students got to school, had their needs met, and felt safe and accepted at school and beyond. That was our mission, and our teachers lived it.

I could not speak to the success of Alliance without speaking about the extraordinary care that teachers showed for our students. If you ask students at Alliance what their favorite thing about the school was, many would say, "The teachers care." This is not an assumption. We would often survey our students using informal questionnaires to make sure we were meeting our mission and to find out their thoughts about the school. The number one thing we saw again and again was, "The teachers really care." Without that care, nothing else would be possible. Here are the stories of some of those teachers and the extraordinary measures they took to make sure that all of our students would have what they need to succeed.

THE PHYSIOLOGICAL

Mari

It only took us three months to realize we needed a full-time social worker. This was not an easy ask. It was unheard of in our district to have a student-to-social worker ratio of 100:1. But, given the poverty, homelessness, trauma, and disabilities that our students were experiencing, and despite our incredibly inadequate budget, we made the decision to shift the guidance responsibilities to advisers and create a full-time position for a social worker. Then we set out to find someone who could help us meet the persistent and real needs of our students and families. When we interviewed Mari, we knew she was the one—she was serious about the work, had more than twenty years of experience, knew every resource that existed within the community, came highly recommended, and cared deeply about our mission.

Choosing Mari was one of the best decisions we ever made. There are some people who walk through the world thinking about how they can use what they find to help others. This is Mari. She never stops thinking about the needs of the students. It was because of her that I started collecting the mini shampoo bottles from my hotel rooms and the little tubes of toothpaste that my dentist gave me. In her office, there was always a cabinet full of everything a student might need. There were backpacks, toothbrushes, T-shirts, tampons, and snacks. The students knew they could go to her for anything, and if she didn't have it, she would find someone who did. I cannot tell you how many times I have received a phone call from a parent wondering where to turn in times of crisis. The answer has always been, "Let me get Mari." There has never been a better safety net for students and families. I don't know if every school social worker has her commitment or will, but if you can find one who does, your community will be better for it.

Coach Velvet

Sometimes it's the people who work with your students every day, and sometimes it's the people who come into their lives at the end of those days. Coach Velvet volunteered as the afterschool basketball coach.[1] Up until then, we hadn't had our own sports teams, because we didn't have enough players to field a team. She got students who had never thought of playing basketball to join the team. That team of novices went from a group of strangers who had never played together to a championship-playing, second-place–winning team. Her involvement didn't stop on the court, either.

Soon after she started coaching, she realized many students were hungry at the end of the long days of school, and the hours of basketball practice only added to their hunger. She started to make sandwiches each day— and served fruit with the sandwiches, because she wanted them to eat healthy foods. New students joined the team when they found out there would be food.

She knew what dignity meant to the students. She raised money to buy uniforms for the team so they could play in style, bought shoes when she saw their shoes were worn out, and made Gatorade for their games and practices, so they could stay hydrated. She even got some of her work colleagues who had been athletes when they were younger to come and play tournament games so the students could practice. Whenever she saw a need, she did what it would take to fulfill it. She told the students she had a donor so that they wouldn't come to expect it, but they never did. They were so grateful, and it was amazing to see how they were able to shine in new ways. Their attendance rates went up. They demonstrated leadership within the school community, and they mentored new students who joined the team. It was truly a testament to the difference one volunteer can make.

Ericka

Some teachers go beyond expectations to make sure a student has a safe place to call home at the end of the day. While not everyone can or should go this far, it would be a shame if I didn't highlight the extraordinary generosity that one teacher, Ericka, demonstrated when a student was dealing with a family crisis and was on the verge of being placed in foster care. This student was an extraordinary young man. He had been a circle keeper for the school's restorative practices class, helped with the school's food pantry, and was in the running to be the valedictorian. Suddenly, he was facing a challenge that threatened everything, and Ericka wasn't about to let him fall through the cracks. She reached out to the social worker and asked what it would take to become a foster parent. And then she did everything it would take to become one. This included forty hours of parenting classes, background checks, and home readiness surveys, as well as regular meetings with social workers and psychologists to support him through the process. She opened her home, bought furniture for his space, made sure he had school supplies, and took him shopping for clothes when he needed them. And when the time came, she also made sure he took his ACT test, encouraged him to apply to college, and helped him write his admissions essays. With her help, he was able to negotiate the challenges in his life, stay in school, graduate, and go on to college.

This was an extraordinary act of care, for sure, and a surprising number of teachers at Alliance, and in many public school systems, have taken on this role or similar ones. Teachers have been foster parents, employers, career counselors, college fundraisers, and surrogate parents for those without families. It is a special gift to students and families to account for these needs, knowing that without the basics, nothing else is possible.

How teachers and schools can meet students' physiological needs:
- Hunger negatively impacts student behavior and academic performance.[2] Make sure no student has to go hungry by having snacks available for hungry students, making breakfast available to all students, and taking away stigma by protecting the anonymity of students who receive free meals.
- Partner with local shelters and service organizations. Have their phone numbers on hand for when students and/or families need them and share the information through newsletters and phone calls.
- Install a washer and dryer in the school and make it available to families.
- Host drives for hats, coats, and mittens, so students have winter clothes when they need them.
- Invite parents with more means to gift an extra school fee, field trip expense, or bag of school supplies when purchasing for their child or children.

- Hire support staff who can work with students and families in crisis, such as social workers, guidance counselors, psychologists, and school nurses.
- Hire teachers who consider care for the whole child to be part of their job.
- Fundraise and connect with donors who can provide funds to ensure the basic needs of students are met.
- Integrate mindfulness practices into the school day, so students can be aware of their needs and communicate effectively to have them met.

SAFETY

Paul

Paul used to tell people that I represented the 50 percent of our students who had been bullied for being LGBTQ, and he represented the 50 percent of the students who had been bullied for other reasons.

I first met Paul at the large urban high school where I taught before starting Alliance. I didn't know much about him at the time, but I knew his students loved him. Close to the end of his first year of teaching, I approached Paul about teaching at Alliance.

You couldn't tell Paul's story just by looking at him. His stories were deeply held, beneath the surface, much like his tattoos, which were not to be seen unless he revealed them. But when I told him that the mission of the school would be to address bullying and teach others how to do the same, he offered himself up immediately and never looked back. As time went on, I would learn about the extent of bullying he experienced as a high school student in Tennessee, and it was then that I understood the depth of his commitment to our mission.

Paul is the one teacher who has been there from the planning days and is still there teaching today. His commitment is awe inspiring. If you ask students about the teachers who have had the biggest impact in their lives, Paul will undoubtedly be at the top of the list. In the early days, many of the students would call him "dad" and me "mom," and they would confide in us about some of the hardest things in life.

One of these students was a young man who refused to go inside a classroom. For months, he would come to school almost every day and sit in the hallway, refusing to be "educated by the man." As many apparently oppositional students are, this student was brilliant, but his refusal to be educated also meant he wasn't going to earn a diploma. Paul built a connection with him, mostly through hallway discussions of literature and philosophy, and slowly found ways for him to complete the expectations of his classes in unique and interesting ways that didn't compromise either of their ethics. When the young man wasn't coming to school, Paul spoke to his parents and learned he was being harassed on the way to and from school, so Paul started to pick him up every morning and take him home from school every day. During those drives, he learned about many of the other challenges the student faced outside of school. It became very clear that much of his behavior was rooted in fear and the need for support, but it also became clear that he also had health issues beyond his control that were going to keep him from getting his diploma on time. At this time, Paul and I learned about the district's High School Equivalency diploma and learned that we could offer it at our school. We put together a plan and helped the student get what he needed academically, so he could take the tests and earn his diploma. We were all incredibly proud when he walked the stage.

In the following years, this student accomplished extraordinary things. He recorded an album, published poetry, and started an organization to build peace in the community through the arts. He recently sent me a message asking me what it would take for him to get into Harvard, where he could pursue his passion for philosophy and possibly become a professor someday.

If it wasn't for Paul's commitment to this student and his unique ability to find a way to work with anyone, this student never would have graduated from high school. Paul is and will always be my work brother, my cofounder, and my dear friend.

How teachers and schools can meet students' safety needs:
- Have the students create classroom agreements outlining what it means to be a member of the community and hold the classroom community accountable to living up to the agreements.

- Use this book as a tool for developing a school culture that is constantly working to ensure students feel safe and accepted at school.
- Create preventive and responsive strategies to deal with conflict, bullying, and safety concerns.
- Figure out the places and times where students don't feel safe, in and out of school, and work with students, families, and the community to develop strategies for reporting problems, getting help, and staying safe.
- Make sure students know who to turn to when they don't feel safe.
- Train your teachers in how to respond to and support students who come to them with reports of witnessed or experienced threats, violence, or sexual assault.

BELONGING

Jill

Alliance students know, without a doubt, that they can call on Jill, our art teacher. When a student's family suddenly became homeless, he called Jill. When another student's sister died in the middle of the night, she called Jill. Whenever I needed a confidante or a friend, I called Jill. Jill has always been the person that everyone would call on, knowing that they would get a response. She is the most loyal and creative person I've ever known. She was also pivotal in creating Alliance's culture of connection and belonging.

Jill is the kind of "twenty-four/seven, every student" teacher that every child needs at least one of. She is ever-present on Facebook and will be the first to head off drama, share information about opportunities for students in the summertime, or connect a suicidal student to support. We jokingly call her Jill-book, because it seems like she has a connection to everyone. If she doesn't know someone herself, she knows someone who knows someone, and she can undoubtedly make the connection. Whenever a new student joins the community, Jill makes sure to introduce the student to peers and make sure he or she feels welcome.

My favorite thing about Jill is that she was 100 percent onboard with any crazy scheme I came up with. One summer, I decided we should paint the walls of the common areas of the school. We had painted these areas before, but it had been several years, the color was fading, and we hadn't thought much about the impact of color on emotion when we had chosen the colors. It seemed like students were often arguing in the lobby, where the color of the walls was orange—an agitating color. So, having read an article about how color impacts mood, I decided a change was needed. This time, we couldn't just pick any colors, we had to pick colors to match the emotional needs of students, spaces, and subjects. Jill and I got together, researched mood colors, and spent a summer painting all of the common areas cloudburst blue with a simple red trim. She got several students to come in and help us, and together, we made it happen. It was a great summer.

She was always reaching out to students, especially those who were shy or on the periphery, and inviting them to be involved in the most amazing opportunities. She collaborated with a local art studio, meeting students there once a week, so they could be exposed to the art community. She was the teacher who partnered with an international artist and engaged her students in a portrait project that made them feel more beautiful than they had ever felt. Another time, she decided her ceramics students should present at the National Ceramics Conference that would be taking place in Milwaukee that year. Not only did they present, but they created a documentary about their experience. There is nothing that Jill wouldn't do to make sure all of her students feel connected and included at school. She is night and day, 100 percent, all in for her students.

Constantine and Corky

Constantine, a math teacher, and Corky, one of our paraprofessionals, were two other staff members who went all out to make sure students felt like they belonged at school. The drag queen basketball competition, first organized by Corky, started as a way to build connections between the straight boys and the transgender girls. The transgender girls had game; most of them had grown up on the basketball courts, and they had a little bit of fire on the court. But it wasn't quite enough game to win the competition, mostly because they didn't have the numbers. With a little bit of support, though, they could put up a good fight. This was where Constantine came in. He and his five Greek brothers filled the drag team with ringers who could put up a challenge for the most talented of players. They all dressed in drag, with the help of their trans teammates, and they showed up on the court ready to play. They may not have made the prettiest of women, but they tipped the basketball scales, making the drag basketball game an event that everyone looked forward to every year. Activities like this were essential when it came to making sure all students felt like they belonged at school, and staff members like these two made it happen.

How schools can meet students' needs for belonging:
- Build relationships in the classroom, through shared stories, group work, games, and lessons that build connections across difference.
- Make sure students see themselves in the curriculum, posters, and messages throughout the school. Think about race, gender, experience, age, etc.
- Have practices and tools to welcome and include students who enroll midyear. These might be support groups, restorative practice circles, peer buddies, adult mentors, handbooks, and so on. Make a special effort to support the children of military parents, who may move often, and immigrant students.
- Host school groups, clubs, and events that students of different groups, backgrounds, and abilities can participate in. Let the students participate in creating and leading such groups.
- Find ways to stay connected with students on social media and beyond, but always treat your social media as if it's another classroom. Anything you wouldn't say to or in front of students should not be shared on social media that you share with them.
- Give students opportunities to feel like the school belongs to them. Allow them to paint, design spaces, create signs, and give tours.
- Make fun a part of the school experience. School is not just preparation for life, it is part of life. Work and play hard to make the journey worthwhile.

ESTEEM

Heather

Heather has been teaching the restorative practice classes at Alliance for the past several years, and that gives her a unique place of love in the student's lives. In her classes, she teaches students to listen deeply, share their stories, and to hold the space for others, and she does this for our staff, as well. Numerous students call her Mama Heather, because she is always going above and beyond for every student. This is a role that she handles beautifully, with grace and a commitment to help students become their best selves. While she is always available to them, she also makes sure to nurture their sense of esteem by encouraging them to lead and master their own experiences.

This doesn't just happen during the school year, either. I spoke to Heather on the phone while finishing this book in early 2018. She had just spent the morning with three of our students who had graduated or left school months or years before. One student had graduated the previous June. Tragically, his younger brother had been shot and killed just days after the 2017 graduation ceremony. He had put off enrolling in college to take care of his family. Another student had graduated two years before, but she hadn't ever considered going to college. The third student hadn't completed high school at all. Despite her love for the school and her extraordinary talent, life had gotten in the way, and she had stopped coming to school and started working for her father as a roofer.

When I spoke to Heather, I learned that on that day, during her winter break, she had taken all of these students to the local community college to register for classes. It all started when one student posted something on Facebook about wanting to go to college but not knowing where to go. Heather jumped at the chance to help and said, "I'll go with you." Two other students saw the thread and responded that they wanted to go, too. Before she knew it, she had a perfect trifecta. In true teacher fashion, as she told me the story, she made it clear that she didn't do anything for them. She simply stood with them each step of the way and asked, "So, what do you think we need to do now?" And the students had figured out their next steps. By the end of the day, the first two students were registered to start college in the fall, and the third student was enrolled in the adult high school completion program at the college.

This is Heather—all of the time.

How schools can meet the esteem needs of students:
- Let the students do the work. If there is a job that can be done by a student, let him or her do it. They can make phone calls, fill out applications, send letters, and host visitors. When the students do the work that is often left to the adults, they gain self-confidence and the skills they need to navigate in the world outside the school doors.
- Provide students with consistent feedback, encouragement, and opportunities to improve. Consider going without grades and make student growth the measure of success, rather than completion of assignments.
- Have your team read *Mindset: The New Psychology of Success*, by Carol S. Dweck, Ph.D.[3] Reinforce a growth mind-set with everyone in the school community.
- Give *all* students opportunities to lead. Some of the best leaders are the students who are rarely given the opportunity to lead. Reach out to find the leader in every student.
- When students ask for help, give them guidance, but try not to do it for them.

SELF-ACTUALIZATION
Jasmine

Jasmine exemplifies the kind of teaching that proves that students are capable of anything when the other needs identified by Maslow are met. A young and enthusiastic science teacher, Jasmine created a science classroom where the students were able to engage in a scientific community. They have created paper presentations on water sustainability, have built a compost bin in the school parking lot, started a recycling program for the school, taught lessons about genetics, and visited the cadaver lab at Marquette University.

They even learned about aquaponics and developed a system in the class-room, sustaining a healthy community of fish and growing their own pep-pers, basil, and other green leafy vegetables. On several occasions, when I visited the classroom, students were eager to tell me about what they were learning and how their experiments had revealed new insights. I loved vis-iting, because it was exciting to see the students so thrilled to be learning.

In every class that Jasmine teaches, you will see students of all back-grounds and abilities challenged and engaged, exploring unanswered ques-tions and proposing new possibilities. This is what's possible when students have what they need to succeed, and this is common in classes throughout the school. In Joel's class, they are finding their blood types; in Chris's class, they are excited about using statistics. Christian's students are hosting so-cial justice fairs, and Paul's students are publishing a book. Jill's students host art shows, while Beth's students call their local political leaders. And several teachers have had their students present at conferences or universi-ties. The work in the classrooms is as challenging as work on the job or the work of college courses I took, and this makes me very proud. Students thrive when they have these types of opportunities, and Alliance teachers illustrate the kinds of teachers who make sure self-actualization can happen.

How schools can help meet student needs for self-actualization:
- Make work challenging and authentic. If your students are learning how to write, have them write for publication. If students are creating art, make their art public. Whenever students have a chance to practice au-thentic work, they have the chance to see themselves in those roles. This is one of the first and most important steps toward self-actualization.
- Give students opportunities to learn from experts in the community and from each other. Bring in guests, visit people on the job, host video conferences, and allow students to share their expertise. This builds knowledge and relationships.
- Provide many opportunities for choice and exploration of new pos-sibilities. List several project examples for how students can demon-strate learning or understanding, and allow students to propose new project ideas, as well.

- Tap into the power of young people. Students have the desire and ability to impact their communities. Give them as many chances as possible to engage in and affect the world around them.

A NOTE ABOUT SELF-CARE

Love yourself first, and everything else falls in line. You really have to love yourself to get anything done in this world.

LUCILLE BALL

In 2008, I attended a peace conference at Lesley University to learn more about strategies for developing peaceful communities. As you can imagine, the people attending the conference were the kind of people who work tirelessly on behalf of others. It's also probably no surprise that there were many teachers in the room. One of the sessions I attended was a workshop on self-care for educators. I needed this session. I had been a teacher for ten years, and in that time, I had provided shelter to many students, become a foster parent, spent a good portion of my income on classroom supplies, shared many lunchtime meals with young people, stayed up far too late far too often, and counseled students through abuse, breakups, tough decisions, and family tragedies. I was exhausted, and I am sure it was obvious to everyone but me.

The speaker told a story about the moment when he realized he had been doing everything backward. He had been working long hours, not taking care of himself, and focusing all of his time and energy on work. He was run-down, sick, and really, really tired. A friend, noting how unwell he looked, pulled him aside and asked, "What the heck are you doing?"

He responded with a list of things he had to do and reasons why he needed to accomplish everything. He couldn't let his students down, because so much was on the line for them. He needed to work this hard so his students could get into college, get good careers, and so forth.

His friend looked at him, gestured at his disheveled suit and the tired look on his face, and said, "Why would they want to do that if this is what a college degree and a good job look like?"

This was his wake-up moment.

He told us we are in the business of selling diplomas. Our primary task is to convince young people to get their credits and graduate. They aren't just listening to us, they are observing us, and if we can't be the model of a healthy, happy life, then we have no business trying to sell those lives to others. The speaker said we have to take care of ourselves first because, "If the students can't see themselves in you, they won't want to be you."

This quote has stuck with me, and I know I am a healthier person because if it. I still work myself too hard, at times, and there will always be some deadlines that just have to be met. But, in the midst of all of the daily demands, I always think about what he said and try to take care of myself, both for myself and so my students can see an image of something they would like to aspire to. With that in mind, here are some tips for practicing extraordinary care for one's self.

How to take care of self, so that you can take care of others:
- Set a reasonable bed time and get at least eight hours of sleep. And practice all of those other positive sleep habits that you know you should do—turn the TV off, leave the laptop in the living room, make the room dark, etc.
- Schedule blocks of time in your week for creating lesson plans and correcting work, and stick to those times. It can be easy to get carried away with these tasks or to find yourself distracted from them, but if you make it a scheduled task, you are more likely to get it done and find more time for other things.
- Do something physical that you enjoy every week. If you like to dance, start a line-dancing group. If you play basketball, find a local social team to join. You will be amazed by how much better you feel after doing something physical that brings you joy.
- Go to the doctor. Too many educators skip doctor's appointments because they don't want to miss school. You know your body. Listen to it. Make your health a priority.
- Carry a water bottle and drink water throughout the day.
- Food is fuel. Give your body what it needs to run efficiently. Eat well, skip the sugar, and cook your own meals. It's surprising how quick

and easy it is to cook at home. Fast food isn't really fast. Time it. You'll see.

- Say "No." It's one of the hardest things for educators to do, but there are others who can help, as well. You don't have to do it all yourself. When you find yourself feeling overwhelmed, practice setting boundaries.

- Build strong and positive relationships with your colleagues, not the negative-teacher-lounge kind of relationships, but relationships that serve the soul. Share lunches, positive quotes, and creative ideas. Plan fun events and get outside of the school together. Every chance you get, surround yourself with the people who make your day.

- If you are finding yourself feeling overwhelmed, angry, sad, or if you just want an objective listener, connect with a good therapist. The work we do is hard, and vicarious trauma is real. There is so much value to be gained from just being heard, especially if your therapist is a good one. If you find you don't like your therapist much, choose a new one. You get to decide how you spend your free time, so don't hesitate to seek out what you need.

EXTRAORDINARY INDIVIDUALS MAKE FOR EXTRAORDINARY SCHOOLS

There are many extraordinary people at Alliance and in schools everywhere, and it is my belief that extraordinary individuals make for extraordinary schools. These individuals care deeply, work hard, and inspire others. If you can find and hire these individuals, you will see the impact of their efforts in the culture and academic outcomes of your school. If you can practice this extraordinary care yourself, you will see the impact in student engagement and love returned. This is a beautiful and reciprocal gift. When a school starts from a place of care, anything is possible, and Maslow has given us a map for how to exemplify such care. Knowing this, there is no reason why all schools cannot become extraordinary, if they put caring at the center of their mission.

6

The Culturally
Responsive School

*Culture is the intersection of people and life itself. It's
how we deal with life, love, death, birth, disappointment
. . . all of that is expressed in culture.*
WENDELL PIERCE

WHAT DOES IT MEAN TO BE
CULTURALLY RESPONSIVE?

As a white woman in a country that has experienced the privilege of whiteness in many ways, I thought a lot about whether or not I had the authority to be writing a chapter on culturally responsive education. I also reminded myself that, as a white woman who has been given the grace and opportunity to learn and lead in communities of color, I have always felt for myself a unique responsibility to lead in culturally responsive ways. Because of this, I have learned a great deal over the years, and I hope this chapter will serve as in invitation for others to consider adopting culturally responsive practices. After all, one cannot be a bully-free school without being a culturally responsive school.

So, what does it mean to be a culturally responsive school? There are as many different definitions of cultural responsiveness as there are differences in cultures. The National Center for Culturally Responsive Education Practices (NCCRESt) defines cultural responsiveness as "the ability to learn from and relate respectfully to people of your own culture, as well as those from other cultures."[1] I appreciate this definition because it centers itself around some of my own core beliefs about cultural responsiveness—it implies an awareness that culture exists, suggests a willingness to learn, and focuses on a deep respect for others. It doesn't mean you always know everything about every other culture, or that you always get things right. It means that you understand that people of different groups have different beliefs, perspectives, practices, and traditions, and that individuals belong to many different groups, so even within groups, there may be different traditions and beliefs. Cultural responsiveness means that you can hold this as truth and be open to the idea that someone may feel or act differently than you, and you can be okay with that, even see the beauty in it. Responsiveness happens at the individual level and at the school level.

Schools have an important role to play in modeling and teaching cultural responsiveness. They are the places where young people step through developmental stages and begin to understand that others may think and operate differently from themselves. Most children are in school when they move from egocentric thought to sociocentric thought, and as they get older, they learn to think more and more abstractly. Schools can help young children and older children learn about culture and become culturally responsive individuals.

Individual educators and school leaders can play a tremendous role in creating a culturally responsive school—first, by developing a deep personal understanding and appreciation for culture and what it stands for in the lives of individuals and communities; second, by creating the schoolwide systems, philosophies, and practices that set a school up to be a culturally responsive place; and ultimately, by working together in becoming a community that holds cultural responsiveness as a community value. By doing so, cultural responsiveness can become part of the way a community thinks, acts, and communicates.

THE FIRST DAY OF SCHOOL

The first day of school at Alliance is a day of hugs and reunions. In the days leading up to that day, I always receive numerous Facebook messages from students who are eager to get back to school.

"When do we start back?"

"What time does school start?"

"I can't wait to see you, Tina!"

"I miss school!"

It feels special that the students look forward to school so much. Perhaps this happens at schools all over the country, but I can't remember this much joy in my own experience of going back to school. I remember feeling terribly nervous and overwhelmed by the thought of returning to school, so it makes me incredibly happy to see our students so excited about their return.

On the first day, when the school was eight years old, the return to school seemed happier than it had ever felt before. As the students walked into the building, they greeted each other, me, and the other staff members with joyful hugs and welcomed the new students with cheerful greetings and offers of assistance. Even the boys who considered themselves the "tough guys" seemed to have softened a bit this particular year. One group of boys, the basketball players, were always hesitant to welcome newcomers, which is not surprising given the fact that they had built a certain level of trust with the staff and with each other, and they were a tight-knit group unto themselves. However, this year, they seemed to let their guards down, and they were quick to welcome new peers onto the basketball court. They suddenly weren't just receiving the benefits of attending a welcoming school, they seemed to understand the power they had in contributing to it.

I was talking to one of the boys at lunch time, and I could tell he sensed it, too. He asked me what I thought about the first couple of weeks of school, and I just raved about what a positive start it had been. I told him how proud I was of the older students who made everyone feel welcome and the new students who brought such positive energy into the first weeks of school. "Us too, right?" he asked, referring to the basketball players and smiling as if he knew something. "We did that."

"Yes!" I exclaimed. "You guys were amazing. The way you made the new students feel welcome on the basketball court was the coolest. I absolutely noticed that."

It was clear that he was happy to be part of what made the start of the year great, and I couldn't help but feel that a small cultural miracle was happening in our building. When we first opened our school, there were some real cultural clashes taking place, especially between our straight boys and our transgender students. We were bringing together groups who didn't typically hang out with each other, yet who shared very similar experiences of ostracism and discrimination. They just didn't know this about each other yet. We had a lot of learning and a lot of teaching to do beyond the typical classroom lessons. Still, we really believed that if we stuck to our philosophy and mission, the school would work for everyone. We knew the key was to get the students to know and understand each other well. The hard part was whether the whole place would erupt into chaos before we ever had the chance.

Luckily, a few students whose lives crossed the boundaries of the different groups became cultural ambassadors of sorts and built bridges between the various groups of students. Black and white transgender students connected with each other, and then helped build the bridges across race groups. Gay students with disabilities connected with their nondisabled gay peers, and new understandings developed. Sometimes the adults helped build those bridges, but as time went on, the students started to learn the language of connection, and they started to do it themselves. This year, for the first time, the habits were in the returning students, and the school seemed to move smoothly into a sense of community, without the normal storming that usually takes place when new groups come together. We were becoming a culturally responsive school.

THE CULTURALLY RESPONSIVE TEACHER OR LEADER

The culturally responsive school community doesn't just happen. It is made up of culturally responsive teachers and leaders who are willing to do the hard work every day. First, it's a personal commitment. When shared, it becomes a community commitment. To get there, individual teachers and leaders must develop the habit of cultural responsiveness. I imagine this level of understanding develops in adults much like object permanence develops in children. It is a developmental process, one that is marked by the constant uncovering of new knowledge and insights. It can be difficult, because you don't know what you don't know until you know. For example, an individual can spend years feeling uncomfortable with someone who doesn't look him in the eye, until he learns that the other person comes from a culture where it is disrespectful to look someone directly in the eyes.

This is the challenge and the beauty of cultural responsiveness. We know that culture is fluid—people are complex, come from more than one cultural experience, and change regularly. In fact, schools are in the business of supporting human adaptation and change. We want children to grow and learn, and we, as adults, are constantly growing and learning, as well. Cultural responsiveness isn't about having all of the knowledge of every culture and community; rather, it is about listening and responding in ways that value all people, beliefs, and ways of being. It is about recognizing that different cultures exist and add endless ways of thinking and being in any community. Cultural responsiveness is about recognizing that one's own interpretation of an action or event is not the only possible interpretation and making the space for every person's individual and complex uniqueness to shine. It is also about recognizing where dominant cultures persist and being open to another possibility.

A Guest in Other Countries

As the child of a military father, I learned this very early. I had the opportunity to travel a great deal when I was young, which was not always easy. However, it taught me a tremendous amount about culture. From the time I was six years old until I was thirteen, we moved from place to place outside of the continental United States, and in each new place we were reminded that we were guests and that we should carry ourselves as such. We took classes, read literature, and learned the beliefs, practices, and cultural norms of the places we called home. We learned there were many ways of acting and believing, and that we could never assume anything about another person's actions, because we might be reacting to a different cultural norm or tradition, rather than a true insult or affront. I remember learning in Greece that we should never wave with an open hand, as this would be considered an insult, and that when people spit on you, it is not an insult, but rather they are wishing you good fortune or protecting you from the evil eye. On Guam, we learned to sniff the hands of our elders and to always strive for peace. As we traveled, we learned many different customs and met people from around the world. At times the customs contradicted each other, so we learned never to judge or assume and to always consider that there might be another possible explanation for someone's actions.

These experiences shaped my thinking and my practices as a teacher. One of the exercises I would do with my students was to put them into groups and give them scenarios where an interaction between two individuals went horribly wrong. I would then have them read the scenarios and discuss, as a group, what happened. A scenario might look like this:

> Mark is an American exchange student in Denmark. In his first week of school, one of his Danish classmates, Sofia, approaches him to introduce herself. They are having a great conversation, until Sofia invites him to meet her in the cemetery after school, where some of her friends will be meeting up. Mark decides not to hang out with Sofia and her friends, and he ends the conversation quickly. What happened?

After some time to discuss what might have happened, the students were invited to look on the back of the scenario (or open an envelope) to learn about a cultural norm, tradition, or practice which may have caused the misunderstanding. In this case, they would learn that in Denmark, cemeteries are treated like parks and are typical places for people to gather and socialize, while in many parts of the US, cemeteries are treated as solemn or spiritual places. They are not likely places for people to gather, unless for nefarious reasons.

The exercise is designed to help students understand there are many cultural norms and at times, these norms lead to misunderstandings between people. My hope was for students to start to think about interactions through this lens, and not be so quick to judge or write off another person.

A "Guest in Service" Mind-set

If you are a white person who has never been in a black church, you need to spend some time in one. And if you find yourself feeling uncomfortable in that space, you know what it feels like to be a black student in a typical American classroom. Most classrooms in America look more like white church ceremonies than black church ceremonies, and they very rarely consider the cultural norms of students in the classroom. This means that many young people are judged harshly for behaviors that would be perfectly appropriate actions and responses in many of their cultural traditions. It also means that classrooms can be uncomfortable and difficult places for many students to navigate.

My travels gave me the opportunity to learn what it felt like to be in spaces where the cultural norms were not my own, and this empathy carried over into my teaching. I like to think of myself as a guest, in service to the students and families I work with and for. For me, this means that school should look more like their cultures and traditions than my own. It also means that I have a responsibility to make school meet the needs of the parents and students I serve.

No one knows a child better than his or her parents and community, and no one wants success for a child more than his or her family. As a teacher, I remembered that these parents were sending their children to me, entrusting me with the most important people in their lives. This was a gift, and I knew I could honor it by working with them to provide their children with an excellent educational experience, one where culture was valued and excellence was defined by their needs, not by my own. I spent a lot of time listening to families, and in doing so, I learned how important it was to them that their children be treated with dignity and be afforded the opportunities often granted to students in wealthier communities. They wanted their children to have freedom, to be treated with respect, and to have the best teachers, as if money and place didn't matter. I heard them and saw how this often didn't happen in our community, so I committed myself to working hard to ensure their children were provided with all of the opportunities that the wealthiest of schools could provide. I committed myself to learning, hiring excellent teachers, and always acting in ways that made students and staff feel like they were trusted and able to accomplish anything.

I could see that we were really doing something special when I had the opportunity to visit the high school in California where my mentor from the Point Foundation was the Head of School.[2] This school was a private school, and many famous people sent their children there. The tuition in 2008 was $35,000 per pupil, the experience was very student-centered, and the teachers they hired were exemplary. If you didn't know all of this, though, you could have easily remarked about how much it looked and felt like the Alliance School. I was happy to see that the climate, philosophy, and teaching practices were similar to those we practiced, and the student experience was much the same. The only remarkable difference would have been the price of the cars in the parking lot. This was why families chose Alliance. We were committed to putting their needs first in everything we did.

In a world where there is so much inequity in educational experiences, and where low-income students and students of color are often served with lowered expectations, lesser opportunities, and very little freedom and choice, I felt very proud that our school could have been placed in that setting, and the education offered would be on par with the education given to the wealthiest among us. The families I worked with knew this, too. They were proud of the school and often recommended it to other families. There were brothers and sisters, cousins, nephews, and best friends enrolled at the school. Keeping focused on being of service to families was the first step in being a culturally responsive school. This service mind-set helped us build relationships with students and families, and it was through those relationships that we learned a great deal about who our students were and what they needed.

New Student Orientation

Before our students even entered the building, we were already trying to get to know them and their families. In 2013, eight years after opening, we started using restorative practice circles during new student orientation. All of the new students would sit in circles with peers and talk with upperclassmen about the transition to a new school, and all of the parents would sit in circles with other parents and talk about what it meant to see their babies off to high school. I had a chance to sit in one of the parent circles, and the experience was quite emotional. We asked a series of four questions and passed around a talking piece so each person had a chance to speak.

Introduce yourself and your child and share why you chose Alliance.
Tell the group what you love about your child.
What are your biggest fears about sending your child to high school?
What are your hopes and dreams, and what can the community do
    to support you and your child to get there?

It was fun to hear the parents talk about what they loved about their children. They were full of smiles and pride, and lots of laughter filled the room. But it was the question about fears that got to the heart of their love for their children. Many parents spoke about wanting their children to belong. Some worried that the work would be hard and they wouldn't know how to support their children. Others worried about bullying, bus rides, and letting go of their babies. The story that hit me most, though, was when one of the fathers shared his fears for his son. He was afraid he wouldn't be good enough as a father. He told us how they didn't talk about love a lot in their family, but how he loved his son so much, and how he wanted everything under the sun for his child. He talked about being afraid to be too stern or not stern enough, but just wanted, at the end of the day, for his son to know that he loved him, even if they didn't say it, and to know that he did his best for him. We could all relate to this father's fears. You saw it in the head nods, affirmations, and teary eyes. I wanted that for my children, as well, and so did everyone in the room. With the final question, we shared our dreams and pledged to support each other, and we really did. None of us ever forgot why we were there together or the depths of each parent's love for his or her child.

What's In a Name?

One way in which many educators fail at cultural responsiveness is in the simple act of learning and respecting a child's name. If you have a child of your own, you likely spent a lot of time and energy thinking about what name you would give that child. Perhaps there were family traditions that influenced your choice, elders that you chose to honor, or special meanings behind the name you chose. When I was looking for a name for my daughter, I looked up the roots and meanings of names. I chose the name Felicia because *Felicitas* meant "my little bit of happiness." When my son, Jeremy, was born, it was important for his father to honor the man who had raised him—Robert. We chose Jeremy Robert because we liked the nickname J.R. We thought about so many things when choosing their names—meaning, history, ancestors, nicknames, and so on. Their names were not accidents, so we wouldn't expect anyone to treat them as such.

In many cultures, it is a tradition to combine the names of important relatives when naming a child. Sometimes, it is the mother's name combined with the father's. Other times it is the grandparents, a significant aunt, teacher, mentor, godparent, or friend. This tradition lifts people up and shines a light on their place in the child's life. It is a special part of many cultures that is often forgotten or belittled by those who don't understand the significance or beauty of such traditions. One of my foster sons combined the last syllable of my name (Tina) with the first syllable of another parent figure when he named his daughter. I will never forget the day he called me to tell me that baby Jenna was here, and that he had combined our names. I didn't believe him at first. I was so incredibly honored and still am, to this day.

Names are important, to families and to individuals, so one of the first things teachers can do to demonstrate cultural responsiveness is to learn the names of all of their students, quickly and correctly. Nothing builds a bridge faster than having a teacher call you by the correct name, especially if that name is a complicated or unusual one to the teacher. It's so important to remember that what may seem complicated to you is likely uncomplicated for your student. Taking the time to memorize and practice pronouncing a young person's name is a powerful way of communicating care and one's ability to consider another culture as valuable. It also conveys respect for the child's family, heritage, and intended place in the world.

Student-Centered Practices

One way to learn about your students is simply to ask. At the beginning of every school year, and throughout the year, I use a variety of surveys and activities to get to know students. I have each student create a notecard with his or her name, a simple picture of him or herself, any nickname, preferred gender pronouns, likes, dislikes, and an interesting fact. I use these cards to help me to learn their names in the first few days of school. We also do activities to help students to get to know each other. For example, we may play a bingo game that invites students to find someone in the class who has traveled out of the country, or find someone who is an only child, or the like. From these beginning activities, I learn some simple details about the students, and they learn more about each other. The bonds begin to form in the classroom. I then begin to develop the curriculum around their interests and aspirations. For example, in one of my English classes, I learned that music was very important to many of my students, so I started every lesson with a song that was connected to the curriculum. I gave each student a copy of the lyrics and started the lesson with a question that connected the song to the lesson and to their personal lives. I also encouraged students to bring me songs that connected to the curriculum, and many of them did. It's been twenty years since I taught that class, and I still have former students telling me they still have their binders filled with song lyrics.

In addition to connecting the lessons to their interests, a powerful practice in culturally responsive teaching is to provide opportunities for students to choose how to show their learning. A student who loves basketball might create a program or playbook for a basketball competition between the Capulets and the Montagues. Using details from the story, he or she can show a deep understanding of the rivalry, the story plot, and the qualities of each family conveyed in the text. For a history unit, a student may create a playlist of music that captures the narrative arc of the events. For every assignment or assessment, it is possible to provide a series of choices for how students can demonstrate their learning, and to invite them to come with additional ideas. This allows students to bring themselves to the lessons in ways that engage them and make them feel like their cultures and experiences are valued.

Cultural Responsiveness in the Curriculum

Students should also be able to see themselves explicitly in the curriculum. In every classroom, students should see on the walls, in the literature, and in the lessons, people who look and sound like themselves. Too often, school curricula reflect the images, stories, and histories of white Europeans. And when others are included, they are introduced as an add-on or as supplemental characters to the stories or histories. There are many ways to counter this and to provide a more culturally responsive academic experience for young people.

When my children were young, I saw this in practice at one of the schools they attended. The school had adopted a global education curriculum framework. The philosophy of the school was that whenever they studied any historical event, they would look at it through the perspectives of everyone who may have been affected by it. They would read first-person narratives written by people of all cultures and communities, and they would talk about whose narratives had been centered in the history books and why. They would interview family members and add their own histories to the ones that dominated the news stories. They learned to see and to counter the dominant narratives through this approach.

Another way schools provide a more culturally responsive experience is by focusing intentionally on the experiences and heritages of students within the school. It is possible to flood the curriculum and the environment with the stories, histories, and practices of the people who attend a school or of the community where the school resides. For example, many schools in Native American communities make native languages, traditions, and stories central to the learning experience. When I visited international schools in Doha, Qatar, the schools clearly reflected the values and traditions of the community. One example was that each of the schools had a *majlis*, a culturally traditional space to receive visitors. The majlis were beautiful, tent-like spaces, with traditional cushions and pillows. One of the schools even had a majlis in the lunchroom, where several students were gathered to socialize and have their lunches together. The pictures on the walls showed men in thawbs and women in abayas doing things such as looking through microscopes or reading books, and teachers from other countries communicated to us that they demonstrated respect for the national customs by wearing loose clothing that covered the arms and legs. Even though the students who attended these schools came from all over the world, the communities deliberately reflected the culture and traditions of the community in which the schools were located.

For schools where there are many cultures and communities, the curriculum should reflect the diversity of the people within the community, and there must be ways for the curriculum to adapt and change to the changing needs of the community. For example, as more Hmong students enrolled in our school, it was important for us to learn about Hmong culture and traditions, and we had to make sure that our Hmong students could see themselves in the curriculum. It was also important for us to reevaluate the curriculum to see what narratives we might have incorrectly been communicating. Had we unintentionally communicated that all Asian students came from the same places and backgrounds? Or spoke the same language? Sometimes, what is absent from a curriculum carries a message just as strong as what is present.

It is important to think about the curriculum as a whole and to review materials often to determine if the literature itself is conveying any beliefs or stereotypes about certain groups. If the only book about African American boys is the story of a boy who is facing the challenge of whether or not to be affiliated with a gang, then what message is the curriculum conveying about African American boys, especially to those who do not belong to this group. African American boys face many challenges and joys in life. Will your students know this if they read the required texts? It is important that the curriculum reflect the diverse experiences of groups and individuals within groups. Otherwise, it only serves to reinforce assumptions about others.

And finally, students can be part of creating the curriculum, as well. Students have their own stories, perspectives, family histories, and experiences that can shape the narrative in the classroom. A story about a wedding may be a unique invitation for students of various cultures to share stories about weddings and the unique traditions of families and communities. They might share pictures, interview family members, or do research on the cultural practices of people within their communities. By inviting students to connect their own experiences to the curriculum, we build our personal classroom collections while also building bridges between individuals and communities that may perceive each other as very different.

The Opportunity to Travel

I love to travel, so I have always tried to give my students the chance to travel, even if that travel doesn't take them far from home. Students need to learn the norms of air travel, of hotel stays, and of other cultures. When we visited New York, my students were stunned by the differences in how people treated personal space and how rarely people talked to each other on subways or on the street. In the Midwest, it is quite usual for people to say hello on the streets and to strike up long and personal conversations with complete strangers. This was not the case in New York, and my students thought people were rude, until I reminded them that they may be perceived as rude for infringing on personal space in a city where it's not the norm to talk to strangers.

Young people, and many adults for that matter, do not realize there are stark differences in cultural norms within nations, within cities, within communities, ethnic groups, and families. As teachers and school leaders, we can do a lot to reduce conflict by teaching about cultural norms. At Alliance, we learn about cultural norms, and we share stories about some of our own cultural and familial norms and times when those norms have been violated. I learned from my students for example, to never reach over someone else's plate or have two people walk on opposite sides of a street pole, and to always wear pressed clothes and follow or proceed my statements about my future plans with "God willing," a practice that is especially important in the Latinx community.

By talking about these cultural norms, it became a sign of respect in our community to practice the norms that had been shared with us. We also learned never to assume that everyone in a group shared the same cultural norms. Where one person may feel strongly about elbows on the dinner table, another person may feel more concerned about not eating until everyone had a plate. Sharing our stories and learning about the experiences of others made us better with each other by giving us the tools to communicate more effectively and teaching us not to assume that someone else's actions were a deliberate insult or attack. They became grounds for connection and for social capital, as well.

THE CULTURALLY RESPONSIVE SCHOOL

It may seem like a daunting task to become a culturally responsive school. After all, there are no absolutes when it comes to culture. But there are some simple things that schools can do to become more culturally responsive, to exemplify and continually practice "the ability to learn from and relate respectfully to people of your own culture, as well as those from other cultures."

Hiring Teachers of Color

There have been many articles and research studies showing the benefits of having teachers of color, both to students of color and to their white peers. Teachers of color have higher expectations of students of color, and they are less likely to judge student behavior negatively.[3] A 2017 study showed that assigning a black male to a black teacher between grades three and five significantly reduces his chances of dropping out of school.[4] Cultural responsiveness calls for an intentionality in hiring practices, so that all students can see images of themselves within the classroom and school community.

It was a challenge to find teachers and staff of color at Alliance. We were a start-up, which made it a risky endeavor, and our mission was a controversial one. But I never gave up on the mission to find and hire educators of color. I knew how important this was to our students. I attended recruitment fairs, posted openings on social media, and deliberately reached into communities of color to find people to join our team. Tameika and Sherri were just two of the people who joined our staff over the years.

Tameika joined our school community when a teacher from another school recommended her, and soon after, her son enrolled at Alliance, as well. She had an amazing commitment to her students, and many of the young people she knew in her previous school followed her to Alliance. She brought great vision and creativity to our staff, and she became an ally that many parents relied on. She was the person who organized many of our schoolwide events, including homecoming, prom, and the Thanksgiving dinner. Tameika also organized the fashion show that brought the mayor to Alliance. In their planning, her students had sent him an invitation, and to their delight, he showed up. He was impressed with the quality of the event and the way the students supported each other, and in a speech to the students, he shared that all schools should be more like Alliance. We were all so proud. With Tameika on staff, moments like this were the norm. Her energy was pervasive and contagious, and her impact was palpable.

Sherri was another educator of color who shaped the experience of education for many of our young people. She came to us as a retired sheriff, and we hired her to be our Parent Coordinator. The students loved seeing and getting to know a black woman who had "made it," as they said. Despite, or maybe because of, her years in law enforcement, she was easy to talk to, and was often the first person that parents would call on when they had a concern about their child or questions about the work. It wasn't unusual for me to find a student working in her office, or someone asking her for advice. It was clear they just wanted to be close to her. We are all moved when we see people who look like us, or who share our personal experience, do extraordinary things. I love every story of a woman in leadership who is the first to shatter a glass ceiling or of a teen parent who starts an organization that makes a difference for others. Just like us, our students need to see visions of themselves on our staff. Because of this, I'm so glad Sherri left retirement for a time to join our team.

There is no doubt in my mind that parents and students feel more connected to the school when they see people who look like themselves on staff. Both Tameika and Sherri had a tremendous impact on our school culture, and in their own ways, they made the school into a much more culturally responsive place. I am grateful for their time and commitment to ensuring that all students have people they feel comfortable going to for support.

Culturally Responsive Discipline

According to several economists and sociologists, Milwaukee is one of the most segregated cities in the United States.[5] One of the hardest things we've had to address over the years are the issues of race that, when left unaddressed, become barriers to understanding between individuals and groups. In our first year, we were still trying to develop our discipline policies and practices, so most of the practices revolved around what each individual teacher would tolerate, and what they would not. Of course, this led to frustrations between teachers and teachers, teachers and students, parents and teachers. One teacher would give a consequence for one thing, and another teacher would not. This group of students got in trouble for something, but that group did not. It was inevitable that the question of race would come into the discussion. The students would always make little comments about race when it came to discipline. The black students would say, "Well, you never discipline the white students." And the white students would say, "Well, you let the black students get away with everything." It was impossible.

One day, I was subbing for a class, and since at the time I was the person who handled most of the discipline for the school, the students decided to use the opportunity to raise their concerns. They started telling me about how one teacher kicked them out of the room for swearing, while another teacher didn't care about swearing, or how one teacher allowed skimpy clothing in class, while another teacher wouldn't tolerate it. At first, I was trying to make a point about knowing your audience and adjusting your behavior for your environment, but they simply weren't going to hear it. This was about inequities, and they just wanted to be heard. I have always trusted young people to tell me what I need to hear, so instead of shutting them out, I decided to engage them in thinking about the problem. I asked if they could help me to understand and develop some solutions. I promised that if they did, I would use their ideas to help us frame our schoolwide practices, which we were planning to discuss at our next staff meeting (it seemed, in those days, as if every staff meeting somehow found its way back to the topic of student discipline). They seemed pleased with this idea.

First, I needed to understand the problem clearly and determine whether or not we were all seeing the problem the same way. I had the students brainstorm every possible thing that they could imagine someone getting in trouble for at Alliance. We made a huge list on the board. Then, on another board, I made a huge chart, and I had them each draw the same chart on a blank piece of paper. At the top, I put the following headings: Really Bad; Bad; Not Really Bad, But People Make a Big Deal Out Of; and Not Bad at All. Then I had each of the students, without talking to each other, put all of the things that we had brainstormed into the appropriate categories in their charts.

The students filled out their charts, and then we had a discussion about where they had placed the behaviors. It was immediately obvious that students in the class had very different perspectives on what was "bad" behavior and what was not, so we used this to spark a discussion about school discipline and about who decides what behavior is "punishable." We decided that if the school was going to be the kind of school the community wanted, then the school discipline policy should reflect the values of the whole community. To capture these values, we decided we needed to have the whole school participate in this exercise, and then we could use what came out of the exercise as the basis for a system of schoolwide expectations and consequences.

Over the next few days, I did this exercise with all of the students and with the staff members at our staff meeting. The difference in perspectives was incredible. It was no surprise why people, adults and students, were getting frustrated. One of the biggest surprises that came out of the exercise, though, was the differences between the perspectives of white students and black students. There were some very clear lines of difference that fell along race lines, and since most of the teachers were white, it was also clear that this could cause some real inequities and very difficult race tensions. While many of the white students were offended by loud behavior and interruptions, many of the black students were offended by public displays of affection and promiscuous clothing. So, when black students would get scolded for being loud, but white students weren't disciplined at all for kissing in the hall, the black students would see it as an example of discrimination, and the white teachers would just see it as the black students trying to shift the attention onto other students.

We had a schoolwide discussion about some of these patterns and trends, and that led to the development of community agreements in each class, so that the perspectives of all of the students and adults could be taken into account in each class. This was very powerful in shifting the conversation from racial differences to community compromise and unbiased expectations, because the students and staff were able to find some common ground and have clear guidelines about what constituted "bad" behavior in any given place.

THE CULTURALLY RESPONSIVE COMMUNITY
Responding to Hate

On June 12, 2016, a shooter walked into the Pulse nightclub in Orlando, Florida, and opened fire, killing forty-nine people and wounding fifty-eight others. At the time, it was the deadliest mass shooting incident ever to take place in the United States, and the fact that it happened at an LGBTQ nightclub on Latin night made it go beyond terrorism to hate-based terrorism. The news of this incident hit very close to home for our school community. Many of our students were Latinx students and/or LGBTQ students, and almost every student in our school could tell a story about a time when he or she had been treated badly based on perceived or real identity. The idea that someone could walk into a place and kill so many people because of who they were or what they believed in was devastating for all of us.

The event happened in the early morning hours of the Sunday before our last day of school. That Sunday, many of our staff members and students spent the day watching the tragic images and listening to the terrifying stories that filled the news. Throughout the day, I received messages from students and teachers, asking what we could do and how we would even begin to think of approaching the next day—a scheduled exam day, followed by a planned six mile walk and outdoor celebration to end the school year.

This day was supposed to be a celebration of our year together and all that we had accomplished, but suddenly it was coupled with tremendous sadness, mourning, and fear. To pretend that it was a day like any other would have been at least a missed opportunity, and at worst a horrific hurt—to staff, students, and our community. As a community, we had to come together to decide how we could approach the day in a way that would give us the space to process and heal, while taking care of our young people's needs to end the school year, as well. After several conversations with teachers and community members, and while saddled with my own sense of grief, I pulled together a plan for the day, crafted the following email, and sent it out to our staff:

> Well, here we are, with one day with students left and three days left to the teacher year. Today has been a tragic day, and I am sure that all of you have had heavy hearts today, as we watch and learn of all the lives lost in the Orlando tragedy. I also know that given the community of young people that we serve, we all feel as if these could have easily been our students, our families, ourselves. This is not the memory that I would hope to have as we step into this final day of school, yet I know that our students will need us as much as ever tomorrow. Several of you reached out to me today to talk about how to approach this day with our young people. Thank you for that. We are going to make this a day of healing and love and still hold on to the celebration of what we have accomplished this school year. We will have our exams in the morning, and at 11 a.m. we will move to the grass behind the school and form a heart shape which we will photograph from the rooftop, a message of love and solidarity with the people of Orlando. Jasmine will have rainbow ribbon pins for all who want to wear them, and we will walk to the Marsupial bridge, where we will write chalk messages of support and then return to the school for our picnic. There will be no water guns, just picnic food, candy treats, raffled prizes, a painted banner, and other outdoor activities, and the buses will leave at 1:30 p.m. I hope that we can do all that we can to find a balance of normalcy and an honoring of the realities of the day.
>
>   Sending love to all of you on this day,
>   Tina

As the students arrived that Monday, they were greeted with signs and messages of love and support everywhere they turned. We met them at the door with rainbow pins and hugs, had counselors ready to support them, and communicated a plan for the day that made space for their learning, healing, and action. Then, we moved through the day in a way that would help them to move from the tragedy, into the school day, to collective action, and out into the summer, knowing they had love and support every step of the way. We held our exams, as planned, and at 11:00 a.m., we poured out of the building and into the park behind the school, where we organized ourselves into the colors of the rainbow based on what we were wearing and stood in the shape of a large heart. I stood on top of the building, guiding students and staff into the heart shape, and then I took a picture of the whole school community. The picture was beautiful, and we instantly started to share it, with each other and on social media. Other people began to share it, as well, and that image became deeply symbolic of our community's solidarity with the people of Orlando. We had taken our sadness and turned it into something beautiful, and while it couldn't change the events that had happened, it made us feel a little bit stronger together.

Cultural responsiveness is made up of moments like this. It is in the ways that a school creates and responds to the individual cultures and the culture of the community as a whole. It is in the moments we pause for, the heroes we celebrate, the stories we tell and don't tell, and the ways in which we acknowledge each other's existence, joy, and pain. Part of the Alliance way has always been to know when our community is celebrating and/or hurting and to respond to such moments as a community. When an unarmed black man is killed by an officer; when a sister community is hit by devastating storms; when our charter contract is renewed; when a student we have known passes on; when seniors receive college acceptance letters; when a fire down the street fills the building with smoke; when an election yields terrible results for our community; when a teacher gets married . . . Moments such as these define us.

We know that to create a safe and accepting learning environment for all students, it is not enough to just do academics. We have a role to play in recognizing and shaping culture, for it is through these moments and interactions that true connections are made. It is this kind of responsiveness that moves Alliance from a place that has culturally responsive practices to a place that holds cultural responsiveness as a community value. It is the idea that we, the staff and the students, truly want to be a place where all perspectives are considered, where power is authentically shared, and where all young people and adults feel like they are seen, heard, and valued. It is built into our practice to reflect, to continue learning, to question ourselves and others, and to be willing to acknowledge when we have intentionally or unintentionally caused harm to another. We do not always see our own biases right from the start. But it is our willingness to listen, learn, and consider another possibility that sets us apart.

This is not just what we do; it is who we are. Our school mantra is: "Be yourself. Get a great education." This means that at the center of our mission is the intention to value all of the selves that people bring to the community. It means we are always stretching ourselves to make room for all of the ways in which people show up, and that we are always learning about others and sharing our stories of self. It means that cultural responsiveness is at the heart of, and is the key to, who we aim to be.

7

The Power of Joy

*I love people who make me laugh. I honestly think it's
the thing I like most, to laugh. It cures a multitude of ills.
It's probably the most important thing in a person.*
AUDREY HEPBURN

WHEN MY DAUGHTER WAS LITTLE, she loved watching old *I Love
Lucy* episodes in her bedroom. We would be sitting in the living
room or cooking in the kitchen, and we could hear her downstairs just
laughing and laughing. The more she laughed, the more we started to gig-
gle, and before we knew it, we were all laughing, and we didn't even have
the television on. Laughter is contagious like that.

Some of the best memories I have of my own school experience, and
some of my favorite memories of teaching, involve laughter. While some
people would argue there is no place for laughter in schools, I would argue
there is no point of schools without it. Schools are not just preparation for
life, they are part of life. They represent a significant amount of time in
our children's lives, and we have the power and responsibility to make that
time joyful. If our children's lives are not filled with joyful memories, then
we have done ourselves and them a terrible disservice.

If that is not enough of an argument, look at the research. A great deal of evidence has been collected to show that happy employees (and hence, happy students) are more productive, healthier, and loyal. A meta-study by Sonja Lyubomirsky of the University of California, Laura King of the University of Missouri, and Ed Diener of the University of Illinois found that in study after study, happiness has a direct correlation with success in work, relationships, and health outcomes.[1] This work is now being attributed in schools, as well.

Martin Seligman introduced the idea of positive psychology as an alternative to the traditional ways of looking at human psychology through the lens of dysfunction and trying to repair it. The field of positive psychology looks for ways to increase feelings of positivity in individuals by focusing on strengths. These theories are now being applied to schools, where the practices are known as "positive education." By using positive education strategies, such as having students write about strengths, focusing on a growth mind-set, and practicing resiliency, schools have been able to demonstrate the connection between positive education and increased academic success.[2]

Even before I learned about the work of Seligman and positive psychology, it made sense to me that happiness was important for learning. When an individual is not happy, he or she is often experiencing negative emotions, such as boredom, fear, anger, sadness, or hurt. As individuals, we tend to avoid situations that lead to these feelings, and at times, these emotions put our brains into a fight-or-flight stance. When this stance is activated, our brains cannot focus on anything else, especially learning.[3] Knowing this, I have always believed that if we, as educators, want our students to learn, we must take some responsibility for reducing negative stimuli and setting a positive emotional stage for learning in the classroom.

SETTING THE EMOTIONAL STAGE FOR LEARNING

When it came time to do my master's thesis in 2009, I felt strongly about this idea of creating an emotional stage for learning. I chose to research and write about emotional antecedents to learning and to investigate ways that teachers can set the emotional stage for learning. I had two purposes for this: to learn more about the psychology of learning, and to share what I learned with the teachers at Alliance. At Alliance, often students had to switch their brains from survival status to learning status once they arrived at school. I knew students couldn't learn when their brains were in crisis mode. However, I wondered if it would be possible for teachers to help students to switch their brains out of crisis mode and into a learning stance.

I dug into the research about emotional antecedents and reactions to stimuli. I was not surprised to learn that all around the world, similar experiences lead to similar facial expressions and emotional responses. It fascinated me to see that many of these responses were connected to sensory experiences. This led me to think consciously about the sensory experiences that students were having in the classroom. I started to consciously use sensory stimuli to make the environment more engaging and calming. What I learned, by combining research with practice, was that for students to feel emotionally safe and engaged, there needed to be a balance of structure and novelty in the classroom. The structure came from things like repeated classroom schedules and routines, predictability of the teacher's presence, and clear expectations for work and assessments. The novelty came from activity that engaged sensory experiences—sound, taste, touch, smell, and sight. These were the experiences that the students deemed "fun." I found that it was possible for me, as the teacher, to set the emotional stage for learning in the classroom and, as the leader, to use similar practices to create this environment for the school. I shared these learnings with the entire staff, with the intention of spreading the practice of creating emotionally safe spaces for learning. Because of this, if you walk through the school, you will see that the teachers are very conscious of colors, smells, sounds, and lighting in the classrooms. You will also notice that the classes have predictable routines.

Adults and students need all of these things: structure, predictability, comfort, clear expectations, novelty, and fun.

FUN AS A PILLAR OF SUCCESS

Every school community needs an element of fun, and people have known this for as long as school has been around. Schools hold pep rallies, provide recess, have show-and-tell days, field trips, and so on. While it seems many of these things have been lost in the high-stakes testing culture and decreasing budgets that are hallmarks of today's public education sphere, the research on positive education suggests that we shouldn't be so quick to cut the fun out of teaching and learning.

Our brains can't function properly without an element of fun, and while many people have focused on high expectations and structure in producing academic outcomes, few have focused on *joy*, which is another key to learning. As a school leader, one must have a finger on the emotional well-being—the culture—of the school and know when a little bit of schoolwide recess is necessary. At Alliance, we had a culture of fun, coupled with high expectations. These two, together, supported the culture of antibullying and academic success that we wanted to—and did—create.

Another organization that used a similar strategy as part of their business plan was Southwest Airlines. If you've ever flown on a Southwest Airlines flight, you've probably noticed the culture was quite different from what you may have experienced on other airlines. On a recent flight, the flight attendant provided us with a stand-up comedy version of the safety precautions, and if you do an internet search, you can find many of these Southwest comedy routines. Southwest is known for hiring people who know how to have fun at work, as fun is considered an essential element of the workplace culture and the success of the airline. Herb Kelleher, the founder of Southwest Airlines, was very deliberate in creating this culture. He focused his actions around three pillars of beliefs: Work should be fun. Work is important. People are important.[4] By reinforcing these beliefs, Kelleher and Southwest built a business where people love to work and where customers come back, time and time again.

Schools can also intentionally build these cultures of fun coupled with success. In an earlier chapter, I mentioned how important it was for the staff to take time to play. An element of play is also important for the entire school community. It makes young people want to attend, relieves stress, strengthens relationships, and builds memories worth sharing.

Recently, when I was talking to a group of students, they were reflecting on one of those intentional moments of fun. "Remember that day when

Tina made us all go outside and hug the school?" one of the students asked. They all nodded and laughed. "Yeah, that was the best," they said.

The activity they were referring to had started as a fun lesson on the power of silent communication. During an all-school community meeting, before everyone could sit down, I handed out five slips of paper to five random students. On the slips of paper were the following directions: "Without talking, get the whole school to go outside and hold hands around the school building." There were several goals of this activity: to get students to recognize their own power, to do something impressive together, and to show how important each person was to creating success for the school. These five students were responsible for getting everyone to move, and before long, the whole student body was moving toward the doors. They used a variety of strategies to get it done. They let people read the paper, nudged their peers in the right direction with nods and smiles, and grabbed hands and pulled people toward the door. In less than fifteen minutes, our whole school was outside, holding hands around the school building.

It wasn't an absolute success. We were very close to being able to connect the circle all the way around the building, but there weren't quite enough people to make it possible. We stretched and pulled and moved closer to the building. We just couldn't close the gap. We were disappointed, but we were still laughing from the creativity of our efforts when we went back in and discussed what had been successful, what had not, and what it would have taken to make it an absolute success. A few students had been absent that day, so we talked about how it would have made a difference for them to be there. We talked about how everyone worked together to get outside, and what a testament it was to the strength of our community that we trusted each other enough to follow each other's lead. We discussed how we strategized, used math, and stretched ourselves to bridge the gaps between us. We learned a great deal from the activity, and it was a day and a lesson they never forgot. Learning doesn't have to be dull. There is room for play and space for laughter. In fact, humor has been shown to increase learning when the humor is connected to learning objectives.[5] This is why, when thinking about school culture, it is important to think carefully about how to build both fun and community building into the lessons and activities.

SIGNS OF A HAPPY SCHOOL

When my daughter was in first grade, she was having a really hard time. I didn't know it at the time, but a lot of students were having trouble with a particular teacher. Every day, it seemed, she was coming home with another story of how the teacher had mistreated her. It was almost unbelievable, so I decided to make a surprise visit to the classroom. My daughter had told me the teacher put her at a desk by herself at the back of the class for talking too much, so I wanted to see for myself if it was true. I was in my teacher education program at the time, so I was developing some very clear beliefs about what good and bad teaching looked like, and this was not my idea of good teaching. I stopped by the school midday and spoke to the principal. I didn't tell her why I was there. I just told her I wanted to check in and make sure Felicia was behaving well. She offered to take me to the classroom.

When we got there, I found that Felicia really did have a desk at the back of the classroom, facing a wall, all by herself. This made me angry for several reasons—first, it wasn't a best practice in education; second, she had always loved school and now she was clearly miserable; and third, she was the only person of color in the room. Her father was Mexican, and in this room full of light-haired boys and girls, Felicia stood out at the back of the room. Then, while I was still at the school, I heard a group of adults discussing how they needed to recruit more families from the neighborhood to the school, so they wouldn't have to accept so many "bused kids." Most of the bused students were students of color, and I was outraged. This was the last straw in a long series of similar episodes, so I decided it was time to go on a search for a new school. In Milwaukee, parents can choose from a variety of schools. I had the freedom to look around, and I did.

I think I visited about twenty different schools, all with varying programs and educational philosophies. There were arts schools, schools for the gifted and talented, and language schools. I learned very quickly from these visits that you can spot a school's culture as soon as you enter the school building. It's in the signs on the wall, the ways people talk to each other, the sound in the hallways, and the voices of the people who work and study there. At each school, I spent quality time in each of the second-grade classes to see what the teachers were like. This was my first experience looking closely at schools and trying to get a sense of the culture and teaching in one visit, but one of the schools really stood out.

It was a small elementary school, in the heart of the city. Some people would have said it was a bad neighborhood, and many people questioned my choice to send my children there (especially my in-laws), but before I even walked through the doors, I could tell that this school was alive with energy. There was artwork on the fences surrounding the school and welcoming signs at the entrance. The name of the school was hung in stained glass art above the main door, and even the security signs seemed friendly. A happy secretary invited me into the office and gave me a place to sit while she called student representatives to the office to give me a tour of the school. While we waited for the students to arrive, the secretaries told me about the school programs, how the students were learning Japanese, about the upcoming second-grade circus, and about what a wonderful principal they had. It was a dramatic difference from what I had experienced at the other schools I visited.

When the two fifth graders came down, they were wearing their honor roll ribbons, and they were excited to be my tour guides. They told me all about their favorite teachers, what they loved about their school, and why my children would love it too. When we visited the classrooms, the students were sitting in groups, not rows, and there was music and art everywhere I turned. The messages celebrated success and focused on the students, and the students and staff genuinely seemed to love their school. The school culture was evident everywhere, and at the end of the tour I had no doubt about where I wanted my children to go to school. I wanted my children to have this special sense of belonging in their school community.

BUILDING PEACE THROUGH LAUGHTER

It's hard to hate the person who makes you smile. Try it. It's virtually impossible.

One of the best memories I have from my first years of teaching was when I taught Edgar Allan Poe's *The Tell-Tale Heart*. For some reason, I had decided that we should bring the story to life by turning a large refrigerator box into floor boards and making life-size, realistic-looking papier-mâché body parts to put "under" the floorboards. I figured I could make it a lesson in research and biology, as well as a literature lesson. Each student had to create an external body piece and an internal organ, and we collaborated with another English class down the hall so that together we could create a whole body.

Of course, this was a completely impractical task, given that we had no sinks or running water in the classroom, and I had forgotten just how messy papier-mâché can be, but the students loved the activity. We used the water fountain between the two classes, and students from both classes moved back and forth between the classes and to and from the fountain. Soon, their hands were covered in papier-mâché, there was water all over the floor in the hallway, and students were making a game out of sliding to and from the fountain. It was a horrible mess, but everyone was laughing and promised to clean it up once our project was complete, which they did together. At one point, the principal came to see what we were doing, and my coteacher had climbed into the refrigerator box. The students pointed at the box, encouraging the principal to look inside. Just as she was about to lift the lid, the teacher popped out, making the principal jump and throw her coffee in the air. The students laughed and laughed. We, the teachers, couldn't stop laughing, either, and after a moment, the principal started laughing, too! I'd be willing to bet that every one of those students could tell you the plot of *The Tell-Tale Heart* to this day.

Laughter is a powerful and necessary ingredient for creating a bully-free environment. There was never any conflict in the classroom when we were laughing. At Alliance, we built our culture using play and laughter as preventive practices in the effort to prevent bullying. This meant that we were actively thinking about how to make joy a part of the Alliance experience. We had a long list of traditions at Alliance, from the annual student fashion show fundraiser, to the drag queen basketball competition (in which many of our teachers participated), to the Maverick Challenge (our annual six-mile walk/run on the last day of school).

There were so many ways we worked to make the days special. On the coldest days of the year, teachers met students at the door with hot chocolate. They used the hot plates from the science room to make it. On Valentine's Day, a couple of teachers dressed up like cupids and handed out hearts to students to make everyone feel special. And my favorite days of the year were the days when "mock chicken leg" was on the lunch menu. This was a breaded meat patty probably made of pork (we never really knew) and shaped to look like a chicken leg.[6] It was my favorite school lunch, so I declared it a holiday—Mock Chicken Leg Day—and created a bunch of holiday traditions. The first was that you had to dress up ("church clothes" style). I would make announcements and hang up posters announcing the upcoming event. On the announced day, I would greet everyone in the morning with the exciting news that it was the "best day ever" because it was Mock Chicken Leg Day, and the shenanigans didn't stop there. I would play the chicken dance over the loudspeaker and give shout-outs to all of the best dressed people, and I would play the music in the lunch line and try to get everyone to do the dance. I'll never forget when one of the boys showed up in a white suit, with a white, brimmed hat and white shoes to match. He showed us all what church clothes were really about! That was the best Mock Chicken Leg Day ever.

These traditions cost little or nothing; they didn't take away from learning time; and they instigated laughter, bringing the entire school community together in the spirit of fun. This is so important, given that laughing has been proven to be such a powerful antecedent to learning. It would be a shame to miss out on such simple and joyful opportunities to impact teaching and learning.

HUMILITY

As you can see from the stories above, you must be able to laugh at yourself a little, especially when it comes to building a positive school culture.

One of the ways I let students (and teachers) know I wasn't afraid to laugh at myself was by teaching a line-dancing class as a gym class. This served many purposes. For one, it let the teachers know I was still a teacher with them; two, it allowed me to build a deeper relationship with students; and three, it allowed me the opportunity to model silliness. Not to mention, it kept me in shape! I had several aims for the students in my class. I wanted them to develop a healthy habit of participating in five days of aerobic activity each week, learn how to work together toward a goal, develop courage, build self-esteem, and see that they could make an impact in their community.

I did this by combining country-and-western and urban line dances with the songs students loved, and then teaching them the dances in our daily classes. We would then take the students' favorite dances, practice them to mastery, develop performance routines, and perform flash mobs throughout the city. Most of the time, we would create these flash mobs with an audience in mind—the local senior center, the art museum, the mall, or the hospital. At times, we participated in larger efforts, like when we participated in the One Billion Rising V-Day activity with the women's center at the local university.[7] This was a flash mob to build awareness about violence against women around the world, and it was wonderful to see the male and female students in my class participating. Another local flash mob, at St. Luke's Hospital, was an effort to raise awareness about the importance of organ donation. We were always dancing in public. Sometimes it was well received, and sometimes it wasn't. When we danced at the mall, we were kicked out for not having a permit, but not before we completed two songs and got a super round of applause from the audience that had gathered (they booed the security guard who turned off our music). And when we performed "Putting on the Ritz" in front of the Milwaukee Art Museum, we did it with top hats and canes, much to the audience's delight.

Of course, I danced with my students at every event. I don't know if they ever would have done it if I hadn't been right there with them. I was just as terrified as they were before every performance, but I reminded myself and them that everyone enjoys a little bit of silliness for no reason at all. There was no way people weren't going to be happy to see us, so we might as well get out there and do it. And besides, it was part of the grade. I told them I didn't believe in throwaway work, so if we were going to do something in class, we were going to do it for real. "Dance," I said, "is meant to be performed." The final grade would be a performance assessment, and the audience would have to be a genuine audience. I always made sure I brought someone along to record the performance so I could assess everyone, and I know they always worked harder to learn the dances because they knew we would be performing them in public.

Having a sense of humility, silliness, and a commitment to public performance gave the students permission to laugh and play in the context of learning. And that ability to be fun, free, and nonjudgmental helped to build the nonbullying culture we created.

OUTRAGEOUS PRAISE

Like laughter and humility, praise is another tool we used to build a positive school culture. A principal I worked with once told me, "People can only hear a critique when they've heard six pieces of praise." As I followed him through his school building, I saw him practicing what I called "outrageous praise." These were not shallow or meaningless comments. He was noticing things and generously passing out genuine praise.

"Tommy, I love how you shared your markers with Javon today."

"Janice, great job at the spelling bee. You really practiced, and it showed!"

"Ms. K, that was a great lesson on fractions. I would love for you to share it with the third-grade team this week."

I have always been someone who is generous with praise, but I learned something important from watching him—how much praise factors into school culture. You could *feel* the culture of praise in the building, and it was contagious. I took this lesson and brought it back to our school community, building it into my practice, sharing it with teachers, and remembering it when it came to teacher evaluations and coaching. This praise was palpable in the school community, and students learned from our modeling to praise each other, as well. It was not unusual for a student to praise or pay a compliment to a visitor to the school, and this would often come as a surprise to our guests. People crave positivity, so it's important to create it as often as we can. When we are conscious of this, we build trusting relationships, so that when we have to offer constructive criticism, it has the potential of reaching its purpose. This is similar to the principle I learned from reading many parenting books and articles—say "Yes," so that when you have to say "No," it sticks.

SAYING "YES"

"Tina, can we...?"

As a school leader, I can't tell you how many times a day, I heard these words. Students come to you a million times a day with requests. My suggestion is, when you can say "yes," say "yes." That way, when you have to say "no," it will stick.

Most of the time, students come with harmless requests. "Can we have a school dance? Can we listen to music in the cafeteria? Can we plan a trip to New York?" The thing that can be problematic is that some of these requests would take a great deal of your time, if you agreed all of the time. The trick for these requests is to say yes and then put it back into their hands. "Yes, you can have a school dance. You are going to do all of the work, right?" You can promise to assist them, to show them where they need to get information, and yes, you will have to do some of the work, but when the students are focused on the things they want to do, they are less likely to be focused on drama. And as a bonus, they will also be less likely to engage in any behavior that will make them lose the opportunity to participate.

This may seem self-serving, yet some of the most magical and fun learning experiences came from the times I said "yes" to students. In 2012, our art teacher, Jill, was getting married. The students asked if they could have a surprise wedding for her during our community meeting time. I knew she would love it, so I told the students they should check with her soon-to-be-husband, and if it was okay with him, it was okay with me. He agreed to it, and they started to plan.

A few students spearheaded the planning, but soon almost everyone in the school was playing a part. The students decorated the gym with handmade flowers and streamers, setting up the chairs in rows so all of the guests could be seated. Yoga mats became the bridal walkway and the students found a plastic bunch of flowers to serve as her bouquet. They planned the music and coordinated food for the reception. One of the students was the ring bearer (carrying a Ring Pop), another acted as the minister, one gave her away, and another served as her maid of honor. Following the ceremony, the students threw paper confetti and the dance class performed a dance to the Bruno Mars song, "Marry You." Throughout the whole event, Jill couldn't stop laughing, but she went along with it and "married" her sweetheart to the students' delight. It was mostly silly fun, but if you think about it, the students likely learned a lot. They worked cooperatively, practiced writing and giving speeches, researched and reenacted wedding traditions, performed dances, and practiced being in community. Most importantly, there wasn't any conflict or drama while the students were planning a wedding together!

This was just one of the times when I said "yes," and it created a space for positive things to happen in the community. When the seniors wanted to create a thrift store out of the donated clothes that were in messy piles in a closet, I ordered them rolling hanger racks to hang the clothes and put them to work. When the freshmen wanted to have a pajama day, I told them they could do it as long as they made the fliers and advertised it, and then I went home and bought a new pair of "professional-looking" silk pajamas, just so I could participate.

Saying "yes" is a powerful thing, and it didn't stop with the students, either. I tried to make it possible for the staff to do whatever they wanted to do, as long as it was good for students. If they wanted buses for a field trip, new technology for their classrooms, paint for their walls, new science lab desks, books, arts supplies, or magnetic paint, I made it happen. I had to do quite a bit of fundraising in the community to make sure teachers had what they needed, because our scarce public school budget was barely enough to cover the salaries of the staff, but I knew it was worth it. Besides, we were lucky to have a few people who believed in our mission and hosted fundraisers for us every year, and occasionally we would receive grants and gifts that made these things possible. It was important to me to make good things possible for students and teachers.

THE LAST DAY OF SCHOOL

When I think about joy, I think about the last day of school. We always made this day a special one at Alliance. The day was filled with activities, such as peace rallies, physical challenges, water balloons, music, and dance. We sent the students off with love, making sure they had access to resources they might need in the summer time, such as locations for free meals, phone numbers for youth shelters, and ways to reach us if they need to. And we made sure to thank them for being part of a unique and special mission as we celebrated completing another year of making school better for young people.

One year, a fire in a large office building just blocks from our school interrupted all of the plans we had in place. The smoke was so bad we had to evacuate our building and be bused to a school building several blocks away. We were so disappointed, but we were determined to make the best of it. We brought our barbecue with us, and ate lunch together in a basement lunch room. After lunch, we went to the gym and set up activities, such as kickball, basketball, and Hula-Hooping. The students danced, played games, and laughed together until the buses came to take them home. Then we lined up to give them hugs and wishes for a great summer as they went on their way. Even in the most unexpected circumstances, we still found a way to celebrate each other and the end of another year.

For many of our students, we are the people they look forward to, and school is like a second home. It's hard to leave home, even when you know that you will return, so transitions are important. When my daughter left home to go to college, I followed her to the airport, hugged her many times, and looked forward to the day when I would see her again. When my students leave school, I follow them to the buses, hug them many times, and look forward to the day when I will see them again. How we say "Hello" and how we say "Goodbye" says a lot about us as individuals, and about the culture of our school. I encourage anyone who is thinking about creating a joyful school culture to think carefully about how you start and end the days, weeks, and years. We are the most influential people in our children's experience of school. We are the ones that can make school a wonderful part of life, one that our students look back on and remember with joy.

IDEAS FOR CREATING JOYFUL LEARNING

Every day is an opportunity to create joyful learning. Ask yourself, "What am I doing today to make the learning joyful?" Here are some ideas, but I encourage you to keep thinking, dreaming, and adding to the list:

- Host school spirit weeks, where students (and staff!) are encouraged to dress up each day according to a different theme.
- Use songs/music that connect to the day's lesson or current events in the world.
- Have consistent routines and procedures for the classroom. (Remember, it is the balance of structure with novelty that creates the space for engagement and fun.)
- Create a "shout-out" wall, where students and teachers can recognize people for doing great things.
- Make learning tactile. Students need to imagine, build, and create every day.
- Each day, try to make sure you do something that capitalizes on a student's strength. For kinesthetic learners, have some movement. For visual learners, have graphic organizers or slide shows. For auditory learners, use recordings, or invite them to write what you say on the board. For artists, provide opportunities for them to draw what they learn.
- Learn the names of every student, and use games to help students remember each other's names, as well.
- Perform dances together. You can do this with students, or you can have teachers practice a dance routine together to perform for the students.
- Celebrate schoolwide traditions, holidays, and special occasions. Host events where the students share their learning with the community.
- Create a birthday board in the classroom or announce birthdays over the daily announcements.
- Arrange to have therapy dogs come to school.
- Invite inspirational guest speakers to share their stories.
- Develop a practice of outrageous praise—make sure that before anyone hears a correction or redirection from you, they have heard at least six pieces of praise.

- Hang up baby pictures of staff and students.
- Say "yes" as often as you can.
- Think consciously about how you will make the learning joyful when you plan your daily lessons, activities, or schoolwide events.
- Focus on strengths as a means for engaging students in the work, and teach and hold a growth mind-set in everything you do.
- Create schoolwide or classroom challenges that will lead to some funny event. I have seen principals dress in funny costumes, participate in pie-in-the-face activities, etc. based on student success.
- Go on field trips.
- Make the environment joyful. Paint walls in colors that make people feel good, decorate spaces, post positive messages, hang student artwork, etc.
- Create books together. Invite students to submit pictures that represent the school or classroom community, and at the end of the year add them to the school yearbook or create a special book for your class.
- Have potluck events for families.
- Use service learning as a method of instruction. Students are happy and engaged when they feel like their work is in service to the community.
- In a high school, do things that the students used to do in elementary school. Have a show-and-tell day, exchange valentines, play duck-duck-goose, or have an Easter egg hunt. High school students are nostalgic for their elementary school years. Ask them to be reflective about their experience: "Tell me what you noticed about yourself or others while engaging in that activity."
- Display outstanding projects or work.
- Write notes to people (adults and children) to let them know how much you appreciate them.
- Have scavenger hunts, talent shows, pizza parties, dances, and more.

  And the list goes on . . .

-
-
-

8

The Democratic
Community

*If we desire a society of peace, then we cannot achieve
such a society through violence. If we desire a society
without discrimination, then we must not discriminate
against anyone in the process of building this society. If
we desire a society that is democratic, then democracy
must become a means as well as an end.*

BAYARD RUSTIN

A T THE CORE OF WHO WE ARE and what we do at Alliance is the
principle of democracy. I have always believed that schools belong to
the people in them, and nothing can be achieved without the will of the
students, no matter how hard we try. They are the ones who have to take
the tests, do the assignments, and even just show up. Learning can't happen unless students want to learn. We may get abject compliance, but we
do not get student learning without some level of engagement and will of
the learner. This is why I fell in love with Summerhill.

FREEDOM AND DEMOCRACY:
THE SUMMERHILL WAY

When I was studying to be a teacher, I had the opportunity to read A.S. Neill's *Summerhill*, which tells the story of an independent English boarding school founded in 1921 and considered to be the first alternative "free" or child-centered school.[1] This school was still on my mind when we were planning to open the Alliance School, and our planning grant provided me with the opportunity to visit the school in Suffolk, England. The chance to see Neill's vision in action really brought home for me the things I believed about education, life, and young people. I had fallen in love with Summerhill when I first read the book, so I was thrilled to see that more than eighty years after the school's founding, the mission and culture was still much as he described it in his book.

When my coplanner and I arrived at the school, we were caught off guard by how surprisingly simple the buildings were. It was easy to imagine that this famed boarding school would have all of the luxuries that wealth and fame would bring to a school, but it was nothing like that. The main building was an old brick building, large but certainly not fancy, and most of the other buildings were various farm buildings and trailers that had been transformed into classrooms for the various subjects. There were young people of all ages at the school, and many of the students took great pride in showing us around. They explained to us that lessons were not compulsory, so students didn't have to go if they didn't want to, but the teachers were really cool and fun, so it made students want to go, because just messing around all day got quite boring after time, and besides, they had to pass their exams. It was great to hear them talk about their teachers as we went from building to building. They had a real love for these people, as individuals, teachers, and mentors.

This was intentional in the school's design. Teachers were not there to force learning on anyone. In fact, that would have been impossible, impractical, and just wrong. If students were going to learn, it had to be by choice, and the teachers were there to mentor them along the way, but only when they were ready. In fact, it wasn't unusual to see students playing outside, rather than attending classes, especially when the students were new to the school. Of course, they had to test out their newfound freedom to see if it was real. But, in the end, the students found that they wanted to be in the classrooms. Older students shared stories of the things they had done in their classes, and the newer or younger students found themselves intrigued, so they *decided* to attend classes. There is nothing more powerful than when a student decides that he or she wants to learn. This premise is at the core of the Summerhill philosophy.

The fact that students were in charge of their experiences at the school was clear in everything we saw, from the lunch menus to the course options and the rooming arrangements. We also heard that the community meeting was the place where student voices really shaped what happened at the school. This was one of the things we hoped to see while we were there, but first, the students had to take a vote to decide whether or not to allow visitors in the meeting. This was another way in which they crafted their own experience of school. We were relieved when they voted yes. We knew there were many reasons why they might not be open to having visitors in their meeting—at times the topics were personal, other times they voted not to have a meeting, and sometimes the students were just tired of having people watching everything they did. I didn't blame them at all, so I was truly grateful that they were willing to share their community meeting time with us.

The weekly meeting at Summerhill is the time when the school community gathers and discusses any issues or concerns of the community members. At the meeting, laws can be proposed or changed. These laws are a list of rules created by the students; these rules govern how the community will act. When we were taking our tour of the school, one of the older students explained to us how once the school community had voted to abolish all laws. It seemed like a great idea at the time, he explained, but the school community quickly started to fall apart. The thing that seemed to be ruining them was the lack of a bed time. Students were staying up until all hours, people who wanted to sleep couldn't sleep, and everyone was tired, crabby, and ill. Finally, at a community meeting, one of the students called on the rest of the students to bring back the laws. "Look at us," he said. "We're a mess. Summerhill is going to fall apart if we keep on this way." The other students agreed and the laws were brought back, to everyone's relief.

The meeting we attended was interesting. It opened with introductions and announcements, and then the chair suggested that if anyone had any issues or proposals to bring up, they should do so. One of the young students, a six-year-old, had a concern. He was upset by the law that said that children under fourteen were not allowed to cook. He really wanted to cook, and he felt the law was unfair, unnecessary, and ageist. A heated discussion between the older and younger students ensued. Some of the students insisted that young students shouldn't be able to cook. It wasn't safe. Others insisted there were some young students at the school who were much more responsible than some of the older students in the school. Everyone agreed with this point. And some of the young students shared some of their own experiences of cooking at home with their families, and insisted there was no reason they should be denied this right when they came to school. It was a fascinating discussion, and one of the most interesting things we witnessed was that the adults stayed out of it. They simply listened and allowed the students to lead the discussion and frame the issues themselves. Perhaps they would throw in a question occasionally, but for the most part, the students carried the entire discussion. I was in awe. Finally, one of the older students made a proposal. She said, "I propose that students under the age of fourteen should be allowed to cook as long as they are accompanied by a student or teacher over fourteen who has had fire extinguisher training." This proposal went to a vote, the students and staff all agreed to support it, and the law was passed.

After the meeting was over, I found the excited young boy outside the building. I asked him, "So what are you going to cook?" and he said, in his heavy British accent, "I want to make risotto." It was beautiful. At that moment, I knew it was one of the things we had to bring back to Alliance.

I also knew we had to bring back the idea of freedom. It's difficult to get students to do what they don't want to do in any school, but in a school that promises to be a place where students can "be themselves and get a great education," I knew the task was going to be even harder. We were bound to attract students who didn't conform to traditional expectations. I joked with some students once that I had the most difficult job of all. I had to take the most oppositional students on the face of the earth and get them all to come to school, take tests, learn stuff, and graduate . . . or be shut down. One of the students said to me, "You really do have the hardest job ever."

STARTING WITH FIRST NAMES

A.S. Neill said, in his book about Summerhill, "More and more, I have come to believe that the greatest reform required in our schools is the abolition of that chasm between young and old which perpetuates paternalism. Such dictatorial authority gives a child an inferiority that persists throughout life, as an adult, he merely exchanges the authority of the teacher for that of the boss."[2] There is a lot of truth in this. If we go through life expecting someone else to tell us where to go and what to do, how do we ever learn to choose for ourselves?

As we visited Summerhill, and later, other democratic schools, we saw a simple practice that represented this shift from paternalism to shared responsibility—the students called the teachers by their first names. People often say it is a matter of authority and respect for students to call teachers by their last names, yet in these places, the students' respect for teachers was profound. It was clear that this small, symbolic statement of how teachers would relate to students—as equals—only made for a stronger connection and working relationship between young people and adults. Rather than making students feel like they didn't have to work for their teachers, it seemed to make students willing to go to the ends of the earth for them, and vice versa. This felt right for our school, so from the beginning, we invited our students to call us by our first names, as well.

This was a bit hard for students who had known us and called us by our last names before we started Alliance. "I just can't do it, Ms. Owen," a few students would say to me with a laugh. But as time went on, the students and parents became much more comfortable with it. Some of the elder parents and grandparents never could completely adjust to it, so they would call me "Ms. Tina," which seemed to create a happy compromise. They could see we used first names to communicate a great sense of respect and a higher expectation for their children, so they said it with a smile and a silent understanding. The students knew it meant something special, as well. Whenever they described the school to others, one of the first things they would say was, "We get to call our teachers by their first names."

GIVING THE SCHOOL BACK TO THE STUDENTS

If the school was going to belong to the students, it only made sense for them to participate in its design and every aspect of its leadership. With this in mind, I started the planning by asking each of the students in my classes at my large high school to create a brochure for the perfect school. You might imagine that students would ask for ridiculous things, like all-day gym classes or no school at all, but they didn't. Students know what they want and need. The brochures highlighted things like arts classes, experiential activities, career focuses, and opportunities to work. The only somewhat indulgent recurring theme I saw was the request for decent school lunches. But, let's be honest. Who doesn't want decent school lunches?

The students wanted things that made sense. They wanted a school that was safe, one where the curriculum reflected their cultures and identities, and one where they could be involved in the decision-making—all things which have been shown to have a positive impact on learning. They also highlighted the things they wanted less of, such as standardized testing, rules that didn't make sense, and bathroom passes.

They created mottos, names for their schools, and logos. With their permission, I took these ideas, coupled them with research and collaboration with other educators, and used them to write the proposal to start the Alliance School. It was one of these students who came up with the motto that we adopted for Alliance, which was: "Be yourself. Get a great education."

It's amazing how the research aligned with students' desires. I don't know if this is because people work harder when their desires are met, or because students intuitively know what they need to be successful. But either way, the students were brilliant when it came to planning a successful school.

THE ALLIANCE COMMUNITY MEETING

The community meetings at Alliance took on many forms over the years, especially as our community grew larger, we changed buildings, and added more grades. We had to adjust to meet the needs of the changing community, while making sure to always build time for the principles of democracy into our days.

In the first couple of years, when we had just one hundred students, the community meeting looked much like the meetings at Summerhill. All of the students and staff gathered once a week in the large open space that served as our art class, library, gym, and lunchroom. Each week, a different student would serve as the chairperson for the meeting. He or she would open the meeting by welcoming everyone and reminding them of our norms:

- Speak when called upon by the chairperson.
- Turn off all electronic devices and listen attentively.
- Stay until the meeting is dismissed.
- Offer sincere praises, apologies, connections, gratitude, promises, reflections, and insights.

We then began the meeting with a performance, guest speaker, or special presentation (by students or people from the community). After that, we had time for any proposals to be brought forth from the advisory meetings. A proposal might be a change or addition to the rules, an idea for a schoolwide activity, or an idea for a new course offering. The students would discuss and vote on these proposals. Then we would have any general announcements that needed to be made, and lastly we would close with an opportunity to share any "praises, apologies, or connections" people might have from the week. This last piece was always my favorite. It was so powerful to see students and staff stand up and recognize the moments and people that needed to be recognized in their lives. A student or teacher might praise someone for a kindness or apologize for a hurt, and someone might share some good or hard news as a connection. People really looked forward to this time. It was a time when people could be heard, be recognized by the community, and build stronger bonds with their teachers and peers.

At times, of course, some individual students would push the boundaries and try to make this piece of our agenda silly or hurtful, but the community quickly made a rule that if you were hurtful in your praise, apology, or connection, you could not come to the community meeting for three weeks. This practice seemed to curb that behavior, as nobody wanted to miss a meeting.

Upon moving to a new building in 2009, we were faced with a huge challenge. We didn't have a space that was large enough to hold all of our students and staff comfortably. We had a gym, but the high ceilings made the acoustics impossible, and when we tried to use a microphone, it just made everything echo. The large open space also made it feel too disconnected. We tried to set up chairs in the second-floor lobby, and we made that work for a year, but as our enrollment grew, we found ourselves cramped and unable to see everyone. We had to accept that the time had come to change the way we practiced democracy. So, we pushed our celebrations, connections, and decision-making into our advisory classes. We still hosted whole-school activities to build community, but they became less talk-based and more activity-based. For example, one of the advisory classes proposed that we have an all-school zoo trip. We voted on it in all of the advisory classes, and with almost 100 percent of the students and staff supporting the proposal, we all went to the zoo together. We had a great day, and we realized democracy doesn't mean that we all have to be in the same room together to vote. It just means we have to make sure everyone's voice is heard.

In the years to follow, this was the way we practiced democracy. Sometimes the votes were about fun activities, such as zoo trips, and other times they were more serious. We would vote on such things as course and schedule changes, new classes, school policies, and whether or not to allow guests in the building, especially media guests. The question of guests came up frequently for a vote. We would often get requests from producers or media representatives who wanted to do a story about the school, but there was no way we could or should let all of them in. It would have been too disruptive to the learning. Our process was that when someone contacted me to do a story, I would invite him or her to write a letter to the staff and students explaining who they were, what the story was, and why they wanted to do such a story. In the advisory classes, the teachers would read these letters to the students and facilitate a discussion around the merits of the proposal. The students and staff would take a vote. The numbers for and against the proposal would be collected and tallied, and an answer would be determined and shared with the community. Then I would let the writer know whether the community had voted to support the story idea or not.

The students always had incredible insights and passionate feelings about who should be allowed to do a story. They said yes to people from CNN and *US News and World Report*, because they hoped our story could be an example for others. But when a producer approached us about producing a reality television series about our school, the students quickly turned down the proposal, saying it would do nothing but bring drama and the wrong kind of attention to our school. If I learned anything from this, it was just how much we could trust our students to do what was right for the school, even when popularity was knocking at the door.

MAKING AND ENFORCING RULES

The students' commitment to the school was clear in how they determined what stories would be written about the school, and in how they made and held each other to the school's policies and rules, as well. When I worked at the large urban high school, teachers were always trying to create rules and policies to keep students from doing anything bad or to punish students for less than stellar performance, so they would be "prepared for the work world." There were hall sweeps, cell phone confiscations, clothing restrictions, and tardy policies, and it was all under the premise that since these things were not acceptable workplace practices, they shouldn't be tolerated in high school. And there were no exceptions.

I remember one time my son was riding his bike to school, and the handlebars broke on his bike. He stopped to fix the bars and arrived at school three minutes late. He was never late to school. He had nearly perfect attendance, and rather than attend a school closer to home, he rode his bike across town to this school every day, regardless of the weather, because he liked its machining program. When he arrived at school, he was escorted to a tardy room for the rest of first period, and then he was suspended from school the next day. The school had a policy that any student who was tardy earned a one-day suspension. They said they did this to teach students the expectations of a job in the machining industry. I had a lot of family members and friends who worked in this industry, but I didn't know of one person who worked in a shop where you would be suspended from work for a day if your car broke down on the way in. I think it was more about punishing kids than about teaching them anything. And the worst part was, the students would see their teachers and administrators breaking these very same rules, regularly and without consequence. This almost immediately created a negative relationship between the adults and the students.

There has to be an understanding that young people are human, and that they make mistakes, have family problems, and deal with crisis, just like the adults in our buildings. We have to create an environment that respects students in the same way we show respect for our work peers, friends, and family members. It's not that we excuse or tolerate bad behavior. We just make room for the everyday occurrences that sometimes come between us and perfection. We have to allow people to be people. To do this at Alliance, we stay focused on having rules and policies that address harm, rather than using rules to control or to punish people for things that are beyond their control.

At Alliance, the students are involved in making and enforcing the rules and policies. You might think that they would be light on rules and soft on offenders, yet it is usually quite the opposite. Students tend to be pretty serious about holding people to their promises. They also tend to get really upset when everyone is punished for the actions of a few, which is an incredibly fair way of thinking about consequences. I remember a time when students were leaving their lunch trays around the building, and one of the teachers introduced a proposal to have all students eat lunch in the lunch room. Everyone was upset. Several students ate lunch with favorite teachers, others would go outside for lunch, and others preferred to enjoy the comfortable couches in the student lounge. Rather than change the policy, I suggested we find out who was leaving their trays out and work with them individually to correct that behavior. Without telling anyone what I was going to do, I numbered all of the paper lunch trays. As students went through the lunch line, I noted the tray numbers next to their names on the lunch list. After lunch, I walked around and picked up all the left-behind lunch trays. Then I had a conversation with each of these students about being responsible for picking up after themselves, and pointed out that their actions had nearly caused everyone to lose privileges. I reminded them that one of our school agreements is, "Leave it better than you found it. Clean up after yourself." I'll never forget how upset one of the girls was; she had given her lunch to one of her peers, and he had left the tray out. She made sure I came with her when she confronted him, saying, "Didn't I give you my lunch?"

"Yes, she did," he replied, sheepishly.

"Don't ever make me look bad again!" she told him.

After that, there were far fewer incidents of lunch trays left behind, and students were able to continue to enjoy their lunchtime freedoms. We had found a way to solve the problem without making a new rule that took away privileges from everyone.

At another time, the district was pressing schools to take away cell phone privileges. In our second or third year, there were a lot of incidents taking place at schools around the city that involved students using cell phones to call people up to their schools to fight. This was creating some dangerous situations in many schools, so the superintendent sent out a message asking all schools to "develop a cell phone policy." We hadn't been experiencing these fights, so when we received the memo we weren't sure how to address it. We decided to do what we always do when it comes to changing policy or practice at our school—we took it to the students. We worked in our advisories to discuss the issues and to come up with a cell phone policy that would address the safety concerns of the district. At the end of many discussions and a couple of votes, we came to consensus around the following school policy:

The Alliance School Cell Phone Policy

Keep your phone off or on silent during class. If you are expecting an emergency call, let the teacher or class know at the beginning of class, and then when you receive the call, step into the hall or stairwell and quietly take the call. When you are done, quietly return to the class without interrupting the learning. If you use your cell phone to fight or to harm others, you will face a central office hearing and may be removed from the school.

The discussion we had in the advisories centered around creating a policy that would be an effective and appropriate cell phone use policy in a work environment, and we used the teachers and staff as test cases. As professionals, how would and should they use their cell phones? Once we had a good description of what we considered to be "professional" cell phone use, we came up with a policy and asked ourselves some questions about it. Would this policy prevent harm? Could we *all* live with this policy? If not, we had to talk about it more. Why not? What needed to change? Why? Once we had a policy that we considered appropriate and doable, we all agreed to abide by it—teachers, students, staff, everyone.

As directed by the superintendent, we printed our cell phone policy and hung posters around the school, so that everyone would know what the policy was and what the consequences were for violating it. This led to a little bit of drama for me as a school leader. I soon learned the intention of the directive was to have the building administrator develop a policy for how cell phones would be confiscated if seen in the school and how parents would be able to retrieve them. I had never even considered this might be what they were asking for in a cell phone policy. One of the teachers from another school was in our building for a training, and she saw one of our posters hanging in the elevator. Outraged by what she saw as a "direct violation of the superintendent's directive," she took the poster off the wall and faxed it to the superintendent. Not long after, I received a call from one of the administrators in his office.

"Is this poster true? Are your students allowed to carry cell phones at school?" I could tell by her tone that my answer was not going to be the appropriate response.

"The message in the bulletin said we should develop a cell phone policy, so we did," I responded, in all sincerity believing I had followed the directive exactly as it had been presented and created a policy that engaged all of the stakeholders. "We met with the students and discussed this at great length. We voted and everyone agrees that this is a good policy for our school. They understand the consequences are tough if they break the rules. Besides," I said, "We don't have this kind of problem with cell phone violence at our school."

I think the last point hit home with her. I don't know what she did or said, but I soon got a message from her to keep our cell phone policy the way it was. We could always adjust it if we found out it wasn't working out.

It became a point of pride for our students that they were able to have their cell phones at school, when many of the schools in the city had absolute bans on all cell phones and electronic devices. They knew the policy was not there to control them, but instead to support them in their learning.

A TEACHER-LED SCHOOL

We try to act as a community, working and deciding together in every way possible, yet every school community still needs adults who can do the official, compliance-related work of school leadership. As we planned the school, we had to decide what this would look like for us. As we studied leadership and learned about democratic school communities, we found several examples of teacher-led schools. These were schools that didn't have principals, assistant principals, or any official administrators on staff. We truly wanted to be a democratic community, so this model appealed to us. We delved into this a little more and found there were many teacher-led models to consider. Some schools operated with one or two teachers taking on roles similar to administrator roles. Others operated without any type of administrative leadership at all, but with systems to fill the roles an administrator might. And still others created a collaborative leadership team.

We decided to use a hybrid of all of these. The planning team suggested I should serve as the lead teacher for the school, because the school had been my vision and I had done an incredible amount of work to get it off the ground. We decided this role would have me serving as the communications person for the staff, making sure that everyone knew what they needed to know on a daily basis. Every teacher would serve in an administrative function. For example, one person would be the administrator when it came to standardized testing. Another would be the lead for all transportation issues. And another would handle all issues regarding special education services. I would funnel the emails, due dates, and information to the appropriate teacher leaders. Everyone would be a teacher, and everyone would be a leader. Even the social worker would coteach a class, so everyone would understand what it meant to be a teacher and what it meant to be a leader.

My day as teacher leader looked something like this:

- Before school and during the first block of classes, I handled administrative stuff. I gave tours of the school, met with parents, counseled young people, found things for teachers, subbed classes, coordinated the day's activities, and so on. This tended to be a quieter time of day, so it was a good time to block off for administrative tasks and meetings. Of course, I always made sure to be standing at the door to greet students and families when they arrived. This is a very important part of setting the tone for the day.

- When second block began, I became a teacher, and other teachers stepped into the administrative role for that block of time. I taught several classes over the years, sometimes to fill a need in the schedule and sometimes because of a student request, including Women in Literature, Spanish, geometry, triathlon, and line dancing.

- At lunch time, I moved throughout the building, visiting classes and the lunch room to socialize with students and teachers.

- In the afternoon, I led an advisory period, worked with the Student Leadership Team, observed classrooms, and/or participated in restorative practices.

- At the end of the day and after school, I met with teachers, responded to student and parent requests, handled the accounting, and planned the professional development activities for the week.

- During each class block, a different teacher handled the disciplinary needs of the school, and when I wasn't teaching, I assisted in this role.

It wasn't always easy to be a teacher and a leader. The hardest part was people would often come looking for me during my teaching period. I worked hard to set clear boundaries around interrupting my instructional time. I didn't want my students to miss out because of the constant demands of school leadership.

The best part of being a teacher-led school, though, was that leadership always felt like a gift from the community. I had no positional authority to make anyone do anything, yet everyone worked hard, cared deeply, and contributed to the functioning of the team. Students, teachers, and parents would often insist on calling me the principal, which I took as a great compliment. Yet in these moments, I always reminded them they were just as much the principal as I was. This was what it meant to be a democratic community.

COMING TO CONSENSUS

For any school or organization to be a democratic community, there must be a process in place for developing consensus. At our school we used a process that involved starting with the problem, sharing ideas for potential solutions (using small groups like advisories or circles), coming up with a proposal, responding to that proposal with concerns or suggestions, revising the proposal, and then voting using a *fist-to-five* process.

A fellow teacher taught me the fist-to-five process, and we have been using it ever since. When it's time to make a decision, somebody proposes an action, and we bring it to a vote. Each person gets to hold up a hand with any number from fist to five fingers, based on how he or she feels about the proposed action. Here is what each number represents:

- *Fist:* "I cannot go along with any notion of this idea. We need to scrap the whole thing and start from square one."
- *One:* "I do not like this idea at all. We have a lot of work to do before I can go along with it."
- *Two:* "I am really uncomfortable with this idea and cannot vote to support it. We need to talk more."
- *Three:* "I'm not certain this idea will work, but I am willing to go along with the team and commit to it wholly."

- *Four:* "I'm a little nervous about it, but mostly I feel really good about this idea."
- *Five:* "I love this idea. Let's do it."

We use this system at staff meetings and in classrooms. It gives everyone a chance to speak and a chance to vote, and it ensures that we never move forward with an idea until everyone is holding up three fingers or more.

THE STUDENT LEADERSHIP TEAM

Several years after founding the school, we created the Student Leadership Team. We always hesitated when it came to creating a student council or student government at Alliance, because it seemed to run counter to the democratic governance idea that we were trying to espouse. How could we have a school president if we didn't even have a school principal? It was clear, though, that students wanted opportunities to practice leadership. So, when a couple of the seniors came to me about creating a student government, I invited them to consider, instead, a leadership team. It would be similar to student government, in that students would petition their grade-level peers to become members of the leadership team. Two to four students (based on the sizes of the advisories) would be selected from each advisory class, yet there would be no hierarchy among the students selected to be on the team. The student leaders would meet once a week at lunch with me, the teacher leader, and would serve two purposes: 1) to consistently find ways to steer the school to better serve its mission and vision, and 2) to provide students with opportunities to grow and develop as leaders.

This turned out to be a great investment, for me and for the students. It was as if I had doubled my staff numbers and suddenly had ten more adults to share the responsibilities with. The students planned schoolwide activities, college visits, and leadership activities. I worked to bring in guest speakers, texts, and opportunities for students to sharpen their leadership skills. When there were conflicts or issues in the school or community, the Student Leadership Team was often the body that worked with me to develop a plan for how to move forward. I was so grateful for their commitment, and there was no animosity toward them from the student community, because their peers always saw them as working hard to bring the student voice to leadership.

During the first year, one of the things the team wanted to do for their own leadership development was to travel. I made it clear, if we were going to do this, that they would have to do the work—the paperwork, the fundraising, all of it. That would become part of their leadership charge, and they agreed. They wanted to do it that way, they assured me, so they could learn what it would take to make it happen. With this commitment, we started to brainstorm. We talked about many different possibilities, and one of the things that came up was the idea of going somewhere to help a community. I told them about a service trip I had participated in with the young people in my church. We had gone to New York for a week and completed service activities in food pantries, homeless shelters, and soup kitchens. Each day, we visited a different site. At the end of the week, we were invited to compare our experiences and think about what service can look like. The students loved this idea and decided they wanted to partner with the same agency to do this work. I gave them the name, and they got to work planning, fundraising, and completing all of the required forms for travel. Of course I had to help with some of the official stuff, but if there was ever a task a student could do, I would pass it back to the team. In May of that year, twelve students, two teachers (including myself), and two parents traveled to New York City to participate in a week of service. It was powerful. Most of them had never been on an airplane in their lives, so the flights alone were a learning experience. In each place we visited, the students engaged in hard work. They helped cook and serve meals, put together bags of food for families, organized clothes, and greeted people from the community. It was challenging work, and the devastation caused by poverty, joblessness, drug addiction, and structural racism was evident in everything we did. But the experience also taught us all how much we could do and how each small act can make a big difference. I was so proud of these students. If there was ever a clear demonstration of leadership, this was it. Not only did they learn about travel and service to the community through this experience, it was clear they learned even more about themselves.

BACK HOME, AT ALLIANCE

A student's experience in school is about life and preparation for life. At Alliance, we try to think about this every day. We ask ourselves, "Have we made sure everyone's voices have been heard? Do we need to take a vote? Are we sharing our power? Is this the most democratic way we can do this?" We try to create and protect democracy in our structures, policies, and ways of interacting. We believe that if we want our students to be healthy, happy, and contributing members of a democratic community, we have to provide them with opportunities to practice being part of such communities. We have to teach them how to share power, explore possibilities, consider other perspectives, question authority, negotiate conflict, and find consensus. We have to model it for our students, and we have to practice it *with* our students. Providing this kind of opportunity to live and grow in community is one of the greatest gifts we can give them. We know one day our children will be our caretakers and the caretakers of our democracy. It's our greatest charge, and the charge we share with everyone reading this book, to think deeply about how we can share and practice the principles of democracy in our schools and everyday lives, so when the time comes, the young people will know how to take care of us all.

9

Restorative Discipline Practices

When you learn something from people, or from a culture, you accept it as a gift, and it is your lifelong commitment to preserve it and build on it.

YO-YO MA

I N THE FALL OF 2005, just weeks after opening the school, I was facing a real challenge. I had never handled anything but classroom discipline scenarios before starting the school, and no one could have prepared me for the level or number of discipline situations I would face as the school leader. It felt like students had to challenge everything, and in a school with a mission of freedom and acceptance, it was often hard to know what to address and what to leave alone.

In true Summerhill fashion, we wanted education to be a choice, not a mandate. However, the realities of putting this theory into practice were a nightmare. While we didn't want to be authoritarian about attendance, and we wanted students to choose to attend class when they were ready, how should we take attendance when students were in school, but not in class?

Attendance was one of the charter contract measures that would be used to determine our success. If a student wasn't in class, we couldn't count him as present, but if we knew where he was and didn't make him go to class, weren't we just securing our own downfall? And what about the loud behavior that developed in communal spaces and disrupted other classes? Our school was small, and there weren't many places where students could go and not be a bother to others. If students chose to sit in the lobby, that was what guests would see as they entered the school. How would that make anyone believe this was a genuine educational institution? We needed to do something, because this wasn't looking like we hoped it would. Freedom couldn't come at the expense of the whole school community. That was never the Summerhill philosophy to begin with.

The staff decided to bring it up at the weekly community meeting, and surprisingly, the majority of students agreed that something needed to be done. They had been *waiting* for us to do something. We needed to come up with a set of agreements for how we would take care of ourselves and each other as a school community, or this school idea wasn't going to work. I invited the students to share some ideas in the large group, and with the discussion started, we went back to our advisories and continued to brainstorm and perfect our thinking. We went back and forth like this for a couple of weeks. At the end, we had developed our Six Agreements, printed at the beginning of this book, which became the guidelines for practice in our community.

The students and staff all signed posters in advisory classrooms committing to the agreements, and when new students enrolled at the school, they also signed compacts promising to abide by the agreements. This made it possible for us to use the agreements as a measure of acceptable behavior and to address behaviors that went against the community's values. If students hadn't been to class, we asked if they were living up to the agreement that "School work comes first," and so Alliance students were expected to go to class. If a student insulted another student, peers would remind him or her that we had committed to "respecting each other's differences." The agreements weren't there for the teachers to enforce alone. That would have gone against our democratic structure. Rather, the commitments belonged to everyone, and above all else, the school belonged to the students. Over time, with the agreements as our foundation, our community's approach to discipline evolved with a focus on three basic tenets: a "no excuses for harm" rule, trauma-informed care, and restorative practices.

NO EXCUSES FOR HARM

We don't have many rules at the Alliance School. The rules we do have are focused around the idea of not causing harm. We don't worry if students chew gum, wear hats, or listen to headphones while doing their work. If a student litters, we ask him or her to pick it up. If he forgets his pencil, we give him a pencil to use. We do not believe that rules and punishments are a means of drilling discipline into students. Rather, they are mechanisms of control, and students only learn to be controlled through such methods. Students learn discipline through practice, with the support and encouragement of those around them.

This does not mean that anyone can do anything without consequence, though. Our mission is to be a safe and accepting place for all students, so we hold tight to the principle of "do no harm." We don't allow for excuses when it comes to harm. If you hurt someone, you are responsible for repairing the harm that was caused, even if that harm was not intentional. Sometimes that harm can be repaired with a simple apology, yet when it is part of a pattern of causing harm, it requires much more of an investment. Because of this, we are quick to document, give consequences, remove a student from a class, or give him or her a break from the community, if he or she continuously chooses to cause harm. Whether it is a verbal or physical assault, there is no place for it at Alliance. If a student deliberately chooses to get into a fight that could have been avoided, or chooses to harm a peer with full intent to do so, that student will face a peer justice council, which could lead to a district disciplinary hearing and likely removal from the school.

In a peer justice council meeting, the peers listen to the charges, discuss the behavior with the student, and come up with consequences for actions, as well as a plan for improved behavior. The council and the student develop a contract with expectations for improvement and the reparation of harm done. The contract can be revoked by the school staff or peer council at any time if the behaviors escalate or continue. This would lead to more traditional consequences, such as suspension or expulsion from the school. Sometimes this is enough to curb the behavior, and sometimes it is not. It is rare for students to find themselves facing an expulsion hearing, yet it does happen at times. At moments like this, when I have had to request an expulsion hearing because a student did not follow through on the terms of his or her contract, parents attending the meeting have traditionally been quick to tell the officer leading the meeting, "The school did everything they could. My child simply would not change his behavior."

TRAUMA-INFORMED PRACTICE

While we are fierce, as a community, when it comes to addressing harm, we spend much more energy preventing it so that we don't have to address it. We do this in many ways. One of the first things we do is spend an incredible amount of energy building bridges for strong relationships. We have talked about this a great deal in previous chapters. In addition to that focus, we invest in making sure our teachers and school community are aware of the signs of trauma, and that they have the tools and supports to address it when they see it. We knew that many of our students had experienced trauma, and we saw the signs of it clearly in the first few weeks of our first year of school. So we started to do research, and we partnered with our school social worker to ensure that all of our teachers were trained in trauma-sensitive practices. We worked to become a trauma-sensitive school.[1]

One of the first tenets we learned about was the importance of holding a nonjudgmental attitude around student behavior, remembering that all actions are the result of underlying physiological or psychological needs. By remembering this, our first reaction to behavior is to think about what need might not being met and to help students get those needs met. With this mind-set, we are able to hold dignity, respect, and care for students at the core of our discipline practices, which means we never hold grudges.

We allow students to start each new day with a new opportunity to try a different way.

We also use a system of "green slips" to track small, yet harmful, words, actions, or inappropriate behaviors. When we notice such patterns or repeated offenses, we do a couple of things—one, we connect that student with the counselor or social worker who starts to check in with the student regularly, and two, we meet as a staff and try to uncover any patterns or see if any teachers have been able to find solutions that work well with and for the student. If the pattern continues despite our efforts, we refer the student to one of our peer justice councils, where peers also work with the student to address and improve the behavior. This is often the most influential intervention when behaviors are persistent.

Finally, we use restorative practices to build a culture that gives young people the space to share their stories in a safe and accepting community. Since speaking one's truth out loud is so impactful, this may be one of the most important ways we support young people who have experienced trauma.

RESTORATIVE PRACTICES

At the Alliance School, restorative practices have become a key part of who we are, a critical element of the Alliance way. This is because the practice sits at the intersection of many of our core beliefs—that young people are powerful, that reparation is more important than punishment, that schools must teach interpersonal skills as well as academic skills, that those who have experienced trauma can excel, that power must be shared, and that relationships are at the heart of preventing and addressing harm. At times, I have heard administrators say they tried restorative justice, and it didn't work. When pressed, I have learned this was often because it was used solely as a disciplinary procedure and not as a philosophical practice. For restorative justice to work, everyone in the school community must own and understand it. It must be practiced in times of peace and in times of conflict. Students and staff must share the belief that harm can be repaired, and they must understand how to sit with and listen to each other deeply. These things take practice.

The Alliance School was a natural setting for restorative practices to grow, because it is a place built on the ideas of shared power and student-centered practice. We have always believed that school is nothing except the cumulative actions of all of the people in it, and when you step back and look at the whole picture, students truly have the most power in any school. For a school to be successful, the students are the ones who must show up, take the tests, learn, and be in community with each other. When adults recognize and honor this power to begin with, young people and adults can see and feel their ownership of and responsibility to the community. We started putting this idea into practice from the very beginning.

THE SCHOOL DISCIPLINE COUNCIL

When we first opened the school, I frequently brought together students to serve on the School Discipline Council. The council was made up of a rotating group of students who would help to handle school discipline concerns. They would review behavioral reports which had been filed by teachers and/or submitted by students, listen carefully to cases, determine causes, and assign consequences for actions that violated our six agreements. Many adults assume students will go easy on each other when given this kind of authority, but we saw the opposite as we watched these students in action. Not only would they be stricter than adults in assigning consequences, their peers were also a lot more likely to listen to what they had to say about the consequences.

For example, one of our students was quite determined to be as embarrassing as she possibly could. Not that she was embarrassed by her own actions. Quite the contrary. She seemed to be thrilled by the fact that she could infuriate her peers and make the adults in the room squirm in discomfort. One day, outside of the school building, she decided that it would be hilarious to insinuate having sexual acts with the fire hydrant in front of the school. She straddled the hydrant and screamed loudly, pretending to orgasm, beside the main street. It just so happened that one of the district administrators was passing by at the time and was appalled to see her in action. Students who had seen her were also fed up and embarrassed. The next day I decided to ask her to come to a meeting with the Discipline Council. This would be an alternative to suspension, because at this point everyone was frustrated and ready to see her suspended. I brought the council together, making sure the students who would act as representatives were people she associated with and cared about, not just honor roll students or staff members. I could have invited people who were furious with her, but that would only have made her happy that her actions had accomplished exactly what she had hoped they would. Instead, when she came to the council, she sat before a group of her closest peers, and a couple of other students who were friends of her friends, all of whom cared deeply about the existence of the school. She was shocked to see them in the room.

They each shared what had happened and how her behavior had impacted them, as well as how her ongoing behavior was impacting them. Some talked about their goals for after high school. Others talked about family members who wanted to attend the school, but whose parents would never enroll them if they saw this behavior. One of the students got to the heart of things when she said, "I know you, and this isn't you. I don't understand why you are acting this way. What's going on?" The girl revealed that this was the way people had always acted at her previous school, so she was just doing what she had always done. She said she didn't like teachers, and so she wasn't going to make things easy for them. The other students explained how these teachers weren't like teachers in other schools, these teachers had created this school for students like them, and they didn't want to lose it. It was a powerful conversation, one where the girl finally looked around her and realized the teachers weren't her enemies, and her peers weren't impressed with her over-the-top behaviors. In fact, they were quite upset by them.

One of the guidelines for the council was that if they were to assign consequences, the consequences had to benefit the school in a way that addressed the harm the school had suffered. In this case, since she had done something that made the school look bad, they expected her to do something to make the school look good. She was a talented artist, so the students assigned her to create a chalk mural in the courtyard in front of the school, representing the values of the school. They also offered to help her do it. This was a turning point for this student. Her behavior wasn't perfect after that, but it was less extreme and a great deal less disruptive.

This was how the Discipline Council operated for the first year. Whenever there was a conflict between students, or a student was repeatedly in trouble, he or she would be assigned to a council. The council was never the same group of students, because this would have taken them out of class too much, and it was better to have students who were connected to the peer being called before the council. But there were a few students who, over time, showed great strength and character as council members, so I would often call on these students to lead the council meetings. During these meetings, I occasionally offered a thought or a question, but mostly I would listen and let the students lead the way. The councils belonged to them, not to me, and they took on the responsibility brilliantly.

There came a time, though, when we hit a wall. A conflict was escalating, and no amount of councils or consequences seemed to be working. This was when we learned about restorative justice.

RESTORATIVE JUSTICE

It was late spring in our first year, and a conflict had been escalating between four girls. I couldn't even quite figure out what the original conflict had been, but it had grown to the point where threats were being made and parents were involved. A couple of these girls were gang affiliated, and things seemed to be getting incredibly dangerous. I was worried about violence and serious weapons, and police officers had already been contacted on several occasions, both by myself and by parents. But the students continued to argue and engage others in the conflict, despite discipline council interventions, in-school detentions, and the officers' warnings. I had recently suspended the students for fighting, and I was on the verge of moving forward with expulsion hearings because the students continued to deliberately engage in harm to each other and the community.

At the same time, our social worker was telling me about a restorative justice training that was going to take place in the summer. It was a long training—four days, eight hours each day. As a year-round school, our summer was a short one, and I was pretty thoroughly exhausted from this first year, but she mentioned several times how it was a tool for solving conflicts and decreasing suspensions and expulsions. In a moment of desperation, I asked her if the facilitator would be willing to come in and address the ongoing conflict that we had been dealing with. She offered to ask, and a few days later we had a plan. I contacted each of the parents and asked them to come in one evening for a restorative justice circle. Each student would have one parent with them, and a few other teachers from the school would be there. They were unsure about it, but they promised to attend, because they didn't want their children expelled from the school.

Patricia (Pat) Lacoque was the facilitator, and she arrived an hour before the families to set up the space. Situated in a large room, she spread a round cloth on the floor and arranged a circle of chairs around it. She then arranged a bunch of flowers, pictures, and knickknacks or "talking pieces" on the cloth, with a candle in the center. She lit the candle, and we talked as we waited for the families to arrive. I wasn't sure what to expect, but I was willing to try anything, so I watched her and waited.

The parents were as unsure as I was. When they walked in and saw the candle glowing in the center of the room, they didn't know what to think at all. One of the parents said to me, "Tina, what kind of voodoo shit are you trying to put us through?"

Despite my own uncertainty, I reassured her, saying, "Trust me. It works."

When another parent arrived, she looked around and said to us, "Shouldn't the police be here?"

It was a testament to how serious the situation had become. I was anxious, but I wanted to believe in this practice. I truly cared about each of the girls individually and didn't want to see them expelled from the school. If there was anything that could possibly make a difference, I was ready to give it a try.

Pat went on to lead the circle, sharing a set of guidelines and then inviting the people in the circle to pass a talking piece while taking turns answering four simple questions one at a time:

- What happened?
- Who has been harmed?
- What needs to happen to repair the harm?
- What are you personally willing to do to address the harm that has been done?

Miraculously, the students, families, and teachers answered the questions with deep honesty and commitment. I was amazed to see how much truth came out when everyone was sitting together, especially between the four girls. It turned out that each of them had twisted the truth a bit in stories to each other, parents, and teachers. When everyone was in the room together, they had no choice but to tell the whole story as it had really happened. Once these truths were acknowledged, it wasn't hard to move past them and find a resolution. By the end of the circle, they were all hugging and apologizing to each other, and so were their parents. The next day, the four girls stood up at the front of the community meeting and apologized to the whole school for the chaos they had caused. It felt like a miracle. The following day, I signed up for the summer training.

RESTORATIVE PRACTICES

That summer, I learned about restorative practices from Oscar Reed and Jamie Williams. Oscar was a large and gentle black man who had been a star football player for the Minnesota Vikings the year they won the Super Bowl. Jamie was much smaller than Oscar, and she balanced his vivacious energy with a solemn strength. She was a fiercely quiet woman with long braids that hung on either side of her face. She had been trained in the practice by indigenous peoples, and she shared with us her deeply embodied knowledge of the circle's origin.

"The circle is a practice that comes to us from the elders," she said. "It is a practice that has been used in native communities for many generations.

When we use the practice, we first thank the elders for this gift." She placed a wooden talking stick in the center of the circle as a reminder of this gift.[2] We would use this talking piece often in the days to come.

Over the next few days, Oscar and Jamie invited us to share stories, play games, create our own talking pieces, and practice leading circles. Together, they were a spiritual force. The training was more than just powerful. It was healing. Many of us had been carrying our personal traumas, as well as the traumas of our young people for years, and in this space the weight of those burdens was released. We weren't alone, and we could set the burdens down in this space. We learned how to facilitate circles, and we learned about the potential for such circles to build relationships. Since building relationships had always been at the center of Alliance's vision for preventing and addressing bullying, I knew the circle practice would become a core practice in our work. Nothing built relationships better than sitting in circle together and sharing our stories.

Once I experienced this, I made sure all of the Alliance staff became trained, and later, I was able to train students, as well. Over time, restorative practices became part of the Alliance way. We used restorative circles like the one described above for a broad range of purposes: to build community, solve problems, and resolve conflicts. Our community-building circles typically engaged a group in answering common questions that built connections between people. For example, one of these circles might have included questions that invited people to share stories about their first day of school. Our problem-solving circles typically engaged the group in a series of questions designed to facilitate brainstorming and coming to consensus. An example might be using the circle process with staff to brainstorm ideas for how to address low attendance rates with tenth graders. The group might pass the talking piece to share what they know about the group, what strategies might work, and to come to consensus on a targeted plan. Repair-harm circles were used when someone had caused harm to the community or an individual. They typically used the same questions that Pat used in her circle with the girls.

I will forever be grateful for Oscar and Jamie's passion for bringing this practice to young people and schools, and I am especially grateful for the many ways in which they shared their practice with me. Over the next few years, I invited Oscar and Jamie to lead trainings several times for my staff and for schools in our community. Each time, I became more comfortable and confident in my own practice, and soon I began sharing the practice with others, as well. It started with me training teachers, but I soon realized that the students needed to own this practice for themselves. This was when we created the first class of Alliance "circle keepers."

THE ALLIANCE CIRCLE KEEPERS

The year after I participated in the training, we kept the Discipline Council and saved repair-harm circles for the most extreme circumstances, such as when the council had tried unsuccessfully to support a student and now family needed to be involved. We were using circles to build community in classes and advisories, but it was still primarily a practice led by the teachers. The students were catching on, though, and after a year, I knew it was time to give the practice to them. I developed a class for students who wanted to learn how to facilitate restorative justice circles. These students, once confident in the practice, would be the circle keepers for the school.

That first year, I taught the practice by creating scenarios and having the students take on the roles in them. For example, one scenario was that a student had told a friend that her father was in prison for a graphic crime. The friend, not knowing this was meant to be confidential information, had shared it with another friend, and it had quickly spread around the school. Now peers were teasing her about her father, pretending to be afraid when she walked by and saying things like, "You're not going to kill me like your father did to those people." It was acutely embarrassing, and she didn't want to go to school at all.

The students in the class played the roles of several people involved in this drama—the student whose confidence had been betrayed, the student who had betrayed it, a parent of each of the students, a teacher, a guidance counselor, another peer who also had a parent in prison, and the assistant principal. We would create more roles based on the number of students in the class, or sometimes a couple of students would observe, take notes, and reflect back what they saw. One student would act as the facilitator and would lead the circle. This is how they would develop their practice.

For the first few weeks, I would develop scenarios, and then once they were more accustomed to the practice, they would develop their own scenarios. Eventually, the students were ready to address some of the real conflicts that were happening in the school, and they did. Whenever there was a conflict, or a recurring issue, students or staff could fill out a form requesting a circle, and the circle keepers would facilitate the needed circle. This worked well, but we were only beginning to understand the power of the circle practice. We wouldn't quite understand that until a few years later when Heather, James, and Yvette joined our community.

Heather, James, and Yvette

The year Heather joined our teaching staff was the year we started to really understand the power of restorative practices. I interviewed Heather in the spring of 2010 for an English teaching position that was open at the school. She was a white woman, a practicing Muslim, and she had been teaching in Milwaukee for several years. I wanted my students to understand a variety of faith perspectives, so beyond her expertise as a highly recommended English teacher, I valued what she could bring to our community's sense of diversity. She told me if she came to Alliance, her colleagues, Yvette and James, were willing to come and be restorative practice facilitators at the school for a year.

The interview committee was thrilled, and we hired Heather for the upcoming year. She would teach two classes of English and would take over my restorative justice class, where she would partner with James and Yvette in the work. I would then begin teaching a physical education class, as this was another need in our schedule. I missed teaching the class, because I loved getting to know the students the way I did, but I knew I couldn't give it the full attention it deserved. I was often being pulled from class to talk to a parent or respond to a central office administrator, and restorative practice circles required a consistent presence that was challenging for me to maintain. I was grateful to have someone who could come in and continue the work I had begun with the students. What I couldn't have imagined

was how much it would grow and develop with the expertise and investment of all of these individuals.

That first semester, Heather, Yvette, and James worked together to transform the restorative justice class from a formulaic ritual to a deeply healing
practice. Yvette and James were an African American couple who had been
bringing restorative justice and playback theater (a form of improvisational
theater using stories from the audience) to schools in Milwaukee. They had
a grant to do this work, and they were happy to come to a school where
restorative justice was already part of the community's narrative. In their
time with us, they were able to bring another layer of restorative practices,
one that was more culturally responsive and iterative. They did this by using a variety of somatic teaching tools to engage the whole mind and body
in the learning process, while working harmoniously with Heather to set
clear learning objectives, intentions, and ritual space for the circle. Rather
than practicing with scenarios every day, the students practiced by sharing
stories, dilemmas, and conflicts from their own lives, building a strong community of practice. When the time came to lead repair-harm circles for incidents that had taken place in the school community, they did it together.
That first year, Yvette and James acted as facilitators, with the students supporting the process, and later, the practice grew, once again.

When the second year started, the grant required Yvette and James to
continue to spread the practices to other schools. Heather took over the
class, continuing to work with partners from the community, and moving
the practice from facilitator led to student led. Like myself, Heather was
confident the students had everything they needed to take ownership of
the practice, and she trusted them to do so. She also felt the school would
only go as far as the students were willing to take it, so she believed it was
important for them to take ownership of this work. Heather taught the
students by inviting them to create and lead their own circles, designing
the rituals and preparing questions for their peers, and the students took
the work very seriously.

The students would often begin the circle with a quote or a reading,
and sometimes these quotes became part of the circle ritual. It was Yvette's
son, Ramsey, a student at the school, who brought the *In Lak'Ech* to Alli-

ance. The In Lak'Ech is a Mayan saying, captured in a poem by Luís Valdez, who learned about the saying from his professor Domingo Martinez Paredes, an expert on Mayan thought and culture.[3] Ramsey heard the In Lak'Ech and thought it would be perfect for a circle he would be leading. He opened his circle by inviting peers to repeat after him.

> You are my other me.
> If I do harm to you,
> I do harm to myself.
> If I love and respect you,
> I love and respect myself.

Something about this saying spoke to the community, and soon it became part of all Alliance circles, in the school and in the community. Whenever the students opened a circle, they did so by reciting the In Lak'Ech. You will still often hear students and/or staff say to each other, in casual conversation, "You are my other me."

Over the course of that year, the students became confident practitioners of restorative practices, sharing the practice in the school and in the community. At one point, one of the students suggested using schoolwide circles to talk about issues and concerns in the community. The circle keepers agreed to facilitate these circles, and a few weeks later, all the students in the school sat in circles at the same time, while the circle keepers led discussions on various health topics. They started with the In Lak'Ech, then invited peers to participate in a game, and then led a circle of questions designed to get students thinking about how to lead healthier lives. This was such a powerful community-building moment that we instantly decided the schoolwide circles should be part of our regular practice. From that day on, the circle keepers have been planning and facilitating schoolwide circles four times a year, based on topics the students determine are important for the community to address.

The growth didn't stop there, though. As time went on, and more and more people in the community learned about the Alliance restorative practices, they wanted to visit and be trained in these practices. The students were happy to lead such trainings, but it soon became challenging to share their practices in the community while still addressing the issues that needed to be addressed within the school. The following year, we decided to create two classes for students—a beginners' restorative practices class and an advanced class. Heather would continue to teach both of these classes. The beginners' class would learn how to facilitate circles and would lead circles within the school community. The advanced class would support the beginners' class and would facilitate trainings and presentations in the community. They would also address some of the issues in the school community, and both classes would plan and lead the schoolwide circles. The staff supported this plan, even agreeing to keep the class sizes smaller in these classes, so students could learn the practices and support the needs of the school. These two classes continue at the Alliance School today, with many visitors coming to the school each year to observe and learn from the Alliance circle keepers.

Now, at every graduation ceremony, almost half of the graduates are trained restorative practice facilitators, and all our graduates are knowledgeable of and comfortable in restorative justice circles. It is something we are very proud of, because this doesn't just change the way people act when faced with conflict, it changes the way people *think* about conflict. Our students are much more likely to consider other possibilities and perspectives, choose reparation over punishment, and be vulnerable with others. These are skills that are invaluable in life, and we are grateful every day to have been gifted with this practice and the right people to grow the work.

SIMPLE AND UNBIASED REPORTING

In order for any of these systems to work, there have to be ways for students and teachers to report bullying and disruptive behaviors, so that the school can document and track the number and frequency of incidents and make sure these behaviors are not allowed to persist within the school community. We had several means for doing this. The simplest way, for small, inappropriate behaviors, was our use of green slips. These were small forms teachers could fill out when a student made an insulting comment or violated one of our other six agreements. If a student received five green slips, he or she would be required to serve a detention, and with ten green slips, he or she would have an in-house suspension.[4] When we first started the school, we used actual slips of green paper for this, hence the name. As time went on, one of the teachers developed an online link where teachers could write out a green slip, and they would be automatically tallied, so we could quickly and easily determine necessary consequences and supports.

For instances that happened outside of the classroom, or patterns not being caught by staff members, we created a confidential "bullying/harassment form" that students could fill out to report an incident. The form asked students about the facts regarding the incident or incidents, who had witnessed these incidents, and what the student thought should happen consequently. This last piece was important, because there were times when a student was friends with someone but wanted the student to stop a specific behavior. The reporting student didn't want the friend to get in trouble, or have a severe consequence, so she or he would often request that a teacher speak to the student or that the reporting student be given a chance to speak to the friend with an adult present. We had designated specific staff members to receive and process these reports, investigating them first to make sure all the facts were correct, and then determining how to proceed with consequences, reparation, or mediation.

In addition to the bullying and harassment form, we taught students they could and should report incidents they saw online. Students could screenshot posts or contact teachers directing them to pages of concern. Knowing what a serious issue cyberbullying is, we addressed all incidents that happened online as seriously as if they happened in the school building, and we were always grateful to students who brought any issues to our attention. Sometimes, all it would take to resolve the issue or stop bad behavior online would be for me to make a comment on the page saying I was witnessing and documenting what was going on, and there would be consequences. Other times, a personal message to the student asking him or her to take a post down would work to stop it until we could address what had already happened. My favorite moments, though, were when I saw students rallying together to report the behavior online or telling friends to stop, saying, "You know this is not who we are. Take that stuff down."

Young people are going to say inappropriate things online at times. It's to be expected. But we can't allow it or brush it aside as unimportant either. We teach students to be better consumers of technology, and better critical thinkers, by modeling what it means to be kind and responsible and by holding them accountable for the good and bad that results from their actions. But we can't assume they will always get it right, because we know too much about child development.

THE TEENAGE MIND

When working with high school students, we are typically working with students between the ages of thirteen and twenty-one. This is a time when the brain is still developing, emotions run high, and impulsivity is to be expected. Young people are going to make mistakes, react without thinking, and say the wrong thing at the wrong moment. They are also trying on new identities at this age and feeling more like adults than children. It is normal for them to challenge authorities and push against rules. Because of this, it is more important than ever that teachers remain patient and trusted adults for them through this turbulent time in life.

At the same time, this is all happening during some of the most critical years of a child's education. Because so much of a teenager's future is built on the decisions they make in these years, this can be a hard time for us, as adults, to remain patient. As parents and educators, we want our young people to do all of the "right" things during these years to set themselves up for promising futures. On the other hand, they want to question everything we say is right, push the limits, and write their own stories into their futures.

I was a master of this at that age. If I had to describe myself as a teenager, I would say I was a bit of a contrarian. Exasperated, my mother used to say things to me such as, "You should be a lawyer," "Do you have to argue with everything?" and "I hope your children are just like you when they grow up." This made my teenage years particularly challenging (especially for her!). I'll never forget the time I tried to convince her that she should allow me and my friends to have a keg party in the house. I don't know where I got this wild idea, but at the time it seemed perfectly reasonable. I told her she would get the beer, and everything would be just fine. I remember lining up my arguments about how young people are allowed to drink in other countries, explaining that we could get permission slips, and trying to convince her that if it was "supervised drinking," nothing could go wrong. I felt so disappointed and wronged when she told me, "Absolutely not!" When I look back at it now, I can't help but laugh at myself. It's a good reminder, though, of what it's like to be young!

PUTTING IT ALL TOGETHER

Issues around discipline will always be some of the hardest decisions that school leaders and communities have to make. Yet, when the school belongs to everyone, decision-making is shared, and relationships are at the core of what you do, a teacher or school leader can leave the building at the end of the day feeling good about the solutions the community came to together. By holding to our three tenets of discipline—no harm, trauma-informed care, and restorative practices—we have been able to find a balance that holds people accountable to the community while continuing to recognize and celebrate the humanity in everyone. This is what makes our mission and our motto possible. They are the keys to making the Alliance School a safe, student-centered, and academically challenging place where students can be themselves and get a great education.

10

Planning for Peace

Peace is a journey of a thousand miles
and it must be taken one step at a time.
LYNDON B. JOHNSON

THE ALLIANCE SCHOOL IS A MODEL of what is possible. It is a model of integration, inclusion, antibullying, restorative practices, LGBTQ acceptance, student-centered learning, twenty-first century expectations, and teacher-led, democratic education. It truly is a place for all students, which shows that when you set the bar at acceptance and high expectations for all, that is what you get. There are still many who say that this is an impossible goal, especially in larger schools or more homogenous places around the country, but I disagree. What we do at Alliance can be done anywhere. The idea is simple. It's about practicing a belief that every person deserves to be treated with dignity and respect. But the *work* is not simple. The work is good, hard work, every single day, and it takes planning.

PLANNING FOR PEACE

If you want a peaceful school community, you have to aim to have a peaceful school community. Peace is not something that happens accidentally.

It is not something determined by the students at your school or the community you live in. Peace is something you have to plan for. The Alliance School is located in the heart of Milwaukee, in one of the most violence-plagued neighborhoods in the city. Our students know what it means to experience violence.

When working on how we would make Alliance the safe and accepting place we wanted it to be, we did a lot of research, and we *planned* to have a peaceful community. One of the most useful resources we found was a selection of writing about peace that is posted on the United Nations website.[1] On this site, they talk about three types of peace work: peacekeeping, peacemaking, and peacebuilding. When I read this, it helped me to think about peace through this framework, and this helped us to shape our vision for how we would create a safe and accepting community for all students. Let me describe the differences between these practices.

Peacekeeping is what an individual, organization, or nation does to prevent violence from happening. An individual might put locks on doors, install security lights, or hire a bodyguard. An organization might install a security system, put metal detectors in place, or hire a security team. And a nation might employ a military, create a weapons system, or build walls at its borders.

Peacemaking is what needs to happen to restore peace after violence has occurred. For individuals, this might mean talking things out, shaking hands, and making some sort of restitution. For organizations, this might mean having meetings with the leadership or the employees of the organizations. And for nations, this might be peace talks, treaties, and negotiations.

While most peace work in schools has centered around these two types of efforts, we learned that the most effective peace work comes in the form of peacebuilding. Peacebuilding is what's done before violence ever happens, in an effort to ensure that violence is less likely to occur. Individuals who welcome new neighbors to the community with gifts of food or simple introductions are peacebuilders. Organizations that partner with other organizations, so their communities can get to know each other, are practicing peacebuilding. And when nations send their representatives around the world to learn about other cultures, they are also practicing a form of peacebuilding.

While many people hesitate to spend money or time on peacebuilding, these strategies are far less expensive and anticipated to be much more effective than peacekeeping or peacemaking efforts.[2] It is hard to convince someone to act peacefully based on an authority's word alone, and preventing someone from acting leaves them with the same desire to act, which means they will often find another way to do it. It is much more effective to get people to share experiences and to choose peace for themselves. This is a foundational idea at Alliance. We put a lot of time, energy, and resources into peacebuilding, so we don't have to put as much into peacekeeping or peacemaking.

A good example of this is our schoolwide circles, led by our circle keepers. We deliberately mix our students up for these circles, making sure there are students of every grade, gender, background, and experience in each circle. These circles build bridges between unlikely peers as they learn from their shared experiences that they are more alike than different. Black students connect with Hmong students. Cisgender students connect with transgender students. And teachers build stronger connections with their students. This is just one of the things we do regularly to create a more peaceful and accepting community.

Planning to build peace is planning to prevent harm. We are constantly thinking about this, and each year we look at how to approach the upcoming year and address any of the challenges faced in the previous year. For example, by looking at our data from green slips after a couple of years, we learned there had always been an escalation of arguments and suspensions the week before Thanksgiving. We recognized in this pattern that holidays are uniquely stressful times for students and adults, so we started to plan thoughtfully to mitigate the stress around these times. We did things such as planning a Thanksgiving potluck at school, so students would not go through the holiday without a family celebration. We kept the lessons structured, but especially engaging this week. Many teachers tend to lighten up on expectations during these celebratory times, yet when students are experiencing stress, they need things to be as predictable as possible. We made sure all staff members were aware of the possibility of stronger emotions during the week, and we offered support to staff members, who may be feeling these emotions as well. Finally, on the day before Thanksgiving, we handed out little fill-in-the-blank notes for people to write messages of gratitude to each other. All of these little things helped us to avoid some of the typical crises and conflicts of that week. They gave students something to focus on, created a sense of family and togetherness in our community, and allowed us to take care of ourselves and each other through tough times. We also found that these practices reduced the number of suspensions and incidents that occurred in those weeks. When you think and reflect consciously, you can plan to make your school days more peaceful.

THE YEAR-ROUND SCHEDULE

As you can imagine, with a school built around a mission of addressing bullying and teaching others to do the same, we thought about everything in our planning and how it would increase or decrease feelings of peace within our community. We thought about peace when we choose our calendar, scheduled students into classes, served breakfast, and more. Understanding that peace is what happens between people and within people, one of the first things we did to keep our students safe was think about how to reduce and prevent self-harm.

In our early days of planning, we learned about high rates of depression and suicide among LGBTQ youth.[3] We also learned, as we started to enroll students for the upcoming year, that many of our incoming students were homeless or in foster care. Knowing many of our students would come from these communities, we were proactive in thinking about how best to serve their needs. We wanted to make sure our students had connections to adults who care all year long, so we adopted the year-round calendar with this in mind.

This is how it worked. The Alliance year-round schedule starts in early August and follows a pattern of nine weeks of school followed by two to three weeks of break. Because we use a block schedule for classes, each nine-week period is a semester. Students attend four classes each day.

The two-week intersessions create many opportunities for students and teachers. This time allows teachers to spend time thoughtfully grading, rethinking curriculum, or teaching classes (for additional compensation). It allows students to rest, work, or catch up on coursework by taking enrichment or recovery classes. It also creates an opportunity for our team to step back and focus on the data and administrative tasks, while taking care of ourselves and each other. Many teachers and families use these breaks to travel, and at the end of each two-week period, everybody is in better spirits. It is like the first day of school all over again, when everyone returns refreshed, happy, and wearing new clothes. Only now, it happens four times a year.

BREAKING UP THE SCHOOL DAY

The student school day in most high schools is long and cumbersome. We are always thinking about what it is like for students to experience the schedule as it is designed. Does it cause unnecessary stress? Allow students time to have their needs met? Incorporate time for reflection? One year, to make this point to the staff, I created a professional development day that mirrored the students' schedule to the minute. Each hour that was scheduled as class time was scheduled learning time for our staff, and the teachers had the same lunch breaks and session breaks as our students had every day. The comments at the end of the day were quite humorous, especially once people knew what I had done.

"The day was too long. I couldn't absorb that much learning in one day."

"We needed to move around more. It was hard to sit still that long."

"I wish we'd had more time for lunch and to just socialize with each other."

"The brain can't take that much in all in one day."

I encouraged the staff to think about what this meant for students and how they could make the day a little more bearable for them. They discussed using more kinesthetic learning opportunities, doing cross-curricular collaborations, and making sure students had plenty of time to talk to each other throughout the day. Just like the adults, students need to move around, talk, and have ways to process all of the learning taking place in each day.

To help students do this, we created longer breaks throughout the school day—including second breakfast, long lunch, and the afternoon break.[4] The first break took place between first and second block. We allowed a fifteen-minute break for students to get breakfast, use the restroom, go to their lockers, and visit friends. We recognized that many of our students weren't hungry at eight o'clock in the morning when breakfast was served, or they were missing breakfast because of late car rides or buses. Our students wouldn't do as well academically if they were missing breakfast, so we divided the breakfast into shifts—an 8:00 a.m. shift and a 10:15 a.m. shift. Students were still only allowed one free breakfast, but they could choose to have it in the early morning or midmorning.

The second break was the lunch break. We had an hour-long lunch break built into the schedule. This made it possible for students to eat slowly, meet with their teachers, talk to peers, catch up on homework, play basketball, or join a club or activity. The lengthy lunch period rarely caused any problems, and it created a healthy brain break for students and staff. This was one of the perks that made students want to remain at our school. Simply giving them a longer, less restrained lunch break made the students feel respected, trusted, and privileged.

Finally, the students had one last ten-minute break between the last two periods of the day. They rarely used this break, because they were typically tired or ready to get to the last class of the day, especially if that class was a favored elective. We often scheduled gym classes at the end of the day, so students could get away with getting sweaty and not taking a shower until they got home from school. This motivated the students to get to class a little bit faster, which was one of the reasons we only needed a short break at the end of the day.

By breaking the day up like this, we helped students develop healthier habits, taught them to socialize with peers effectively, and encouraged them to reflect on their learning throughout the day. We also made them much happier. It's amazing what a simple break can do to boost morale.

THE END OF DAY RELEASE

While much of what we seem to have control of happens within the school's walls, some of the threats to our peace came from outside of the school. Over the years, we shared our campuses with several other middle, high, and elementary schools. The chaos of end-of-day releases can become a nightmare if we don't think them through and plan for a peaceful release. Before each school year started, I learned the release times of the schools around us and scheduled our day so we wouldn't be releasing at the exact same time as the others. This saved on traffic problems, city bus crowding, and interschool mingling, all things that can lead to unnecessary tensions and potential arguments or fights.

Sometimes, part of planning for peace means building relationships with students that aren't yours. At one point, a group of eight to ten middle school students from a neighboring school had taken to running into our building at the end of the day and calling students homophobic names. I had contacted their principal about it, and he promised to hand down consequences, but I knew it would take some time to identify the culprits and deliver on the consequences. Since they had done this a few times already, I was pretty certain they would do it again. The next time they came in, I was ready for them. I made several copies of an article about our school from *People* magazine. It was titled, "A School to Feel Safe: Bullied at Their Old Schools, Junior High Kids of Every Stripe Find a Welcoming Haven in Milwaukee."[5] Then, I waited for the students on the steps to the school. When they ran around the corner and up the steps, I was there, and I instantly started handing out the articles.

"What's this?" they asked, looking puzzled.

"It's an article from *People* magazine about our school," I said. "You clearly don't know who we are or what we are about, so I made these for you."

One or two of the students dropped the articles and walked away, saying "I'm not taking this."

But most of the students had questions.

"Wait. Your school was in *People* magazine?"

"Hey, isn't that you in the picture?"

"So, you're not just a gay school?"

"Do you have to be bullied to go to this school?"

I explained to them that anyone could come to our school, bullied or not, but at our school we didn't allow for bullying to continue. Our mission was to put an end to bullying and to teach others to do the same. One of them asked if we could come teach some things at his school. We talked for a little bit and then they ran off to catch their buses, most of them carrying their articles with them. And they didn't run into our school ever again. A couple of them must have talked about our school to teachers, because a few days later one of the teachers came over to talk to us about enrolling students for the following year.

I could have responded to this misbehavior in many ways. I could have blocked their way, threatened them with consequences, or even called the police. They would have found a way to continue to threaten and harass us. Instead, I thought about what might change their behavior for the long run. I thought, "If I could help them understand the mission of our school better, maybe they would stop coming in here and harassing our students." My goal from that point on was to get them to understand us, and that's what I did. This was another one of those moments where a little bit of relationship and a deeper understanding went a long way. It's up to us to make those moments happen.

PLANNING WITH DEVELOPMENT IN MIND

We have insults, arguments, and occasional fights at Alliance, just like any other high school. You can't have the impulsivity and self-consciousness of the teenage years without the conflict and emotion that comes with it. Usually what happens is someone posts something obnoxious on Facebook, and someone assumes, either correctly or incorrectly, that the post is about him or her. In order to save face, that student then feels he or she must confront the person who posted the comment in front of everyone, in order to show that he or she won't be "punked" by anyone. More often than not, the issue stems from a friendship turned sour because one friend is hanging out with another friend more, or because someone is now dating someone's ex. Or maybe someone gets angry about a rough play in the heat of a basketball game, or a sideways comment about someone's answer in class, and the two are ready to fight in an instant. These are the types of conflicts that blow up quickly and can feel out of control or dangerous in the moment of confrontation. I am sure most people who have worked with teenagers can attest to this. I have seen young people go from perfectly calm to picking up a chair and getting ready to throw it in the heat of a moment. What makes Alliance different is the way the school community plans for and responds to such behavior.

We know students are going to act impulsively, so we spend a good amount of time teaching students at the beginning of the school year about the teenage mind, and how they can help their peers in times of conflict or stress. In the first two weeks of school, we set aside two days to teach students about how we do things at Alliance. Over the course of these two days, the students participate in mini workshops or lessons; we handle some of the administrative tasks of starting the school year, such as distributing lockers, and we spend time teaching students about emotions, bullying, intercultural facts, how to get help with conflict, how to participate in circles, and what the consequences are for engaging in harm to one's peers or the community. Because of this, our students know that if they choose to willingly engage in conflict or bullying, they will face serious consequences, which may include suspension or expulsion. They also learn that there are plenty of people, staff and students, who are willing to help them resolve conflicts, so it rarely comes to that.

I stated earlier that bullying is a systems problem, fueled by the action or inaction of the community that surrounds those involved. It is the system that determines whether a solitary incident of impulsive behavior will stop at that or develop into a bullying problem. At Alliance, the work we do in advance—teaching students about the school's resources and building relationships between people—takes over in times of conflict or crisis. Students truly care about their peers, and they understand that people can blow up or make poor decisions in moments of anger. They don't want to see the people they care about hurt or expelled, though. Because of this, our students are quick to separate their peers and calm them down, encouraging them to breathe and not do anything that will get them hurt or kicked out of school. I have seen students pick up peers and carry them into separate rooms, just to keep them from fighting.

In many other schools, this is not the case. I have heard stories about schools where groups of students will gather around and cheer on a fight, recording it and making sure security guards and adults can't get to the center to break it up. This behavior is extremely dangerous for the students and for anyone close to the altercation. That is not the kind of environment any young person or adult can feel safe in.

At Alliance, the students take their ownership of the school and their commitment to each other seriously. They are quick to help their peers in moments like this, and they trust that if they lose their cool, their peers will help them out in return. And the educators are just as committed. I have watched staff members talk to an angry student, helping him or her to calm down and remember what's important. I often hear them say, "I care about you, and I don't want to see you make a bad decision." This is often the thing that deters a student in a moment of heated anger.

You can't ensure that no adolescent will ever get angry. The person who figures out how to do that will be a wealthy individual, for sure. But having knowledge of adolescent development, cultural norms, and your community's strategies and resources makes it possible for teachers and school leaders to help young people meet these moments with a healthier response.

THE MAVERICK CHALLENGE

Young people do the strangest things, often thinking it will impress their peers. I remember being in seventh grade, riding the bus, when a group of students on the bus started talking about cussing and decided to direct the conversation to me.

"Tina doesn't cuss," I heard them saying. And the banter went back and forth as they tried to decide whether or not I was the cussing type. I didn't know these kids at all, so my heart was beating fast the whole time. Finally, they turned and asked me directly.

"Tina, do you cuss?"

I don't know what compelled me to say it, but I looked at them and said, "Shit, no." Then I stuck my nose up, turned my head, and looked out the window, trying the whole time to appear cool and unbothered.

They all busted out laughing and didn't pay me any attention after that.

To this day, I still feel a strange mixture of pride and embarrassment when I think back to that moment—pride for coming up with a witty response in the moment, one that made them leave me alone, and embarrassment that I was so concerned with appearing cool that I would *cuss*, something I wasn't known to do, even in my Goth days.

Children everywhere do foolish things to impress their peers. Some of these things are more serious than others. For a while, a tradition had developed in many Milwaukee schools where students would plan to fight on the last day of school. The increased use of social media made the videos of these fights spread quickly, and many students schemed to have their fights recognized and shared. It was a terrible ritual that had lasting effects on many students' lives, and left many other students afraid to come to school on the last day.

We were talking about this in my running class one year, and many of the students were concerned that something like this could happen at Alliance. I encouraged them to think about what we could do to ensure it didn't happen. We decided we should do something to make the last day a schoolwide celebration of peace, rather than an open invitation for chaos. So we planned a Peace Rally and created activities around the end-of-year celebration. Our class planned to make our final exam a six-mile walk/run to the lakefront and back, and we made it so the whole school could participate, and everyone who finished would win prizes. We christened it the Maverick Challenge (because our mascot was a penguin named Maverick). After the challenge, we had our Peace Rally—an outdoor picnic with music, games, food, and activities, all centered around the idea of peace. We invited families, community agencies, our neighbors in the senior housing across the street, politicians, and friends in the community. Everyone who attended signed a nonviolence pledge for the summer.[6] The Peace Rally was a big success and became something we did every year to end the school year. There weren't any conflicts or issues. We were all so busy running, eating, and having fun together that if there had ever been the possibility of conflict, it dissipated in the excitement of the day.

SENIOR-DESIGNED GRADUATIONS

While in that case it was possible to spot a potential problem and avoid it altogether, I never could have imagined that a conflict would erupt at a graduation ceremony. But it did, and it made us think about how to plan for more peaceful graduation ceremonies from that day forward. Most graduations call for a serious keynote speaker. Usually that speaker is someone who is well-known in the community and has a special connection to the school. One year, I invited one of our school board members to be the keynote speaker. I knew he cared deeply about our mission, would speak passionately, and had great wisdom to share with the graduates. Unfortunately, not many people got to hear his speech. A couple of over-exuberant family members continuously screamed their graduate's name throughout the speech. When another guest looked back and told them to hush, the loud guests became argumentative and started to threaten the woman who hushed them. I was able to intervene and get them to wait outside for their graduates without it causing much of a scene, but it was not a proud moment for me. I was embarrassed to have this kind of display on such a special day. I left that event feeling deflated and determined not to ever let that happen again.

When I thought about how to do that, I realized that our graduation ceremonies were long, boring, and *white*. That is, they followed a tradition that was Eurocentric and did not reflect the cultural values or practices of the community we were in. I knew that black churches were typically places where members shouted praises and participated actively in the sermons and prayers, while white churches were typically quiet, with scripted responses and prayers. Our graduation ceremony felt like a white church, and most of our students were students of color. I started thinking, "Why are we trying to have a traditional graduation ceremony, when it goes against everything we know and do as a school?" I was the senior adviser at the time, so I took the opportunity and decided to shake things up a little. I had to, because I did not ever want to experience a graduation like that again.

I wondered what would happen if we expected the graduation ceremony to be as student-led as we expected the school to be. It seemed unnatural for our graduation to be hierarchical and adult-led, when our school was all about student leadership. And if the students were the ones doing the planning, wouldn't it reflect the values and practices of the community better? And if they were doing the speaking, wouldn't the guests be more likely to give them the floor? I decided to give the graduation back to the students. The next year, I invited the seniors to plan and lead the ceremony. They would be the MCs, give all of the speeches, choose the music, and find ways to make it their own. I'm glad I followed my intuition on this one.

That year, we had one of the most beautiful graduations ever (a sample graduation script is included in appendix B). The students did everything. One student sang "Seasons of Love" from the musical *Rent*. Two students did a poetry performance. A DJ was there to play music throughout the ceremony, and we chose special songs for when the graduates crossed the stage. The students created a flower ceremony to honor the people in the room who had "raised them up," and, to my delight, no one in the audience shouted when the students were speaking. It was fabulous, and from that day on, these uniquely creative (and culturally responsive!) graduation ceremonies became part of the Alliance tradition. One year, a group of students performed a line dance. The next year, the circle keepers led the guests in saying our traditional circle opening, the In Lak'Ech. In later years, the seniors lined the stage with teddy bears for the next year's incoming ninth graders. Every year, the ceremony had a unique sound, style, and tradition, one that reflected the students and families attending. And every year they were beautiful, heartfelt events.

THE ALLIANCE BIG BUDDIES

The teddy bear exchange between graduating seniors and incoming freshmen was one of my favorite activities, because I was able to see the impact on both ends. The graduating students processed in at commencement, each carrying a teddy bear that was either new or had meant something to them growing up. This made for some adorable photos. When they reached the front of the auditorium, the students placed their bears on the stage before walking to their seats. Once everyone was seated, an assortment of large and small teddy bears and stuffed animals lined the stage. (A note in the commencement program explained what the stuffed toys were for.)

At the end of the ceremony, I collected the stuffed toys and saved them in my office for the right moment. The following year, a few weeks into the school year, I gathered some of the students who were now seniors and asked them to help me hand out the bears. The ninth-grade English teacher knew we would be coming, so she wasn't surprised to see us at the door. We told the students about the gift from the previous graduating class, and then we walked around and gave every student a bear or stuffed animal. It was like Christmas at the Alliance School. You might imagine that high school students would be too cool for teddy bears, but this wasn't true at all. Every student was excited to receive one. Suddenly, every one of them was like a five-year-old, giddily clinging to his or her stuffed toy. As the day went on, I saw that a few of the boys had given their bears to their "special girls," but even this created a little bit of extra joy in the halls. There was no shame in keeping your bear or sharing it with someone special.

I loved this idea, and I was always encouraging the older students to think of ways to support their younger peers. One year, a group of seniors came up with the idea to have older students become "big buddies" for younger students who were having trouble adjusting to high school. The big buddies would sit with their little buddies at least once a week during lunch and could be called upon when a student was dealing with a conflict or issue. The older students took great pride in watching out for their younger buddies, and the younger students were grateful to have someone older to connect to and look up to. Many of these relationships stayed strong well beyond the high school years, and I am certain that some of our most challenging freshmen students could credit their big buddies for keeping them in school and focused on the important things. I cannot stress enough how important these healthy and positive relationships between older students and younger students have been.

MODELING PEACE

Just as I expected the older students to model peace for the younger ones, the best way the adults in the building can create peace is to model it themselves. Whether you are a teacher, school leader, parent, or district administrator, your actions set the tone for how and whether peace will be practiced and exemplified in the school. One cannot use threats and coercion to achieve peace. These acts are already violent in their nature. They demonstrate a use of one's power to induce fear in others. This is exactly what bullies do. The administrator who threatens to write people up, the teacher who threatens to kick students out—these actors model the use of power to gain control. They are creating rules for how the system will operate.

On the other hand, the teacher who invites students to create compacts, the parent who encourages conflict resolution, and the leader who assigns agreed-upon consequences without threats or lasting judgments—these individuals model what it means to be in community. When we interview teachers for the Alliance community, we look for people who share power, discipline with dignity, and know how to differentiate between a student in trouble and a troubled student.

I also modeled this expectation for peace in our community. One of the things my students will tell you is that I was just as disappointed with a student who didn't do anything to mitigate a conflict as I was with the student who engaged in one. If a student knew a fight was going to happen and didn't tell anyone, or if someone saw something on social media and didn't report it, I would often let them know I found them just as responsible for the outcomes as anyone else—"You could have done something, and you didn't." This can be a heavy responsibility, but I also made certain that it was safe to speak up. No one's identity would ever be revealed for speaking up, so there was no reason not to help stop a conflict. Sometimes, new students were shocked by the idea that they were just as responsible for stopping conflicts as they were for staying out of them, but as time went on, they started to understand why I felt this way. I would often remind them: we are a community, and that means it's everyone's responsibility to keep our community safe. It's not okay for us to wait for someone else to do the work that we can do ourselves. And doing that only allows other people to control our destinies. We are the best peacebuilders for our school, and for our lives, and we have to practice that, always.

THINKING ABOUT PEACE

As you can see in this chapter, you can wait for bad things to happen in a school, or you can think consciously about when and where bad things might happen, and then imagine what kinds of things would make them less likely. Some people do this by using peacekeeping efforts, such as security guards, cameras, and locked hallways and bathrooms. In one school where I worked, we had to call security guards to escort students to the bathroom when they needed to go. This peacekeeping strategy was meant to keep problems or messes from developing in the halls. At times, it probably did. It didn't change the overall culture of intimidation and bullying, though. Peacekeeping measures are only temporary fixes. If people want to cause harm, they will find a way. It's also true that these methods tend to be resource heavy and reduce feelings of trust within the community, something that increases the likelihood of violence in the long run.[7]

The more effective strategy is to think consciously and proactively about how to change the way people feel about causing harm. That is what we did at Alliance. You will likely find, as we did, that you are able to predict patterns of conflict or harm in advance, just by thinking about adolescent development or looking at events in the community. And you may find that you can look to your own data and past incidents to determine where additional planning is warranted. However you think about it, by imagining what's possible and probable, you can begin to plan proactively to prevent harm. It may be through some of the practices described in this chapter—conversations, schedules that reduce stress, or cleverly designed activities—or it may be through unique ways that you discover and devise after reading this chapter. There are many, many ways to plan for peace. The secret is to ask yourself, "What can I do today to make it more likely that people won't want to cause harm in the future?" I hope you will take me up on this challenge, and I wish you peace in your planning.

11

Leadership

People don't buy what you do; they buy why you do it.
SIMON SINEK

WHEN I BEGAN DREAMING about the Alliance School, the thought of leadership was far from my mind. All I knew was the school needed to exist. The issue of bullying was too real, and it felt like a matter of life and death to start a school where all students would be safe and accepted. I hadn't thought much about who would lead it or how that leadership would look. In the proposal I had begun to write, I described a democratically led school where all of the staff, students, and families had a role in the leadership. This was a nice thought, and it was enough to get our planning grant approved, but when we dove into the real work of opening the school, every document required a signature from the head of school and the central office wanted to know who to call with questions.

When the time came to decide on a leadership model that would answer these questions, the discussion was a short one. We came together as a planning team, and I was immediately asked to step into the role of lead teacher.

"It's only right," they said. "The school was your idea."

I was grateful for their faith in my ability to lead. I knew I wouldn't let them down, for two reasons—one, because they had given me this chance, and two, because to fail them would be to fail at our mission, and I wasn't about to fail the young people who needed us the most.

From the beginning, it was our intention to be a democratically led school. Our model depended on it, and I didn't believe there was any other way it could work. If young people and adults did not see the work as their own, nothing could happen. Because of this, I was very intentional about ensuring all of our decisions would be made through consensus. I would use discussion and decision-making protocols, and in the end, nothing would move forward without consensus.

This way of thinking was a blessing and a curse. It quickly taught me the value of shared leadership, something that would help me in every leadership role moving forward, yet it also left open a lot of questions about authority. Someone needed to design those protocols and decide what would come before the staff and when. Someone needed to take the reins and move us in the right direction. Leadership is necessary, even in a democratic space, and it took me a while to figure this out.

In the first couple of years, I struggled with the question: what *right* did I have to lead in a democratic community? I was hesitant to make any decisions without consensus, and I realized that there was a lot of power and responsibility in my position, even as I tried to push that power and responsibility out to others. Each day, I was being faced with hundreds of mini decisions, and I felt like I was betraying our vision to answer them without the group's consent. But I soon realized that people were waiting for me to lead, expecting me to lead, and I felt I was letting them down by not taking on that charge. I found it was impossible to call a meeting for every decision that had to be made. I had to make some decisions, and I had to trust that their consent was in their choice to make me the lead teacher. I could honor their choice by making decisions that aligned with our mission and serving them and the community to the best of my ability.

With this realization, I stepped into the leadership role, and once I gave myself permission to lead, I found the work of leadership exhilarating. I loved being of service to the teachers, students, and families by finding creative ways to meet their needs, and I loved seeing the results of that leadership. I felt the joy that comes from serving others, and even though the work was hard and the hours long, I felt a great sense of fulfillment from my work. This kind of "radical servant leadership" served me as it served them.

RADICAL SERVANT LEADERSHIP

For me, leadership has always been about service. My role is to make sure the teachers, staff members, and students have what they need to do the best work they can do, and I truly enjoy this work. I can't imagine any other purpose for my leadership. I learned in my master's program that this is called servant leadership. This style of leadership has been described throughout the ages in works of literature and poetry, but it became popular in modern day leadership circles when Robert Greenleaf wrote an essay about it in 1970.[1] I was glad to hear that there was a body of writing and research supporting what I felt intuitively at my core and what I had been practicing in my first couple of years of school leadership.

As I dug into the idea of servant leadership, I found I had one hesitation. While I wanted to be of service to the teachers, staff, and students, I did not want to be serving people with the wrong tools or actions. If you give people everything they want, you don't necessarily give them what they need. I wanted to always be questioning myself and my team, asking, "Is this the best tool or practice for our students? Is there another possibility? Have we considered all of the potential consequences?"

Whenever there was a decision to be made, I led the staff to get at the root of a problem by using protocols to bring the problem to the staff, brainstorm possible solutions, and discuss the solutions until we found the best possible direction for the community. One example of this was when a staff member proposed using bathroom passes to limit the number of students leaving the classroom at any given time. This was a contentious issue because it challenged the philosophy of freedom in our community. We brought this idea to one of the staff meetings and had a lengthy discussion about it. First, we identified the problem—with our philosophy of student freedom, too many students were leaving class, often at the same time. This made it challenging for the teacher to continue the lesson, and it also created disruptions in the hallways, where gathering students could be loud, distracting the students who were still in class. We never liked the idea of hall passes, for a few reasons. Mainly, they put the student and teacher back into a paternalistic relationship, where the student has to ask for permission to get his or her basic needs met, and the teacher is put in the position of having to grant or deny that permission. It also interrupts instruction when a teacher has to stop teaching to sign a hall pass, and this often happens several times in a block period of learning. Finally, we didn't want to assign a rule for practice to all teachers. Some might not be dealing with the same problem, or they may have developed solutions that already work for them.

We discussed the problem and the possibilities. In the midst of the conversation, one teacher shared her process with the staff. She had drawn a chart on the chalkboard closest to the door, and when a student needed to use the restroom, he or she would fill in the chart with name, time of exit, and time of return. The students were expected to be back in the classroom within ten minutes, and only one student was expected to go at a time. Students were able to take care of their needs without asking for permission, and the teacher was able to continue teaching without interruption. This system seemed to work well for the teacher and the students, so many of the teachers decided to adopt it for themselves. We decided as a group that it was not necessary—and would have gone against our mission—to require hall passes, but that we could address this problem that was impacting teaching and learning by trying something slightly different—and without creating a rule that could impact another teacher's practice in a negative way.

This way of getting to the root of problems and coming to agreeable solutions gave everyone a chance to consider how a proposed practice aligned with our philosophies, whether there might be unintended consequences of the change, and if this was a solution we all could live with. In my final paper on leadership for my master's program, I called this style of leadership "radical servant leadership." In an interview for the *New York Times Magazine* in 2009, activist Bill Ayers was asked to define himself politically and said, "I think I am a radical. I have never deviated from that. By radical, I mean someone trying to go to the root of things."[2] This resonated with me. I imagine a radical servant leader to be someone who serves people by helping them to get to the root of things and then providing them with the resources and supports necessary for the right kinds of change. As a leader, I aim to serve my community in this way.

HIRE THE PEOPLE YOU NEED, NOT THE ONES YOU WANT

I have also learned that this holds true when it comes to hiring, as well. When we first started the school, we were interviewing and hiring people who believed strongly in our mission and had strong reputations as teachers. This was a good way to make sure we all shared similar values, but it wasn't enough. By hiring people who were a lot like ourselves, we were missing out on the opportunity to fill critical needs in our skills and abilities. At a district workshop, I participated in a *SWOT*—Strengths, Weaknesses, Opportunities, and Threats—analysis for the district, and I recognized the power this analysis could have for our community, as well.

In a staff meeting, I led the staff in an exercise to identify our community's SWOT. (You can find an example of this exercise in appendix B.) We found we had strengths in problem solving, creativity, and mission focus, but we were weak in communication and diversity on our team. We believed it was important for students to see themselves in all of us, so we wanted to make sure we had more African American and Latino staff on our team, since many of our students belonged to these communities. We also realized our growth was providing us with an opportunity to hire someone with skills in fundraising, portfolio development, and community outreach, and we acknowledged that a threat to our existence was the lack of understanding around our mission. Too many people were calling us the "gay school," when our mission was centered around addressing bullying and being a safe and accepting place for *all* students, including, but not limited to, LGBTQ students. We had to do a better job of getting the word out around the city.

Once we outlined our needs, we created open positions and designed interview questions around filling our particular needs. This was a great success. We found and hired a diverse group of people with unique strengths, abilities, and backgrounds, and this made it possible for us to serve our students better, while also dividing up responsibilities better in order to meet our mission. We also found it was much easier to collaborate when everyone wasn't fighting over the same preferred tasks.

TIME

The type of collaborative, radical servant leadership I have been describing takes time, which is something many leaders don't think about as a powerful leadership tool. They believe school schedules must be the way they have always been. Or they tell themselves that state, local, and district requirements dictate the use of time. But this is a missed opportunity. Even with dictates, traditions, and expectations, there are many ways school leaders can craft time intentionally to support teachers and learners. And they must do so. It is impossible to do the kind of collaborative work necessary for strong leadership without deliberately building opportunities for collaboration into the schedule.

At Alliance, we built our weekly school schedule so students have a half day one day a week. During the part of the day when the students are not in attendance, our staff meets for professional development, team building, problem solving, and administrative planning. This allows us to do the collaborative work necessary for building consensus. In a large school, where the hours are set by a district, a leader may not be able to set aside a half day of time for the whole community to meet every week, but he or she can think deliberately about how to create the time for teams to meet consistently and in blocks of time that make sense for teams to work together. Some schools do this by using elective classes or release time for teachers to meet, and others extend the day four days a week to create a half day of classes or no classes at all on the fifth day, so teachers can meet. The important thing is to think consciously and creatively about how and when teams will meet to do the collaborative work of shared leadership.

Another conscious choice we made about time is the use of block scheduling for classes. The job of teaching has changed dramatically in recent years, with teachers being responsible for inclusive education, differentiation, standards-based grading, and student assessment outcomes. To do this kind of teaching well, teachers need time built into the schedule to plan, collaborate, and assess. It is the school leader's responsibility to create and protect this time for teachers. We have used block scheduling from our start for several reasons. We know the longer blocks will better support the kind of teaching and learning we are planning, as well as the relationship building that we see as a critical part of our school mission. The block classes also lead to smaller class sizes and more focused instructional time, with fewer student transitions and less planning and grading responsibility for teachers. This means they can dedicate more time and energy to quality teaching for the classes they have. In our four-block schedule, classes are eighty to ninety minutes long, and teachers typically teach three out of four blocks each day. Teachers are able to use the fourth block for planning and assessment, while also serving as administrative support during that time period. While planning for a ninety-minute block takes some skill in itself, as teachers have to learn how to structure the block to help students go deeper into topics over longer periods of time, the benefits of such a schedule far outweigh the challenges for us.

Another way in which I think about time is in the scheduling of classes. I have traditionally created the first draft of the schedule myself, because I know how important this task is (an example of one of our schedules is included in appendix B). I consider this an act of service on behalf of teachers and students. Some teachers prefer morning, lunch, or afternoon prep periods. And students prefer end-of-day gym classes, so they don't have to stay sweaty throughout the day. I try to accommodate these types of preferences when possible, because I know I will have better teaching and learning if I work with peoples' preferences. If a class requires a lot of materials preparation, such as a chemistry or ceramics class, I try to schedule those classes after prep periods or at the start of the day, so teachers can consciously set up the classroom without rushing between classes. I start with the freshmen core classes, because this group of students is a cohort that moves together. Then I build in the other core classes, taking into account what I know about the teachers, students, and classes. Finally, I add electives and enrichment classes. I bring drafts of the schedule to the teachers and ask for input, doing this several times, until I have a schedule that feels good to everyone. When a preference cannot be accommodated, the teachers are never upset, because they know how hard I tried to meet everyone's needs and desires. This act of leadership in itself has a powerful impact on teacher satisfaction and retention rates, because teachers feel like their concerns are addressed, and the work feels more sustainable.

In a larger school, this careful attention to the schedule may be a little more challenging for a principal or school leader, yet several schools have been able to replicate this practice by using house models, where the students are divided into houses or families. The administrator, dean, or head for each house knows the community well, and he or she becomes responsible for working with the programmer to create a schedule that meets the needs of the staff and students. No matter how large a school is, it is possible to create smaller communities within the school and to invite teachers into the process of creating the schedule. This is a small leadership gift that many teachers appreciate.

So far, all of this discussion has been about how to schedule other people's time. But another essential act of leadership is how a school leader schedules his or her own time. I had to learn, over time, how to do this. When I first started leading the school, I worked until I couldn't keep my eyes open. For the first couple of years, this meant that I rarely fell asleep before one in the morning, and I was back at school at seven o'clock. This was not sustainable. I was tired, sick, and overwhelmed. In a democratic school, this shouldn't have been my reality, yet I was trying to be all things to all people. I had to learn to delegate, ask for help, give the work back to people, and schedule my time wisely.

One of the ways I asked for help was by making the workload visible. In a staff meeting, I gave everyone a picture of a bucket and had them write all of the tasks they had to do on sticky notes and add the notes to the bucket.

I wrote mine, too, and it was soon clear that my bucket was overflowing. In an instant, the team started to take some of the sticky notes out of my bucket and add them to their own. It was such a relief. That moment really showed me it was okay to ask for help and assured me that nobody wanted me to feel overwhelmed.

Another thing I learned to do was to set some boundaries around taking on work. One of my professors described this as "giving people back their monkeys." I later learned this was a leadership practice described by William Oncken Jr. and Donald L. Wass in an article for the *Harvard Business Review* in 1999.[3] Oncken and Wass described this time management skill as a way "managers can transfer initiative back to their subordinates and keep it there." This was something I had to learn, because I was drowning in monkeys. It was not easy, especially at first, but when I didn't hand back the monkeys, I found myself taking on all the tasks that people came to me with. "We need to order the graduation caps and gowns," someone would say, and I would add it to my to-do list. "Do we have a plan for exam week?" another person would ask, and I would start laying out a plan for the week.

So I tried a new tactic. If someone came to me with something that needed to be done, one of my first questions was, "Is this something you can do yourself?" This small change made a big difference. I also worked with the staff to outline the tasks of leadership and divide them more evenly, with individuals taking ownership for pockets of work. For example, one person became responsible for all things related to transportation, and another became responsible for all things related to standardized assessments. When a task needed to be done, I could forward the email or send a quick message to the person who owned that portion of the work, and when a task fell outside of those responsibilities, I learned to invite the team to figure out who would take it on. It usually became the responsibility of someone whose task load was low at that moment. I didn't always remember to do these things, so I still had quite a list of tasks, but when I did do this well, it saved me a lot of time and energy, time that could be used for other things.

BE A WALL OF POSITIVE ENERGY

If you ask people who know me to describe me, they will likely say, "She's always smiling." Young people need this, and adults need it, as well. In the toughest of times and in the easiest of times, I know I set the tone for the building. I realized at one point that even the clothes I wore set a tone. If the students liked what I was wearing, it always seemed to put them in a better mood. "I love this," they would say, with a smile, and they would head to class in a better mood than the one they started with. Over time, I started dressing for the moment, wearing serious clothes on days when they needed to be more serious, and fun clothes on days when we needed a break in the monotony. I found this was also a great time to plan a spirit week, when everyone would be dressing up each day. The students and staff will pick up on and multiply whatever energy I am sharing, so it's important, as a school leader, to convey a sense of strength and calm, helping people to believe that we will get through whatever the challenges are before us. It's also important to encourage the staff to remember this and to model it, as well.

This was also the case when it came to interactions between the central office and the school. I realized I was the translator of the messages coming from the central office. I would often reframe what I heard so the messages would be more likely to be received well by our school community. People don't respond well to commands, except in crisis, and unfortunately, a lot of commands tend to come from central offices. When I spoke to my staff, "You have to . . ." became "We have an opportunity to . . ." and "You must . . ." became "The district has generously shared these resources with us . . ." I don't know if the staff always bought my nuanced language, but I know they appreciated my positive spin on things and the fact that I never, *ever* told them we "had to" do something "or else."

There were many, many moments over the years where positive energy carried us through. I will be the first to acknowledge that it takes a lot to be this kind of wall for so many people. To do so well, one must have outlets for the energy being absorbed. This is why self-care becomes so important. I made sure to have a personal therapist, so I could vent and process challenges, as well as a community of school leaders and educators whom I could call on just to talk about the work. People who haven't been in school leadership can't really imagine the unique challenges of this kind of work, so it helps to have people in your corner who can relate. Today, my spouse is the person who reminds me to put the work down and do something outside of education. It isn't easy, because I am so passionate about my work, yet it is so important, and I am grateful. At the end of the day, a school leader is responsible for the everyday experiences of young people and adults, and that is a lot to carry. It's nice to know that we don't have to be in the work alone.

PUBLIC PRIDE AND PRIVATE PROBLEM SOLVING

When I started teaching, in a large urban high school where 99 percent of the students were African American, the students used to always say, "Don't front my life off." When I asked them what they meant by this, they explained that I could correct or redirect them without letting everyone else know, that I didn't have to "put their personal business out there in front of everyone." This was especially the case when it came to addressing poor behavior. If I called them out on their actions in front of others, they were sure to "get in their feelings" about it, becoming angry, defiant, or upset. Yet, if I quietly pulled them aside, used notes, or spoke to them outside of the classroom, they responded much more agreeably, saying, "Okay, Mrs. O. I get it. I'll chill."

It isn't much different with adults. At first I found it much harder to approach adults about concerns, because I was still so conscious of the fact that there was no difference in authority between us. The reality was, though, that sometimes something just needed to be said, and since the community had granted me the authority of leadership, sometimes I had to be the one to say it. I found the adults were no different from the students. They never wanted to be called out in public, they never wanted everyone to be punished for the actions of a few, and a private conversation often got the problem solved.

A good example of this was at the end of one school year at Alliance, when we had a teacher who was close to retirement. He had plenty of sick days left, so he was taking them at will. It wasn't against the rules, but it was hard to fill the void when he wasn't there. The substitute teachers weren't that great, if they showed up at all, and the students were missing out on the quality instruction he could impart. I avoided this conversation for a while, feeling like it wasn't my right to speak to something that wasn't against the rules, but soon the impact on everyone in the school community was too clear. I decided to speak to him. I told him, "I know you have the right to take these days, but when you are not here the school really suffers, and it's incredibly hard for me, as I often end up dealing with all of the issues that arise. I hired you, knowing you would retire at the end of the year, because so many people raved about what a great teacher you are. I need you to be that great teacher until the end. Otherwise, it's unfair to the kids and the staff here." I don't think he had realized how different or difficult things were when he wasn't there. "I had no idea," he said to me. He shared that he wouldn't want to make things difficult for me or the staff or students in any way. He promised to commit himself to teaching with his full heart for the last few weeks of school and to end the year on a positive note. A simple and private conversation had an incredible impact and opened a door for even more conversations.

I also held to this principle when working with my superiors or the district as a whole. Even when I disagreed with an administrative decree or practice, I never spoke negatively of the district or my superiors. If I had something to say, I said it to them in a private conversation or through one of the many feedback mechanisms. As far as the district went, I knew we were on the same team and had battles to fight together. It didn't make sense for us to be publicly in opposition to each other. I also knew my disagreement didn't mean I was right or understood all of the circumstances behind a decision. I assume first that everyone's intentions are good, and then try to air my concerns in ways that allow people to maintain a positive rapport in the community. I know this commitment to "team first" is appreciated.

HUMILITY AND GIVING CREDIT WHERE IT'S DUE

I did not want to write this book, and I really did not want to write this chapter on leadership. I wondered for a long time how I could write a book and be recognized for the work which had been done by so many people. I knew the book needed to be written, because there was no doubt in my mind the practices had saved lives, but I didn't know how to write it in a way that would capture the shared imagination that brought the school to life. I collected stories along the way, writing down the things I thought were essential, and I even tried to get the whole staff to write the book with me one year, but I finally had to accept the fact that if the book was going to be written, I had to write it.

I was wrestling with this while attending classes at Harvard, so I decided to visit one of my professors who had, herself, written a book. I asked her how she dealt with the fact that she might earn income by telling stories that belonged to many. She told me two things. First, she assured me with a humorous tone in her voice, most books don't bring in a lot of money, so don't let that be your barrier. And second, she asked me, "Have you talked to your teachers and students to see how they feel about it?" This was a revolutionary thought for me. I hadn't even considered asking them about it. I went home and started to ask them immediately. I even shared some of the stories with the students I had written about. They were honored, not angry at me for writing about them. One of the students only had one request— "Can you use my real name, rather than a pseudonym?" The teachers were excited, as well. "Please write the book," they told me. "Somebody needs to tell the story, and no one can do that better than you."

I was humbled, honored, and committed to bringing the book to life after that. Just like I had to learn that the staff had gifted me with the opportunity to lead, I had to realize they had gifted me with permission to tell our story. The stories and practices described in *The Alliance Way* are a gift from them to me and from me to all of them. I tell their stories with permission first, and always with great love, respect, and care.

This humility is genuine. It is understanding that every success is the accumulation of thousands of tiny acts by many individuals. It is recognizing that the students spend most of their time with the teachers, and that is why they come to school. It is believing that the work is done by the students, and any positive academic outcomes are there because the students got the work done. It is honoring the parents and caregivers for the roles they take in getting the children to school every day. And it is acknowledging the community for their continuous support and generosity. It is so important for a leader to give credit to the people who have done the work, and a lot of work goes into making a school great. This is not to say that leadership is not important, because it is, but leadership is an accumulation of all of those acts together, and a great leader knows this and makes sure everyone else knows it as well.

Over the years, Alliance has won many awards and has been recognized in many places. Whenever I get the chance to speak, I acknowledge all of the people who made it possible. I thank the students, the staff, the parents, the community members, and my family. I often call myself the cofounder of the school, because I know I did not do it alone, and when writing my acknowledgments for this book, I had many people to thank. People appreciate this acknowledgment of their work. It is the most honest kind of praise, because truly, a school's success belongs to everyone.

COMMANDS ARE FOR CRISIS

I don't believe in telling people, and especially grown people, what to do. It strips a person's dignity to be ordered around, and most people resist being told what to do. There's only one time when commands are effective, and that is in crisis situations. When the district adopted a behavior management system, we were tested on this principle. Those leading the project wanted every school to put the following "agreements" on the walls: "Be safe. Be respectable. Be responsible." For us, these were not agreements. These were commands, and we didn't believe in talking to people like this. We had already developed our six agreements, which were posted on the walls, and our school culture was strong. We argued that these should serve as our agreements, but we were told it was impossible. The district had made "fidelity of implementation" part of a plan to meet a state directive to improve school culture, and this meant every school, even those with great school cultures, had to have the same agreements on the walls. There would be people coming to check.

We had a long discussion about how to handle this. It went against our values as educators, yet we didn't want to be the one school standing between the district's success and failure. We decided to post the agreements, but to do so in our own way. Rather than filling our halls with commands, we changed the wording, giving the agreements a more respectful tone. We wrote: "At Alliance, we honor: safety, respect, and responsibility." Then we discussed with the students what it would look like to honor these things. Even though they were high school students, they still wanted to be able to earn prizes and rewards for exemplifying these behaviors, so at their request we created a prize box that students could go to when they had repeatedly been recognized for modeling commitments to safety, respect, and/ or responsibility. They voted to add snacks to the prize box, as high school students will often do, so we added snacks, along with other trinkets and gifts that high school students would appreciate. Teachers then made it a point to recognize students when they were demonstrating safety, respect, and responsibility. There is something about this simple act of changing the language from a command to an invitation which is a matter of protecting the dignity of young people and adults. Besides, if you can move people without commanding them, you know the people are with you.

TRUST

After studying leadership, I have come to believe that one of the most important pieces of my leadership was leading from a place of trust. When I talk to teachers I worked with at Alliance, they tell me one thing again and again about my leadership: "You trusted us." This is important. I didn't realize how true and how important it was until I came to study at Harvard. In my classes, I learned how trust is vital in the world of business and in leadership. In an article by Paul J. Zak, for the *Harvard Business Review*, I read the following statement:

In my research I've found that building a culture of trust is what makes a meaningful difference. Employees in high-trust organizations are more productive, have more energy at work, collaborate better with their colleagues, and stay with their employers longer than people working at low-trust companies. They also suffer less chronic stress and are happier with their lives, and these factors fuel stronger performance.[4]

Most of the teachers at Alliance have been there for more than ten years, staying in a highly challenging field, with less than appropriate resources and little public recognition. They tell me they stayed because they felt trusted and valued.

I am definitely someone who starts from a place of trust, especially when it comes to teaching and learning. There is no way I can possibly know everything there is to know about teaching pedagogy and practice for every subject, especially since the fields are ever-changing. I have to trust that the teachers we have hired will remain current in their practice and be the most informed people in their content areas. They know better than I do how best to teach their subjects. If I find a new resource or professional development opportunity, I will share it with them, yet I trust them to be able to determine what is best for the young people.

Just as I trust them to know the classroom best, they trust me to manage the affairs of the school building. In the weeks before our building opened, a facilities person came to me with the master keys. She said, "These keys open everything. If you lose these keys, the whole building will have to be rekeyed, which will cost $50,000." I put those keys on a ring, and I wore them on my arm every day, being very careful never to lose them. I was just as careful with the finances and budgeting. The staff trusted me with this level of authority, so I couldn't imagine how I would not trust them with the work they knew best.

This trust ran through all of the work we did together. When we were making decisions, I trusted their opinions. If the group didn't like an idea that I felt passionate about, I trusted the group knew something I didn't, and I let it go. If the teachers wanted to go on a field trip or adopt a new curriculum, I trusted they had done the research and knew what was best for young people. And when a teacher wrote an article or spoke to the press,

I trusted he or she knew what was important for our school and would always aim to make our school and our young people look good. I couldn't have been available to the children and families the way I needed to be if I had been spending my time micromanaging the staff, and besides, the staff never would have tolerated it. People don't stay where they are not trusted. As Paul Zak says, "It's not about being easy on your employees or expecting less from them. High-trust companies hold people accountable but without micromanaging them. They treat people like responsible adults."[5]

WHEN TRUST IS VIOLATED

The hardest thing about sharing trust so generously is there are times in leadership when that trust will be violated, and it hurts. When this happens, I know I am not alone. The teachers relish this trust, so they are just as disappointed as I am when someone violates it. It feels like an assault against everyone, not just against me, as the leader. I have dealt with a few, though not many, incidents of misconduct over the years, where staff members acted in dishonest ways, and every time it rattles me to the core. How could anyone cross these lines when children are at the heart of our work? I will never understand that. But people do, and when they do, I take seriously my responsibility to hold them accountable.

I do several things to prepare for these unfortunate circumstances. At the beginning of the year, I take time to go through the district's Code of Conduct thoroughly with the staff, not just having them sign it, but reviewing it with them as a community and making it clear that anyone who violates the code will be held accountable, per the contract. Throughout the year, I keep my doors open and give people the chance to talk to me early if they are having problems. I support the staff's participation in the union. I believe teachers should have these protections. If I have to move forward with a misconduct hearing, I want to know I am following proper protocol and not rushing to a rash decision. For the times when I have had to address more serious violations of the Code of Conduct, I have worked closely and quickly with upper management. I would never allow someone who might be a danger to students to remain in the school building for an additional moment, if there was something I could do to prevent it. My personal mission in starting the school was to protect students, and I practice this in every way possible.

The circumstances requiring such interventions are rare, yet sadly, it is likely that a school leader will have to address an issue like this at some time in his or her leadership. Remember to use the tools available to you, ask for help when you need it, and keep careful records of everything you do. And most importantly, remember why you do what you do. It's about helping young people, and this starts with making sure the other adults are as committed to and accountable for this mission as you are.

TEACHER EVALUATIONS

Truly, there are only two types of employees in the workplace: those whose actions are hurtful or destructive (very rare), and those whose actions come from a place of sincere intent. For the first group, it is the leader's responsibility to use the systems that are in place to remove them from the workplace, and for everyone else, it is the leader's responsibility to help them to be the best educators they can be. This is why the topic of teacher evaluation is such a puzzle to me. I will never understand why systems have put so much energy into merit pay and evaluative grading systems for teachers, when the real purpose of teacher evaluation should be to help people improve.

At Alliance, we developed a peer evaluation system based on this mindset. Since our goal was to improve our practice, we worked together to do so. Every teacher would choose an improvement goal each year. Sometimes these goals were based on feedback from the previous year's peer observations, and sometimes they were based on the teacher's own sense of what he or she needed to improve in practice. The teachers shared their goals at a staff meeting early in the year, and then developed a plan for how to improve their practice and achieve those goals. Throughout the year, the teacher would participate in professional development opportunities, research best practices, and observe peers. At the end of the year, at one of our final full staff meetings, the teacher would present his or her learning to the staff, showcasing what was done, what was learned, and what impact it had on student outcomes. The individual teachers would each fill out a small form evaluating the presenting teacher. The evaluations were based on whether or not he or she met the goals for personal growth as an educator, the strength of the presentation, and the impact on student outcomes. At the end of the presentations, I would collect all of the forms and turn the peer comments into a summary evaluation for the teacher. This evaluation was shared with the teacher and went into his or her file with the district.

What I loved most about this practice was the fact that we all learned from each other through the process. Whether it was from the peer observations or the presentations at the end, there were always insights to gain from watching and listening to one's peers.

LEADING FROM THE HEART

It's hard to know the right answers to all of the questions that come up each day. I always told myself: if I could end each day knowing I had done my best and acted from the sincerest of intentions, no matter what happened, I could live with the decisions I had made. This always seemed to work out for me, and at the end of the day I could leave the work behind and know that everything would be okay. I also like to think about leadership through the lens of restorative practices. In restorative practice circles at Alliance, we typically use the following set of guidelines or norms when we sit in circle with each other:

- Listen from the heart.
- Speak from the heart.
- Respect the talking piece.
- Trust that you will know what to say.
- Respect confidentiality.
- It's okay to pass.

As I thought about how to sum up the work of school leadership, these guidelines came to mind. I imagined how powerful it would be for school leaders to hold these guidelines close while practicing leadership. They are, after all, very similar to the practices I've described throughout this chapter. What if we all could practice listening and speaking from the heart, using protocols to discuss issues, trusting ourselves and others, respecting confidentiality, and knowing when to call on others for help? If we did all of these things, wouldn't it make the hard work of school leadership just a little bit easier? I can't speak for everyone, but I can say holding these principles close has made the work of school leadership tremendously rewarding to me.

12

When the Creeks Rise

I finally figured out that not every crisis can be managed.
As much as we want to keep ourselves safe, we can't
protect ourselves from everything. If we want to embrace
life, we also have to embrace chaos.
SUSAN ELIZABETH PHILLIPS[1]

IF THERE IS ANYTHING that doesn't come through clearly enough in these chapters, it's how much chaos there is in this work. There is nothing easy about education, democracy, leadership, or addressing bullying. For us, taking a well publicized stand against bullying meant dealing with additional trouble. Every day the work was filled with questions, challenges, and crises that needed to be addressed. No matter how blessed you are as a school leader, accidents, tragedies, and incidents will happen. You will do your best in every situation, and at the end of the day you will have to know it was all you could do.

LOSING CURTEAH

When Curteah and her mom came to visit Alliance during her eighth-grade year, I was stunned to hear that she had been the target of cruel bullying.

Curteah used a wheelchair much of the time, usually using it more like a walker than a chair, and she had significant health challenges, requiring her to be in and out of the hospital many times over the years. It was surprising to me to learn her peers had been so cruel. I didn't know if we would be able to make the accommodations she would need to attend Alliance. This was going to be the first time we would have a student attending who would bring a personal-care assistant with her. Curteah and her mother were very excited about Alliance, though, and their optimism was contagious. We all decided to give it a try.

Despite the absences in her early years of school, Curteah did extraordinarily well at Alliance. She stayed on the honor roll, was voted onto the Student Leadership Team, and even participated in my line-dancing class, which we both loved. When she was tired, she rested, but most of the time she was up and dancing with the rest of us, and not using her chair. Often it was easy to forget she had health problems, because she never allowed herself to do less than anyone else, and she didn't want to be treated differently. During a skate party we held for students on the honor roll, Curteah was excited to participate, first skating by pushing her wheelchair, and then giving it a try without the wheelchair by holding the arm of a teacher. Her smile lit up the room when she did it on her own.

She attended Alliance through her junior year, doing very well in her classes every semester and making plans to attend college. It never occurred to us she might not make it, even though the doctors had never expected her to live past her middle school years. She visited several campuses with us, each time considering how accommodating they were, as well as the programs they could offer. When the Student Leadership Team planned our service trip to New York, I thought for sure Curteah would come with us, because she had been a big advocate for the trip, but this time she decided the travel might be too much. She was a little bit tired, she said. She still helped with all of the fundraising, but when the time came to turn in permission slips, she shared with me that she had decided not to go.

Things didn't seem unusual when we left for New York, so nothing could have prepared me for the call I got one evening while we were there.

I was standing in the hostel with several students and a parent chaperone, after a long day of service, when my phone rang. It was one of the teachers from Alliance, and I imagined she was just calling to check on us. Instead, she said to me, in a voice that sounded like she had to force the words out, "Curteah passed away today. It was her heart. She had internal bleeding and nobody knew it." When I heard it, I fell to my knees and started to cry. While there are some things you can plan for in life and leadership, other things just take the wind out of you. This was one of those things.

By this time, the students had gathered around me and were asking what was wrong. Reaching for their hands, I told them, "Curteah passed today." They reacted as I had, with gut-wrenching grief and tears. I have never seen anyone cry as hard as we all did that day.

When we finally stopped crying and sat for a moment, the stories seemed to pour out of us.

One student started with the memories, "Remember when Curteah did that presentation in ninth grade? She had a PowerPoint and posters and a typed report. She made us all look like slackers that day. We had to step up our game after that!"

Another chimed in with, "She gave me my first tour of the school."

And another made us all laugh when she said, "Remember when she told off Jahari because he wouldn't stop making ridiculous sounds in class. She let him have it!"

As we told the stories, it almost felt as though Curteah was there. We all joked that she had worked so hard at fundraising she was going to come on this trip with us one way or another. We just wished this wasn't the way she decided to do it.

It was hard to figure out what to do next. We discussed going home early, but we felt like she would be really upset with us if we did. She had worked really hard to make this trip possible. We all had, and there were people who were counting on us. And we didn't know where we would possibly find the money to go home early, if we decided to. Then again, we talked about how it felt almost impossible to go on with the trip, knowing she had passed. It was a hard night. In the end, we clung to what Curteah would have wanted and promised to finish the trip as a way to honor her. We also promised ourselves and each other to do something for her and her family when we returned.

Since we took the trip during Spring Break, when we returned to school, all of the students and staff were returning together. The circle keepers organized schoolwide circles for us to talk about Curteah and what she had meant to the school community. Since her favorite color was blue, the students made blue-ribbon pins for everyone to wear, and they hung handmade blue-ribbon posters around the school. They even made a special quilt for her mother, signed by everyone at the school. At Curteah's funeral, her family arranged for everyone to release blue balloons into the sky in her memory.

Losing Curteah was hard. She would often come to my office or catch me in the hall. When she did, she would hang onto my arm, and would play with my bracelet, turning it in circles around my wrist. Sometimes I would have a million things to do, and I would have to hurry away. Her passing made me wish I would have stayed just a little longer. I can still feel her arm through my arm, her hands turning that bracelet, and it will forever be a reminder to me that our time is not promised. We have to spend time with the people who give us every bit of themselves, giving them our full attention and love, because we never know when that time might be cut short.

THE HARDEST PART

I often tell people the hardest part of teaching at the Alliance School is taking home the stories of the students. I have taken home many stories over the years. Young people shouldn't have to go through the things our students go through, and yet they do, again, and again, and again, it seems.

One morning, the year our school opened, a young girl came to me at the beginning of the day. She was just fourteen and visibly terrified. She asked if we could talk somewhere where no one would see her. When we went into my office, she told me a story that gives me shivers to this day. The night before, she had been standing on a porch with her boyfriend when he started arguing furiously with the person they had come to see.

She tried to encourage him to leave, but the argument just got louder. Suddenly, and without warning, he took a gun out of his waistband and shot the man through the head and through the heart. And then he turned and walked away. Stunned, all she could do was walk away with him. She didn't know what to do. She told me she knew he was in a gang, but it seemed like everyone she knew was in a gang. But the people she knew didn't go around shooting people like that. And besides, she said, he was so sweet to her. She couldn't have imagined he would ever do such a thing. She sat up all night, horrified by what she had seen and terrified that he might do the same thing to her. She wanted to do the right thing, to contact the police, to tell them what happened, but she was afraid—afraid for herself and for her family.

As she told me the story, she cowered behind the door of my office, sitting below the window where no one could see her, rocking back and forth, crying, and startling every time there was a knock at the door or a sound in the hallway. She was certain every knock at the door was him, coming for her. We contacted the police together and made a plan with them to use a different exit from the building to get her out of there safely. The precautions they took made me certain her fears were justified. The detectives met us at the loading dock and quickly escorted her away from the school. Days later, I heard she had been placed in a witness protection program, something I had only heard about in movies and television shows. She never returned to Alliance as a student. However, she did come to see us once, two years later, to say hello and see how we were doing. I was so happy to see her and to know she was all right.

Over the years, I have been called upon to help many students report abuses or crimes. Most of them weren't as serious as this one, but any abuse or violence is devastating to a young person. As someone who experienced abuse growing up, I know how hard it is to speak up and ask for help, so I have always been committed to supporting young people when they take this courageous step. I finally spoke up at the age of thirteen, after years of abuse, by confiding in a counselor at church and then participating in the legal process that sent my father to prison. I have always felt that the act of speaking up made me stronger. By taking my life into my own hands and putting an end to the abuse, rather than waiting for someone else to do it for me, I had taken back some of my power.

Since this had been so healing for me, I have always encouraged students who disclose abuse to make the necessary calls themselves, with me promising to be there to support them through the calls and whatever comes next. I assure them I am a mandated reporter, so I have to make the call even if they do not, but I give them the chance to make the call themselves if they want to. Because of this, I have been there when students have reported all kinds of abuses, from sexual abuse to domestic violence. In the days that have followed, I have gone to court with young people, helped them find counselors, and even fostered some of them. It's a shame how much so many young people go through, and it's especially shameful when it is at the hands of the people meant to protect them. Teachers are often the first people that young people confide in, and it's important that we take that role seriously. It's also important that we take care of ourselves, as we experience the vicarious trauma of being first responders in many of our students' lives.

MILK AND COOKIES

I think the most effective school leaders must acquire a gift for calming people down in heated moments. It's definitely something we are called to do often. I have spent a great deal of time over the years calming down students who were angry at peers, parents who were angry at children, and teachers who were angry at spouses. My most challenging moment, early on, was when I had to calm down a large group of angry protesters.

I was working at my desk one late fall day when the phone rang. It was a news reporter asking about the protesters.

"Are the protesters there yet?" the over-anxious woman asked.

"Protesters," I said. "There are no protesters here."

"Oh, well, I'm sorry then," she said. "I must have misunderstood."

I hung up the phone and decided to take a look outside, just in case there was anyone out there. When I got to the courtyard, I saw a man with a news camera packing his stuff up and walking away. "How strange is that?" I thought.

It had been four years, and our school had existed up until that point without serious protest, despite the fact that we had been explicit about being an LGBTQ-friendly school. Occasionally, the students would tell me about a lone individual handing out religious pamphlets on the street in front of the school, but other than that, we had remained fairly unbothered. So there was no reason to expect that anyone would be out there now. Still, it was rare for the news crews to show up without reason. I couldn't help but be a little nervous.

I walked around to the other side of the courtyard and out onto the main street in front of the school. There were a couple of men standing just a few yards away from the courtyard entrance, signs leaning against the wall, as if they were waiting for someone. Then, as I looked around, I realized more people with signs were coming from all directions and moving toward the courtyard entrance. The signs said things like:

"Homosexuality – AIDS."

"Tell MPS not to teach kids how to be gay."

"NOT with my tax dollars."

I grabbed the few students who were hanging out in the courtyard and suggested they come inside the building. "I'm not sure what's happening here, but it doesn't look good," I said.

When we got inside the building, I went right to the phone to call Roseann, the public relations director for the school district. I had worked with her often, as the school had been covered in the press quite a bit, but this was the first time we had faced any type of serious protest. When Harvey Milk High School opened in New York, protesters had come from all over the country and lined the streets with angry signs, and students had to be escorted into the school building by armed security guards for several weeks. While Alliance wasn't exclusively a school for LGBTQ students, we knew the fact that we were LGBTQ-friendly also had the potential to bring controversy. I didn't know who these protesters were, or how many had gathered there by this point, but I knew it was not something to take lightly.

I picked up the phone and gave her a call.

"Roseann, there are protesters outside. And they have lots of signs."

I felt confident she would know what to do. It certainly wasn't the first time there had been a protest in the school district. And she had plenty of experience dealing with the media. I thought she was going to reply with something reassuring, like "Don't worry, honey, we'll be right over."

Instead she said, "And you're going to go out there and give them milk and cookies and make everything alright, like you always do, aren't you?"

I didn't know how to respond. I sat quietly for a moment and thought about what she was saying. It was true, I had done my fair share of convincing challenging people of the merits of the school. Once, I had even called in to a local talk-radio show when they were discussing whether or not there should be a school to address bullying. I'm not sure how many people I convinced, but I did receive thank-you letters from people after the call, and at the end of the call, the host said something like, "Well, you can tell her heart is in the right place, but is it right?" I considered that a small win, given that this particular host wasn't typically in favor of anything discussed on the show. This was all great, but up until this moment, I hadn't had the experience of having to face an angry mob of challengers like this one.

In my head, I thought through all of the worst-case scenarios: "What if they have guns? What if they're crazy? What will happen to my children if something happens to me?" At this time, my own children were twenty and sixteen, and I knew they would be devastated if something happened to me. When I heard Roseann's reassuring voice, though, I knew I had to put my fears aside and go out there and talk to these people.

"People," I thought to myself. "They're just people. You can handle this."

"Yes. That's what I am going to do," I said to Roseann. And I grabbed my coat and headed outside.

In that short amount of time, the group had grown to close to fifty people, and many of them were trying to speak to students, handing them biblical pronouncements and false statistics about homosexuality, HIV, and AIDS. As one of our students attempted to walk by, one of the men held up his Bible in front of her and said, in a deep, preacher voice, "If a teacher gives you a textbook, how do you know it doesn't have AIDS on it?"

"Because I had health class," she replied, shaking her head and shrugging her shoulders. She walked around him and into the school, and I'm pretty sure I heard her mumble, "Idiot."

By then, many of our students had started to gather outside to see what all of the fuss was about. Teachers were encouraging them to stay inside, but they were bold in their desire to protect the reputation of the school. "Did you see their signs?" one of the students asked me, pointing at a particularly homophobic one. "And you call yourself Christian," the student said to the man carrying it. "I'm a Christian, and that is not Christian."

I could see that most of the protesters were carrying signs that said things about sixth graders and homosexuality, and I suddenly realized that they were there because of our middle school. Up until that year, we had only been a high school, but at the request of several of our parents who had middle school children who had experienced serious bullying, we had decided to expand our enrollment to include a middle school program. They were here to protest that.

Well, actually, they were there for two reasons—our proposal to open a middle school program, and the district's proposal to adopt a new human growth and development curriculum. For some reason they had combined these two issues into one, and they were now protesting what they believed was the creation of a middle school that would teach kids how to be gay. It was outrageous and bizarre.

It didn't take me long to find the leader of the group and to get a copy of the press release he had sent out to the media regarding a protest at noon today (which explained why the press had been there and then left). "We oppose the creation of the MPS middle school of Alliance to teach homosexuality," he said to me, as he waved the press release vigorously in my face. He was a squat, older gentleman, with a round, yellowed face, squinty eyes, and white hair combed back from his face and over his ears. The straight lines between his chin and his cheeks strangely made his mouth look like the mouth of a wooden puppet.

I took a breath for courage and introduced myself to him as the founder of the school.

"Do you know what our school is about?" I asked, as kindly as I could. By this time, a group had gathered around to witness what was happening.

"You people want to make middle school kids gay," he said. I could tell he was used to creating a kind of circus atmosphere. He seemed to enjoy it. He spoke with his hands waving wildly, gathering his followers in, making sure they heard everything he said.

"Oh no," I replied. "We wouldn't do that. Why would anyone want to do that? It certainly wouldn't make life easier for anyone." I said it jokingly, and it caught him off guard a little.

"Well, MPS is going to make you teach it. It's in the curriculum," he said.

"I certainly wouldn't teach anything that I didn't agree with," I said. "Even if it was in the curriculum."

His changed demeanor seemed to suggest he was somewhat calmed by the idea that I would not give up my personal values for a district mandate. I focused on changing the subject back to our school.

"No, our school is about putting a stop to *bullying*," I said. "We teach our students that it's not okay to hurt anyone for any reason, even if you don't agree with them. Our school is for anyone who doesn't believe in bullying."

"So, you're not teaching kids how to be gay?" he asked, one eyebrow raised and looking at me with skepticism.

"No. We teach kids math, science, social studies, and English, and then we tell them the one thing we won't tolerate here is hurting any one of your fellow human beings in any way. It's okay to disagree about things, but it's not okay to hurt people."

This seemed to be making sense to him. He took a step back, looked down, and put his fingers to his chin, as if he was thinking about what to say next.

"Well, what if I was being harassed because I was stating my beliefs as a Christian?" he said.

"If you were being bullied for being a Christian, I would protect you, too," I responded. "Our mission is to be a safe and accepting place for all students, so we don't allow anyone to cause harm to anyone. You can believe what you want, but you just don't get to hurt people because they believe differently from you. Besides, I'm a Sunday school teacher. What would it look like for me to allow a student to be bullied for being Christian?"

After hearing this, a couple of the people who had gathered close by seemed to be starting to understand the mission of the school a little better. Some of them started to reveal their own stories about being hurt or bullied as a child. One man started to tell me about a time when he was sexually assaulted in a movie theater.

"What happened to you never should have happened," I said.

A woman started telling me about horrendous bullying she experienced in middle school and how the adults did nothing to stop it.

"We wouldn't let that happen here," I told her. "That's why we want to start a middle school."

As we stood there and talked, I learned many of these people had needed a school like Alliance when they were young. A few of them even shook my hand and thanked me for what I was doing, apologizing for having been so wrong about the mission of our school.

A couple of days later, when the items went before the school board, the protesters were there to speak on the human growth and development curriculum, but they didn't say a word about the middle school proposal. In fact, they invited me into their circle so they could pray for me. The proposal for the middle school moved forward, without question, and the following year the Alliance Middle School program was founded.

The whole situation was a testament to the power of listening and speaking from the heart. I was able to put my own fears and judgments aside to listen to the stories of these protesters, and when I did, I heard their fears. In return, I was able to share my own passion for addressing bullying with them. This was something they could relate to, as well. While we didn't agree on everything in life, we could at least agree that no one should ever experience harm because of who they are or what they believe in. Years later, I told this story to a reporter, and somehow it became part of the story that I *actually* gave the protesters milk and cookies. This story has now been repeated so many times, it's becoming legend. Since this is a moment of full disclosure, let me say there were not any real cookies or milk, just metaphorical ones.

THE PROTESTORS RETURN

These protesters seemed satisfied with my explanations of the school's mission, and they probably wouldn't have come back, if it wasn't for an invitation from the media. When they returned, it was because they were invited by French reporters who had come to the United States to make a documentary about our school. When the reporters asked if we had ever had protesters, I made the mistake of telling them about the group that had been there just days before. They must have wanted to get this on tape, because the next day, the French reporter seemed to be hinting that we might have protesters that afternoon. I tried not to think much of it, because it felt like such an impossibility, given the way we had come to an understanding just days before, but I could feel myself preparing a bit for it, just the same. Sure enough, a small group of protesters appeared that afternoon. The group was much smaller this time, and I even noticed that one person who had protested the week before dropped off one of the guys and then waved at me, looking almost apologetic as he did, and drove away.

This time, the students were angry. They had trusted me when I said things were okay between us and the protesters, and they hadn't expected to see them return. The signs the protestors brought were nastier this time, and they seemed to draw the ire of the students who came outside to argue with them. "You call yourself a Christian?" the students yelled. "Do unto others as you would have others do unto you." I couldn't help but feel a small swell of pride watching these students stand up for what they believed in, and I was especially proud of the non-LGBTQ students who stood up for their LGBTQ peers. But I was also worried about what this protest could breed.

I could see that a large group of students from a neighboring high school was gathering across the street, perhaps seeing this as an opportunity to unleash their own hateful diatribes and appearing emboldened by the signs of the protesters. I turned to address the Alliance students who were outside and impressed on them the need to go back into the school. They didn't want to go back, especially if I was still outside, but with a little prodding, they heeded my request and turned and went into the school. I followed them to the doors. As I walked I could see the swarm of students from the other school starting to cross the street. Just as I closed the door behind the last student, I turned, and there was an angry mob of students, looking like a pack of wild animals, ready to bust through the doors and tear the school apart. I turned to face them, and with the instinct and ferocity of a mother bear, I held out my hand and said "NO. GO BACK TO YOUR SCHOOL." The group seemed to scuffle their feet a bit, and then they turned and went away. Soon I saw teachers from their school coming across the street to round them up and bring them back to where they belonged.

By now, I was furious with the protesters. I went over to where they were standing, and I unleashed my fury. "See!" I cried. "See what your hateful signs have done. YOU DID THIS. YOU BROUGHT THEM HERE." I was shaking as I pleaded with them. "Your words mean something. You did this. You made those people believe that this is what we're about, and you know us. YOU know better. SHAME ON YOU!" I roared.

As I looked around, I could see that both the protesters and the French reporters could see the danger they had posed for the school. What was meant to be a display for the cameras had almost turned into a dangerous mob situation. "You're right, Tina. You're right," the protesters I had come to know just the week before said, apologetically, as they tucked their awful signs under their arms and walked away from the school. "We didn't mean for that to happen."

Finally, feeling as if the danger had passed, I went inside the building and I couldn't hold it back any longer. The tears began to flow. Several of the students came over to hug me and to tell me that it was going to be okay. I think seeing me cry upset them even more than the protesters had. "They made Tina cry!" they said, with a tone of outrage. "No one makes Tina cry and gets away with it." I couldn't help but laugh at their defensiveness for me. "I'll be okay," I said. "I'm just really mad, that's all."

That was the incident that made us all very cautious when it came to reporters, especially documentary reporters. I never would have imagined someone would call people and ask them to come protest, just so they could get it on tape. Since then, we have had many requests by producers hoping to do documentaries and reality shows about the school. We discussed and voted on every proposal, but we have turned down many since that day. As the students said when someone wrote asking to do a reality show about our school, "They are just going to bring drama to the school, and we don't need any of that." In the end, it wasn't that the French crew produced a bad documentary. As a matter of fact, the film was great, and we received a lot of positive messages from people all around the world who saw it. But getting to that moment was harsh, and I would never want to put the school at risk again the way we did that day.

LEADERSHIP AND POLICY CHANGE

Of course, the challenges for school leaders don't always come from outside the district. At the time of these protests, we had a district leadership team that strongly supported the mission and philosophy of the school. I knew I could call on them when there were crises like this one, and I trusted them to help me to make sound decisions. It felt like our visions were aligned. The central offices, at this time, were filled with people who believed in school autonomy, shared decision-making, and interoffice communication. That didn't last long, though. Since most superintendents only remain in their positions for three to five years, it's probably not surprising to hear that our district leadership team changed more than once over the years. When this happened, the constant challenges of new leaders, changing political winds, and federal reform efforts made it hard to know what was expected of us from one day to the next. One moment, we were the golden child of an autonomous system, and the next moment we were the disobedient children of a new centralization effort. One moment, small schools were all the rage, and the next moment, they were economically inefficient and being shut down. One moment we were being honored for high achievement, and the next moment we were being scolded for not meeting federal targets. It was hard to tell up from down during these transitional times, and even more importantly, it was hard to survive through these leadership changes.

To meet some of these challenges head on, a group of us decided to create the Teacher-Led Network, a network of schools committed to collaborating, sharing resources, and advocating for the needs of teacher-led schools. Together, we were able to fight for equitable budgets, change the charter school evaluation process, and develop a shared year-round, Montessori, International Baccalaureate calendar. With this calendar, we were able to host professional development opportunities for the network, create shared enrichment classes for our students during intersession breaks, and collaborate to use data improvement cycles to improve student outcomes. We were also able to keep an eye on school board agenda items and bring teams together to advocate on behalf of our schools.

Luckily, one of the things that stayed constant over the years was the composition of the Milwaukee Board of School Directors, and their commitment to addressing the issue of bullying. Most of the board members could think of times when they didn't want to go to school because of bullying. It is an issue that too many people understand personally. This helped us to keep strong ties with the individual board members, and I will always be grateful for their continuous support. Maintaining positive relationships with the school board is an important aspect of school leadership, so it truly helps when your mission is something they believe in as much as you do.

WHEN THE DISTRICT VISION CHANGES

No matter how supportive your board is, though, a change in district leadership can have serious consequences for a school. As new superintendents saw the need for more centralization, many aspects of our mission and vision were tested. For example, in the last few years, we have lost a little bit of our graduation luster, as the district has moved to make the graduation ceremonies more standard and traditional, in the non-Alliance sense of the word. We fought this and continued our tradition the first year, only to be forced into standardization the following year. Since that year, every one of the district graduations takes place at the same place according to the district's schedule. The adults do most of the speaking, while the district's leadership team sits on the stage in their caps and gowns, giving a speech or a comment here and there. There are no teddy bears, DJs, or student performances in these ceremonies. The ceremony is scheduled during the school day, which means most of the teachers cannot attend because they have to stay back with the students who still have school to attend. It also makes it difficult for many families to attend. This is probably the thing that upsets everyone the most. At one point, the students were ready to boycott the graduation ceremony altogether, but the teachers encouraged them to enjoy their moment walking the stage and promised them that it would be recorded, so most of them did. Still, it was disappointing.

This was one of the many ways in which the centralized nature of the district was beginning to threaten what made us tick. They also were pressing on us to eliminate our time for teaming, take away block scheduling, drop the year-round schedule, reduce the number of restorative practices classes, stop doubling our freshman English and math blocks, and so on. Everything was becoming a fight, and if we couldn't do the things we knew were making our culture strong, how would we ever be able to meet the mission that inspired us? This was one of the first times I started to think outside of the district box for other ways to maintain and spread our mission, vision, and practices. That wouldn't be the last time, though.

WALKING AWAY

In the summer of 2015, the district started another new initiative. They decided to double the leadership in schools across the city by placing a second administrator in every school. Since Alliance did not have a principal, they decided to assign an assistant principal to the building. We were not given a chance to interview or discuss this with anyone, despite the fact that our contract clearly outlined our status as a teacher-led school with the ability to interview for all positions. Without any regard for our contract, they placed someone at the school. This was frustrating. Besides the obvious violation of our contract with them, we had been asking for a security guard for years to help us monitor who came in and out of our building (all security staff were assigned and distributed centrally), but we had been told over and over again there was no money, and we didn't need one because our school culture was too good. Suddenly the district had enough money to *give* us an assistant principal, a position that was much more costly and hard to fill.

I was personally outraged for this reason and many others. First, we were a teacher-led school, and the sudden placement of an assistant principal in the building brought up all kinds of questions about hierarchy. Parents were confused about who they should talk to. Students didn't know how to feel about calling one person by her last name while they called me and all of the other teachers by our first names. And there were issues to address regarding the official chain of command. We were able to have it clarified through contract talks that I was the leader for the school, and the assistant principal was there to assist us, but despite my commitment to making it work, and acknowledging the fact that she turned out to be a wonderful friend and ally, the absolute disregard for our model of leadership made me realize it was time for me to consider new possibilities.

I had already been feeling restless and believed I needed a new challenge. There was a part of me that felt as though the school could run itself. Everything had been working well, and the teachers and students knew what made it work the way it did. I felt like this was the time to step outside to fight for our mission, as well as to think about how to share our mission and practices with others. I had already been actively sharing our practices in other schools and networks. I had given keynote speeches in Toledo, Ohio, and Buffalo, New York; helped people start schools in other cities; trained a Catholic schools network; done presentations for numerous colleges; collaborated to publish articles; and answered requests from teachers, parents, and leaders around the world. And despite the clear needs of my own district, I could see I wasn't going to be invited to share our practices with our leaders any time soon. The people making the decisions just didn't understand what made Alliance work.

While considering other ways of spreading the work, such as teaching evening classes at the local university or starting another school, I received an email from the Harvard Graduate School of Education. I was on their mailing list to keep up with newly released research in education. In the email was a description of the Ed.L.D. program, a doctorate program in education leadership modeled after a medical residency—with two years of coursework and a year in practice. When I looked into it a little further, I learned it was a fully funded program. Anyone who was admitted would receive a financial aid package that covered tuition, housing, personal expenses, and medical care for the full three years. It sounded like a dream. I had never imagined applying to Harvard, but suddenly it felt possible. My wife had just retired after twenty-eight years in law enforcement, so I showed her the website and said, "So, what do you think?"

She said, "Why not? What have we got to lose?"

I took a chance and applied, while also applying to a couple of other doctoral programs, knowing I would be happy whether I was accepted or not, because I loved working at Alliance. My only hope was that by stepping into a position of leadership I could nurture and share the practices that made our school successful. I didn't know what would happen. I sent in my application and then went back to work and waited. In March of 2016, I was talking to some teachers during parent–teacher conferences. My phone started to ring, and when I looked down, I saw a Massachusetts number. My heart started to beat fast. I excused myself and stepped into the copy room to answer the call.

"Is this Tina Owen-Moore?" the voice on the other end of the line asked. He then told me the admissions committee was hoping I would accept their offer to join Cohort Seven of the Harvard Ed.L.D. program. He said I had some time to think about it, but I should let them know soon.

"I'm coming!" I replied, almost too excitedly and with tears in my eyes. "I mean, of course I'm going to accept," I said, wiping away the tears. "I wouldn't have applied if I wasn't going to come!"

He laughed and told me he was glad to hear it, and told me I would receive my official invitation in the next couple of days.

I hung up the phone and danced around a little bit in the dark and cramped copy room. I couldn't contain it. This was one of the most surreal and amazing moments in my life, and I knew I couldn't share it with anyone that night, except my spouse. I would have to wait until the right moment to tell the teachers and the students. I pulled myself together and went to look for my wife, who was attending parent–teacher conferences that evening because she was the basketball coach. I pulled her into my office and whispered, "I got in!" She picked me up and spun me around. "Congratulations!" she said. "Let's do this!" A year later, I was studying alongside many incredible people at Harvard University.

There comes a time when many of us have to decide whether to stay or leave, and this was my time. It was not an easy decision for me. I loved my students, my staff, and the work I did every day. I only wished I had the district's support and understanding, so I could continue to do what I knew worked for young people and share our mission and practices with other schools in the district. If this had been my environment, I likely would have stayed in the district until I retired. But the universe has a way of pushing us to where we are needed. As the district hired assistant principals and planned graduation ceremonies, while piling on more and more initiatives that challenged or eliminated the very practices that made us successful, I knew it would take me stepping outside of the district to keep the Alliance mission and practices alive.

This proved to be a powerful insight. In many ways, my acceptance at Harvard provided a new lens for those looking at our work, as so many of our practices align with research around what the academy has learned works to prevent bullying in schools. And while the Alliance community has made some small changes since I left, when I visit I have been happy to see that the core of the vision is thriving and the mission remains strong. Knowing this, I have been able to confidently step away and take on the challenge of sharing the practices that brought this vision to life. I still go back every now and then to celebrate and be part of the community where it all began, but I know my work now is to spread that mission to other schools and communities. Through this book, my current academic work, and my future endeavors, I aim to do just that. I believe that every community can make every school a safe, student-centered, and academically challenging environment to meet the needs of *all* students. I know together, we can make every school a bully-free school.

APPENDIX A

Ten Things School Leaders Can Do Today to Prevent and Address Bullying

1. Have your teachers trained in peacemaking circles and restorative justice practices. Alliance teachers use circles in the classroom regularly, so that the students are comfortable with them. When minor conflicts arise, these circles are an incredibly effective way of ending the conflict before it turns into violence or bullying.
2. Address name-calling immediately. Never let hurtful comments go unchecked. If you hear a student call another student a name or say something hurtful, express your disapproval. If this type of behavior is repeated, report the behavior to the parent and the administrator. If the behavior continues, report it again.
3. Have advisory classes or activities where students focus on team building and relationship strengthening, so that students form strong bonds with their peers. These classes and activities are the cornerstones for relationships in the school, so be very deliberate in your planning and in assigning teachers to advisories.

4. Involve students in decision-making for the school. When there are major changes being considered, have the students discuss the changes and vote on whether or not the changes should be made. Students need to feel that the culture of the school belongs to them and that they have the power to make the school experience positive for everyone involved.

5. Create a bullying/harassment form that students can fill out when they feel that they are being bullied. Be sure to make the forms readily available, and make the process for turning them in simple. The staff members who receive the forms should be comfortable addressing the complaint and following through with investigating and assigning consequences.

6. Have a student discipline council or restorative practices class that handles repeated incidents of bullying or disruptive behaviors. This council or class should be made up of a diverse group of students at all academic levels who meet with students, discuss behaviors, determine consequences, and mentor the student to improve behaviors.

7. Encourage students to start diversity clubs and gay/straight alliances, and then support the efforts of the clubs. The presence of these clubs sends a strong message about the school's acceptance of all people.

8. Encourage students to bring bullying to your attention. Cyberbullying counts, too. Either have them send you the messages that they see online (if you are a social media user), or have them print out what they see and bring it to you. Provide safe and anonymous ways for students to do so. Some kids will not report bullying if they believe that they will be named in the process, so be careful to listen and address the bullying without making the witness the new target.

9. Teach students about different cultures, beliefs, and practices, and teach them how to work with people who are different from themselves. This is not something that students automatically know how to do, and it is the most important quality for the workplace.

10. Be sure to say, "If it happens again, please come tell me again, so that I can know that my intervention didn't work, and I need to take

more drastic measures." Sometimes, when students report bullying and then it happens again, they think that the administrator did
nothing, and the administrator thinks that it stopped, because nothing else was reported. Be sure to encourage students to come back if
the behavior continues.

Sample Documents

THE ALLIANCE SCHOOL STAFF MEETING AGENDA

The following agenda was created for a staff meeting after our first intercession break of the school year. It illustrates how we sought to use much of our time together for teaming, building connections between staff, and modeling a caring culture for our students, in addition to teaching and learning. During this staff meeting, we focused on self-care, for our students and for ourselves, and used the first-quarter data to evaluate our practices and plan for the new quarter.

October 29, 2012

Welcome back from intersession break!

Morning 9:00–11:00 a.m.
1. Connections
2. Housekeeping—Schedule for the two days, things to accomplish, logistics, etc.
3. First Quarter Data and results of PBIS discussion with Sheila/Staff Activity

Staff Activity

At Alliance, the staff and students are really great at showing love, respect and care for others, but how do we show love and respect for ourselves? In the PBIS meeting with Sheila, we realized that a lot of our biggest worries at Alliance have to do with students who are making choices that put themselves at risk, so we thought that it would be important to start to have a conversation with students about showing love for themselves as well as they do it for others.

- Brainstorm: In groups of three to four, on a large note paper, brainstorm some ways that you take good care of yourself. List things that you do and things that you don't do. For example, I follow my gluten-free diet, and I don't smoke.
- Share some of the things you came up with.
- Why is it important for us, as teachers, to take good care of ourselves?
- If the students can't see themselves in you, they won't want to be you.
- Write a letter to yourself reminding yourself of some of the things you want to do this semester to take good care of yourself. Put it in a self-addressed envelope.
- Circle: How can we get our students to start to internalize this message of caring for self as well as others?
- Assignment: Create a lesson plan around this idea of self-care that fits in with your course curriculum. Bring it back to the afternoon meeting.

Afternoon 1:00–3:00 p.m.
1. Lesson Plan sharing
   Dissemination Grant Activities:
2. Retreat Plan
3. Plan for ISU visitors on November 8th and 9th

ALLIANCE SCHOOL DISCIPLINE POLICY

The Alliance School Discipline Policy was created with the goal of decreasing negative behaviors by first encouraging, then documenting, and then disciplining. The goal is for the advisory classes to work together toward increasing positive behaviors in the school community.

These are the teacher procedures for different actions:

Negative Actions (repeated swearing, cell phone use, walking out of class, students in common areas rather than classes, etc.):

> First, teachers and staff members will try to use gentle reminders not to swear, use cell phone, etc. When the gentle reminder is not effective, the staff member will have the option of using a sighting form. Here are the steps for using the form:
> Fill out a **green** sighting form.
> Give forms to advisers.
> Advisories will chart the incidents and come up with plans and goals to reduce.
> If an adviser notices that an individual is receiving a lot of sighting forms, the adviser will call the student's parent or guardian to talk about the problem behavior. These calls will be documented in ESIS.

*When an individual has been sighted twenty times in one quarter for negative behaviors, he or she will be asked to participate in a peer justice council with a group of peers. The adviser will give the sighting forms to the lead teacher, and he or she will arrange a council meeting. The peer justice council will work with the student, come up with consequences, and refer the student to other resources. The council can also request a central office hearing if no other actions are successful.

Think It Through

At times, a student might just need a little time-out. At these times, a teacher can fill out a Think It Through sheet and send it with the student to another teacher's classroom. The teacher there will let the student in; the student will fill out the form; the teacher will check in with the student and sign the form; and the student will return to class and give the teacher the signed slip. The teacher will keep a file of Think It Through sheets.

Non-negotiables

The following actions call for immediate and serious consequences and will result in a one-day suspension and/or a peer justice council:

• Threatening or harassing others, physically or verbally

If a staff member witnesses these actions, he or she will fill out a "72" form and bring it to the teacher in charge. The teacher in charge will determine whether an in-school suspension, an out-of-school suspension, or a peer justice council meeting is warranted. The staff member will receive a copy of the administrator's disposition.

Positive Actions

The Alliance School staff also plans to recognize positive actions in the school community. These are the procedures for documenting positive actions.

Fill out a **purple** sighting form.

Give forms to advisers.

Advisories will chart the incidents and come up with plans and goals to increase.

If an adviser notices that an individual is receiving a lot of positive sighting forms, the adviser will call the student's parent or guardian to tell him or her about the student's positive contributions to the school environment. These calls will be documented in ESIS.

All teachers will have their own discipline policies to address things such as tardiness, attendance, work completion, etc. If detentions are assigned, they will be handled by the teacher or staff member assigning the detention. At Alliance, because of our mission, students have a lot of freedoms. Teachers will make efforts to use discipline strategies only for behaviors that are hurtful or disruptive, and intervention strategies for behaviors that are affecting the student's chances to graduate.

THE PEER JUSTICE COUNCIL AT ALLIANCE

At the Alliance School, circles are part of everything we do. We begin each staff meeting with a circle of connections; we use circles to resolve conflicts; and our Student Discipline Council uses a circle process, as well. What follows is a description that the students on the Discipline Council helped to write.

The Discipline Council at Alliance

The Discipline Council was created to allow a forum for students to work with other students who are chronically disruptive or who commit serious acts (arguing, fighting, destruction of property, etc.) within the school. The council is made up of six to eight students. The students are chosen for the Discipline Council based on their relationships with peers, their abilities to resolve conflicts, and their examples of positive behaviors. The diversity of the group is a key to the group's success, because the council works best when a student who comes before the council can count on the fact that there will be at least one person who he or she can relate to personally.

The Meeting

The Discipline Council meets when there is a serious incident, such as a fight or argument that disturbs classes, or a series of disruptive behaviors. Teachers or students can make recommendations for who should come before the Discipline Council. Council meetings typically take two to three hours, so the council works best if it is reserved for serious and/or chronic problems. There is one teacher who is on the Discipline Council with the students. This teacher serves as an equal member on the council.

The council begins with a report of what has happened and/or why the student has been asked to come before the Discipline Council. This is usually done by the teacher, but could be done by a student, as well. The council has a few moments to go over any incident referrals, harassment forms, and/or witness statements. The council addresses the following questions with the student:

1. What happened?
2. Who was harmed?

3. What needs to be done to repair this harm?

4. What each person is personally willing to do?

The council listens to what the student has to say, talks to him or her about how it hurts the school or the student, determines consequences for the student, creates a behavior improvement contract, and works as a mentor to that student in following days and weeks. They often find that there are other things that are going on in the student's life, so they also help connect students with resources, or interventions with the social worker can be set up. The consequences can range from cleaning the school, to going to anger management classes, to teaching younger students how credits work, but the goal is to have a consequence that benefits the school and/or the person who was harmed. The council also has the ability to recommend a central office hearing, where the student could possibly be removed from the school, if all other efforts fail.

There are a few guidelines for the Discipline Council:

- What is said in the council stays in the council (confidentiality)
- Mutual respect
- Restorative consequences, not punishments

STAFF RETREAT AGENDA

At Alliance, we used semiannual retreats to strengthen connections between staff and to give us the opportunity to go deep into the work without interruption. In 2009, we hosted a staff retreat to outline our practices as a staff, and to plan for curriculum alignment and collaboration. This is the agenda for that meeting, as shared with staff in advance of the retreat.

Sunday, June 21, 2009

4:00–10:00 p.m. Retreat Arrivals

Check in

Check in any time Sunday evening at the hotel registration desk. Let them know that you are with the Alliance School and will be staying in the Entertainment Cabin. They will give you your key, waterpark passes, etc.

Dinner

Home-made pizza night! We will bring the dough and makings for pizza. If you have any special favorite toppings, bring them along, but we will have the basics—cheese, pepperoni, onions, sauce . . .

Connections & Optional Movie

Monday, June 22, 2009

7:30–9:30 a.m.

Breakfast

Tina will be making omelets and pancakes. If you'd like to make or share anything else, feel free!

9:30–10:00 a.m.

Walk and Stretch

Take a quick walk and stretch and get ready to dive into the work of the day. This is your own time for reflection and energy-building.

10:00–11:00 a.m.

Modeling Behaviors

This scenario-based activity will focus on what it means to model a value and how we can do this in the classroom.

11:15–11:45 a.m.
Procedures Brainstorm
This will be a quick brainstorm of things we need to develop procedures for. The following day, we will work on developing those procedures.

11:45 AM–1:00 p.m.
Light Lunch
Since breakfast will be big, we will have a light lunch of soup and salad.

1:00–3:00 p.m.
Curriculum Alignment and Collaboration
This is where we focus on developing practices for content across the curriculum, planning our service learning goals for the year, and aligning curriculum to ensure that students are meeting academic goals and benchmarks.

3:00–6:00 p.m.
Water Park/Fun Break!

6:00–7:30 PM
Dinner
This night will be a summer barbecue night. We will make sausages, hot dogs, veggie dogs, and more. If you have a favorite side dish to share, this is your chance to reveal it.

7:30–10:00 p.m.
Honest Conversations
This will be a time to reflect on what pushes our buttons, what gets us stuck, and what brings us joy. It will also be a time to think about ways we can support each other in these things.

Tuesday June 23, 2009

7:00–9:00 a.m.
Continental Breakfast

9:00–9:30 a.m.
Awards & Prizes

9:30–11:00 a.m.

Procedures

In this activity, we will outline schoolwide procedures to ensure a good start to the school year.

11:00 a.m.–Noon

Pack & Play

We must check out of the resort by noon, so this is time to pack up. Feel free to spend the afternoon at the resort, though, or hang out in the Dells.

SWOT ANALYSIS

The SWOT Analysis is the tool we used to identify our strengths, weaknesses, opportunities, and threats, as we planned to hire new staff members. We used each new or open position as a chance to address needs identified in the analysis.

Strengths

- Faculty with Master's, PhDs and MFAs
- Full time social worker—Mari!
- Cooperation, staff works well together
- Staff understanding of student issues and empathy
- Sense of humor
- Great energy and motivation
- Young staff/old staff—staff retention
- Great ideas/great motivation
- Strong social justice focuses
- Safe place/safe community
- Technology and art
- We eat family style
- Relaxed atmosphere
- We all *care!*
- Extra time spent with students before and after school
- We are all friends
- People-friendly
- Compliance/financial and performance
- Students learn how to knit
- Everyone knows all students' names
- Staff knows how to step up— leadership—active with students
- Community involvement
- PR—positive reputation
- Relationship building
- Promotion of opportunities—students and staff
- Block scheduling
- Flexible staff
- Time for PD/collaboration
- Walk the talk/great role models
- Inclusion
- Alternative assessments
- Student empowerment, choices
- Integrated curriculum
- Staff and students WANT to be here
- We are a chosen family

Weaknesses

- Discipline inconsistencies
- HS students with insufficient primary level math and reading skills
- Lack of extra programs—music, sports, dance
- Poor facilities
- Money
- Parental communication/involvement
- Philosophy conflicts with district requirements
- Access to technology
- Kitchen/food
- Assessments
- Portfolios
- Gallery
- Communication between staff
- Student alternative needs
- Class availability
- Procedural inconsistencies
- Retention rate at ninth grade level
- Truancy
- Long advisories/Wednesdays
- Finding student opportunities for service learning
- Foreign language
- Student reading and math scores
- District-enabled transience
- Over-extended staff (lack of balance)
- WKCE/benchmarks

Opportunities

- Publishing
- Gardening/"green" school
- Portfolios
- Sports (Gym)
- Music—Conservatory, Riverside, grants
- Computers—A+ certification, tips/techniques, programming
- Dance—ballroom, fine arts
- Cheerleading
- Behavioral Interventions
- New space—stage, gym
- Inclusion
- Creativity
- Afterschool programs—Schedule E
- Classes during summers and interim breaks
- Riverside HS sports partnership
- Milwaukee music/theater
- Art schools/campus
- Community partnerships
- Middle school
- New energy and staff
- Outside space
- Collaboration: Arts Center, PQ, Boys and Girls Club, Elks
- Become a "model" school
- Time to talk about deep student stuff
- Tina time
- Fundraising
- School spirit
- Varied classes
- College connections
- Branding
- Notability, social justice, technology
- Building visibility

Threats

- Labels "alternative" or "gay" school
- Professional growth, staff retirements
- IDEA/NCLB
- Lack of diversity
- Community/public intolerance
- Current student struggles/poor role modeling
- Teacher apathy
- Front door security
- Redundancy/too many teachers with similar skills
- Money/budget cuts
- Selves
- Test scores/charter review
- Student attendance
- Communication
- Inconsistent procedures and follow-through
- District discipline policies
- HR process
- Standardized tests
- Gangs
- Racism
- Urban versus world views
- Not enough students

HIRING LOOK-FORS AND INTERVIEW QUESTIONS

As a result of the SWOT analysis, these were some of the qualities we committed ourselves to looking for in the interview process, as we felt they were keys to our success.

Important things to look for when hiring (collateral responsibilities):
- Diversity
- Content knowledge
- Ability to work with parents and community
- Foreign language teaching expertise
- Service learning philosophy/experience
- Commitment
- Understanding of urban education issues
- Flexibility/willingness to take on varied responsibilities
- Portfolio assessment experience
- Spirit of cooperation
- Belief in school mission and vision

Interview Questions 2009

1. Tell us a little bit about yourself, why you want to work here, and why you are leaving your current school.
2. Tell us about a time when you had to adapt to a new environment. What was that experience like for you? What were the outcomes?
3. Many of the students at Alliance come from diverse backgrounds and experiences, including gay and lesbian students, students with disabilities, and students from a variety of socioeconomic backgrounds. What experience do you have working with students from these or other diverse populations?
4. What kinds of approaches have you witnessed or employed to maintain a positive school culture or environment?
5. You are walking down the hall and a student cusses at you. What do you do?
6. Share a story about a time when you gave up power to meet the needs of the group.

7. Some of the Alliance core values are democratic education, student empowerment, freedom and responsibility, acceptance of differences, teamwork, fun, and community. How do you see yourself ensuring that these core values are maintained?

8. Describe a time when you worked really well with a team or an individual. What made this situation so positive?

9. Have you ever been a champion for any programs, causes, or campaigns? Tell us about your roles and responsibilities in those efforts.

10. What experience do you have in using portfolios for student assessment?

11. What unique skills or talents can you bring to the Alliance School community?

12. Do you have any questions for us?

STUDENT-LED COMMENCEMENT SCRIPT

From 2011 through 2016, the Alliance graduation ceremonies were planned and led by students, as part of our philosophy to be student-led and our goal of planning for peace. Here is the script from the 2011 ceremony.

This evening's ceremonies will be hosted by Jasmine, Alliance School Early Graduate Senior.

Intro of Vitamin C, "Graduation Song" (a few bars)

Introduction—Constantine P.: Welcome families and guests of the Alliance School Class of 2011. We are hoping that tonight's ceremony will be as unique as the Alliance School experience. Throughout the ceremony, please refrain from yelling or making noise while the speakers are talking. We would like to see every graduate have the opportunity to shine tonight. Thank you. Now let's begin tonight's celebration. Please rise and join me in welcoming the Class of 2011.

Processional—Class of 2011 enters to Vitamin C, "Graduation Song"

Middle School Entry

High School Entry

Constantine: Welcome our Host for this evening's ceremony, Jasmine.

Music for Jasmine coming to the microphone: Lupe Fiasco, "Superstar"

Jasmine: Welcome to the 2011 Alliance School graduation ceremony. We're glad you're here. Once again, we'd like to ask you to help us make this event the most memorable event possible, by saving your applause and cheers for when each graduate walks across the stage. We will make sure to leave plenty of time for applause between the graduates. Now, let's bring to the stage Shaniqua to lead us in song.

Inspirational: Shaniqua, "Seasons of Love"

Jasmine: Thank you, Shaniqua. If there's 525,600 minutes in a year, that means we've spent 2,102,400 minutes together over the past four years.

That's a lot of minutes, and it's only the beginning. We know that the friendships we've made here will last a lifetime. Now, here to bring you some opening remarks about the Class of 2011 is someone who has known us for all of those 2 million minutes. Please welcome, Paul M.

Opening Remarks: Paul M.
(At the end of his remarks, Paul calls Chavon to the stage for a special recognition.)

Music for while Chavon is coming to the stage: "Like My Mother Does" (just a few bars)

Special Recognition: Chavon
(Chavon will give a speech about the mothers and others who have stepped into those roles over the years. After her speech, the song Kristy Lee Cook, "Like My Mother Does" will play and the graduates will all come and take flowers from the front of the stage and bring them to their mothers or other female role models.)

Jasmine: Thank you to all of the mothers, and the fathers, and to all of the special people who helped us get to where we are today. Graduates, please stand up, turn around and give a round of applause to all of the people who helped you get this far.

(Graduates stand and applaud. While they give their round of applause, the song Boys II Men, "Thank You" will be played.)

Jasmine: Now, the time has come for us to honor the eighth graders who will be moving on to high school next year (Jasmine's words for the eighth graders). Eighth graders, please rise and line up in the center rows.

Music while the eighth graders line up and while they're being called across the stage: The Weepies, "Can't Go Back Now"

Eighth Grade Presentation of Completion Certificates: Alicia M. & Sean L.

Music for after the eighth graders receive their certificates: Kanye West, "Good Life"

Jasmine: Please give our eighth graders a big round of applause. (Pause for applause). There are many talented students here at Alliance. We have singers and poets and artists and accountants among us tonight. We wish we could share all of their talents with you, but we would be here for days if we tried. We would like to share just a bit of the talent from the Class of 2011. Please help me welcome to the stage two of my fellow graduates, Cayla and Jordan, who will share some of their poetry with you in honor of tonight's events.

Music for when the poets are coming to the stage: OneRepublic, "Stop and Stare" (Chorus)

The Poets: Cayla & Jordan

Jasmine: Thank you, Cayla and Jordan. Now, I'd like to invite Kendra, our Class of 2011 Valedictorian, to the stage. Kendra represents a lot of firsts for Alliance. She is the first African American to earn the title of Valedictorian for Alliance. She is the first student to have 100 percent attendance for all of her four years. Well, she did miss one day in those four years, but only because her mom nearly tied her down when she was terribly ill. If she could have had her way, she would have been at school that day too. She was the first female student to try out and make it onto the Riverside Wrestling team. And, she is the first student to complete over one hundred miles in the triathlon class three years in a row. Kendra is one tough woman. Kendra also has a great smile, a gentle spirit, and a never-give-up attitude. We have been lucky to have her as part of our senior class, and we are honored to be giving her this honor tonight. Congratulations, Kendra.

Music for when Kendra is coming to the stage: KT Tunstall, "Suddenly I See"

Valedictorian Speech: Kendra

Academic Awards: Mari S. & Jay F.
    Science
    Social Studies
    Math

English
Service

Rising Above Award: Catherine V.

Music while student comes to stage for the Rising Above Award: Kate Perry, "Firework"

Jasmine: Congratulations. Now, let me invite Chelsea, Class of 2011 Salutatorian, to the stage. Chelsea also has earned a number of firsts. She is the first Alliance graduate to earn the Honors Diploma. To earn this, a student must have a 3.5 or higher, 80 percent attendance or better, forty hours of community service, and must take at least three advanced courses in her four years at Alliance. Chelsea is also the first student to earn the Alliance Service Award. She is smart, hard-working, and has a passion for making the world a better place for everyone. Please join me in welcoming Chelsea.

Music for when Chelsea is coming to the stage: Eve, "Who's That Girl" (Chorus)

Salutatorian Speech: Chelsea

Jasmine: Thank you, Chelsea. Well, it's not every school that brings in a DJ and a comedian to celebrate the commencement, but we figured that if you're going to sit for an hour, we might as well make it fun and do this thing Alliance style. Tonight, we have for you, the comedian, Chastity. Chastity has been performing for nearly twenty years. She is a performance artist, playwright, choreographer, and former Michael Jackson impersonator. She was a finalist in the MGD Miller Comedy Search in Chicago and appeared on BETs *Comic View* with Bruce Bruce. She has been on TV and radio and tonight she's here to join us in our celebration. Please help me welcome Chastity.

Music for when Chastity is coming to the stage: Michael Jackson

Message for the Graduates: Chastity

Lisa: Thank you, Chastity. Now is the moment that you all have been waiting for. Tina and Jill, will you please join me on the stage and help me to greet the 2011 Alliance School graduates. Graduates, please line up in the center aisle.

Music for while Jill and Tina come to the stage and while graduates cross the stage: Rent, "Seasons of Love," and transitioning into Nicki Minaj, "Moment 4 Life" (just the Chorus)

Presentation of 2011 Graduates: Lisa K.
(Music playing softly while graduates are announced)

Music for while Tina is coming back to the stage: "Seasons of Love"

The Naming of the Tocarra Wilson Awardee, Tina O.

Graduation Declaration & Acceptance of 2011 Graduates

Tina O.: Guests, please remain in your seats while our graduates have their final stroll down memory lane.

Music for the recessional: "Seasons of Love" and Will.I.Am, "It's a New Day"

Recessional: 2011 Graduates

(Graduates will walk out to "Seasons of Love" and then will come back in to "It's a New Day.")

ALLIANCE DRAFT MASTER SCHEDULE

A draft of the Alliance School A Day/B Day Block Schedule proposed for the 2014–2015 school year.

Semester 1	A Day—Monday/Thursday	B Day—Wednesday/Friday	C Day—Tuesday
8:30–10:00 a.m.	Biology 9 Sem 1 (9A)—Jasmine Spanish 9 Sem 1 (9B)—Crystal Economics—Chris AP Art History Sem 1—Jill Poetry—Paul Restorative Practices Sem 1—Heather Physical Science Sem 1—Joel World Geography Sem 1—Christian	US History 9 Sem 1 (9A)—Christian Geometry 9 Sem 1 (9B)—Chris AP Art Studio Sem 1—Jill Myth & Folklore—Paul Pre-Calculus Sem 1—Constantine Restorative Practices Sem 2—Heather Spanish 1 Sem 1—Crystal	Staff Professional Development & Collaboration 8:30–11:40 a.m.
Break: 10:00–10:15 a.m.			
10:15–11:40 a.m.	Biology 9 Sem 1 (9B)—Jasmine Spanish 9 Sem 1 (9A)—Crystal English 10 Sem 1 (10A)—Stephanie Physical Science 10 Sem 1 (10B)—Joel AP Statistics Sem 1—Chris Algebra Sem 1—Constantine Adv Restorative Practices Sem 1—Heather American Gov—Christian	US History 9 Sem 1 (9B)—Christian Geometry 9 Sem 1 (9A)—Chris English 10 Sem 1 (10B)—Stephanie Physical Science 10 Sem 1 (10A)—Joel Environmental Science Sem 1—Jasmine Comp Musicianship—Constantine Adv Restorative Practices Sem 2—Heather Latino Literature Sem 1—Crystal	
Lunch: 11:40 a.m.–12:40 p.m.			Lunch: 11:40 a.m.–12:10 p.m.

Semester 1	A Day—Monday/Thursday	B Day—Wednesday/Friday	C Day—Tuesday
12:40–2:05 p.m.	English 9 Sem 1 (9A)—Stephanie Algebra 9 Sem 1 (9B)—Constantine Algebra II & Trig Sem 1—Chris Drawing & Design Sem 1—Jill AP Language Sem 2—Paul Anatomy & Phys Sem 1—Joel Creative Movement—Tina	Writing Lab 9 Sem 1 (9A)—Stephanie Health 9 (9B)—Joel Chemistry Sem 1—Jasmine Geometry Sem 1—Chris Painting Sem 1—Jill AP Literature Sem 1—Paul US History Sem 1—Christian	12:10-1:00 p.m. A/B Day Period 1 1:05–1:55 p.m. A/B Day Period 2 2:00–2:50 p.m. A/B Day Period 3 2:55–3:40 p.m. A/B Day Period 4
Passing: 2:05–2:15 p.m.			
2:15–3:40 p.m.	English 9 Sem 1 (9B)—Stephanie Algebra 9 Sem 1 (9A)—Constantine Biology Sem 1—Jasmine Fiber & Fashions Sem 1—Jill Lifetime Sports—Paul World Geography Sem 1—Christian (Get Fit Stay Healthy) Yoga—Heather	Writing Lab 9 Sem 1 (9B)—Stephanie Health 9 (9A)—Joel Chemistry Sem 1—Jasmine Sculpture Sem 1—Jill Independent Study Math—Constantine Spanish 2 Sem 1—Crystal Composition—Paul	

Semester 2	A Day—Monday/Thursday	B Day—Wednesday/Friday	C Day—Tuesday
8:30–10:00 a.m.	Biology 9 Sem 2 (9A)—Jasmine Spanish 9 Sem 2 (9B)—Crystal AP Art History Sem 2—Jill Economics—Chris Psychology—Paul Restorative Practices Sem 1—Heather Physical Science Sem 2—Joel World Geography Sem 2—Christian	US History 9 Sem 2 (9A)—Christian Geometry 9 Sem 2 (9B)—Chris AP Art Studio Sem 2—Jill Short Fiction Sem 2—Paul Pre-Calculus Sem 2—Constantine Restorative Practices Sem 2—Heather Spanish 1 Sem 2—Crystal	Staff Professional Development & Collaboration 8:30–11:40 a.m.
Break: 10:00–10:15 a.m.			
10:15–11:40 a.m.	Biology 9 Sem 2 (9B)—Jasmine Spanish 9 Sem 2 (9A)—Crystal English 10 Sem 2 (10A)—Stephanie Physical Science 10 Sem 2 (10B)—Joel AP Statistics Sem 2—Chris Algebra Sem 2—Constantine Adv Restorative Practices Sem 1—Heather American Gov—Christian	US History 9 Sem 2 (9B)—Christian Geometry 9 Sem 2 (9A)—Chris English 10 Sem 2 (10B)—Stephanie Physical Science 10 Sem 2 (10A)—Joel Environmental Science Sem 2—Jasmine Comp Musicianship—Constantine Adv Restorative Practices Sem 2—Heather Latino Literature Sem 2—Crystal	
Lunch: 11:40 a.m.–12:40 p.m.			Lunch: 11:40 a.m.–12:10 p.m.

Semester 2	A Day—Monday/Thursday	B Day—Wednesday/Friday	C Day—Tuesday
12:40–2:05 p.m.	English 9 Sem 2 (9B)—Stephanie Algebra 9 Sem 2 (9A)—Constantine Algebra II & Trig Sem 2—Chris Drawing & Design Sem 2—Jill AP Language Sem 2—Paul Anatomy & Phys Sem 2—Joel Creative Movement—Tina	Writing Lab 9 Sem 2 (9B)—Stephanie Lifetime Sports 9 (9A)—Joel Chemistry Sem 2—Jasmine Geometry Sem 2—Chris Painting Sem 2—Jill AP Literature Sem 2—Paul US History Sem 2—Christian	12:10–1:00 p.m. A/B Day Period 1 1:05–1:55 p.m. A/B Day Period 2 2:00–2:50 p.m. A/B Day Period 3 2:55–3:40 p.m. A/B Day Period 4
Passing: 2:05–2:15 p.m.			
2:15–3:40 p.m.	English 9 Sem 2 (9A)—Stephanie Algebra 9 Sem 2 (9B)—Constantine Biology Sem 2—Jasmine Fiber & Fashions Sem 2—Jill World Geography Sem 2—Christian Lifetime Sports—Paul (Get Fit Stay Healthy) Yoga—Heather	Writing Lab 9 Sem 2 (9A)—Stephanie Lifetime Sports 9 (9B)—Joel Chemistry Sem 2—Jasmine Sculpture Sem 2—Jill Advanced Composition—Paul Independent Study Math—Constantine Spanish 2 Sem 2—Crystal	

Notes

Preface

1. Matt Dickinson, "Research Finds Bullying Linked to Child Suicides," *Independent*, June 13, 2010.
2. Bryan Vossekuil et al., "The Final Report and Findings of the Safe School Initiative: Implications for the Preventions of School Attacks in the United States," US Secret Service and Department of Education, July 2004, https://tinyurl.com/mgy6gj6.
3. Dewey Cornell et al., "Perceived Prevalence of Teasing and Bullying Predicts High School Dropout Rates," *Journal of Educational Psychology* 105 (1): 138–149, doi:10.1037/a0030416.

Introduction

1. I founded the Alliance School in 2005 with a group of teachers, students, family, and community members. In 2016, I left the school to pursue my doctorate degree at Harvard University. Throughout the book, I use the present tense when referring to the Alliance School, because I still remain actively engaged in the community and its work. Where it is necessary to distinguish a past context versus a present context, I refer to the school in the past tense.
2. "What Is Bullying," https://www.stopbullying.gov/what-is-bullying/index.html.
3. Dorothy L. Espelage, "Ecological Theory: Preventing Youth Bullying, Aggression, and Victimization," *Theory Into Practice* 53, no. 4 (2014): 257–264, doi: 10.1080/00405841 .2014.947216.

Chapter 1

1. The full poem can be found at https://www.poetryfoundation.org/poems/52702 /the-bridge-builder.
2. Robert Sylwester, "Art for the Brain's Sake," *Educational Leadership* 56 (1993): 3, http://www.ascd.org/publications/educational-leadership/nov98/vol56/num03/Art -for-the-Brain's-Sake.aspx.
3. Ingrid Obsuth et al., "A Non bipartite Propensity Score Analysis of the Effects of Teacher-Student Relationships on Adolescent Problem and Prosocial Behavior,"

Journal of Youth and Adolescence 41 (2012): 1661–1687, doi: 10.1007/s10964-011 -9665-3.

4. Melissa E. DeRosier, "Building Relationships and Combating Bullying: Effectiveness of a School-Based Social Skills Group Intervention," *Journal of Clinical Child & Adolescent Psychology* 33, no. 1 (2004): 196–201, doi: 10.1207/S15374424JCCP3301_18.

5. Thomas C. Frohlich and Sam Stebbins, "The Worst Cities for Black Americans: All Are in the Midwest," 2015, https://www.huffingtonpost.com/entry/worst-cities-black -americans_us_5613d10ee4b0baa355ad322f.

6. *Milwaukee 53206*, directed by Keith McQuirter (New York: Transform Films, 2016).

7. I AM: International Foundation. Retrieved from *Exploring Identity Through Art and Film,* https://www.iaminternationalfoundation.org/.

8. John Hattie, *Visible Learning: A Synthesis of over 800 Meta-Analyses Relating to Achievement* (New York: Routledge, 2009).

9. In 2016, I left Alliance to study in the Ed.L.D. program at Harvard University's Graduate School of Education. The Ed.L.D. program is a three-year doctoral program in education leadership, preparing educators to be systems-level education leaders.

Chapter 2

1. At Alliance, we developed a schedule that allowed us to spend a half day each week in staff development and collaborative meetings. We also had district staff development days throughout the year. In later chapters, I share some ways school leaders can make time for teams to meet when using different schedules.

2. Stephen C. Lundin, *Fish! A Proven Way to Boost Morale and Improve Results* (New York: Hyperion, 2000).

3. Tom Rath, *StrengthsFinder 2.0* (New York: Gallup Press, 2007).

4. Rath, *StrengthsFinder 2.0*, iii.

5. Edward Anderson, "The Genius and Beauty Found Within: The Clifton Strength-Finders Theme of Talent," https://www.k-state.edu/strengths/resources/The_Genius _and_Beauty_of_Strengths.pdf.

6. Mikhail Lyubansky, "New Study Reveals Six Benefits of Restorative Justice: School-Based Restorative Practices Do More Than Just Reduce Suspensions," *Psychology Today*, May 18, 2016, https://www.psychologytoday.com/us/blog/between-the-lines /201605/new-study-reveals-six-benefits-school-restorative-justice.

Chapter 3

1. Ratemyteachers.com is a website where students can anonymously rate teachers and/ or professors: https://www.ratemyteachers.com/tina-owen/555144-t.

2. The Harvey Milk High School is a small, public high school in New York City designed for, but not exclusively serving, students who identify as lesbian, gay, bisexual,

transgender, or questioning. The school was founded in 1985 but became a fully accredited public school in 2002.

Chapter 4

1. Centers for Disease Control and Prevention, "Lesbian, Gay, Bisexual, and Transgender Health," https://www.cdc.gov/lgbthealth/youth.htm.
2. *Nabozny v. Podlesny*, 92 F.3d 446 (7th Cir. 1996), https://en.wikipedia.org/wiki/Nabozny_v._Podlesny
3. "Jamie Nabozny: Safe School Advocate," http://www.jamienabozny.com/.
4. The most recent surveys did not allow students to identify as transgender, so results only note disparities for students who self-identified as lesbian, gay, or bisexual on the 2015 survey.
5. The Centers for Disease Control and Prevention (CDC) conducts the Youth Risk Behavior Survey (YRBS) every other year in schools in the United States. The website lists disparity data for LGB students based on results from the 2015 report. https://www.cdc.gov/healthyyouth/disparities/smy.htm.

Chapter 5

1. Coach Velvet started as a community volunteer and later became my wife.
2. National Education Association, "Facts About Child Nutrition," 2018, http://www.nea.org/home/39282.htm.
3. Carol S. Dweck, *Mindset: The New Psychology of Success* (New York: Ballantine Books, 2006).

Chapter 6

1. Christiann Dean, *Empowering Skills for Family Workers: The Comprehensive Curriculum of the New York State Family Development Credential* (New York: Cornell Empowering Families Project, 1996).
2. The Point Foundation is a scholarship organization that provides academic support and mentoring to promising LGBTQ students and allies. Students receiving the scholarships are considered Point Scholars. In 2007, I applied and was named a Point Scholar. I received tuition assistance for my master's degree program, as well as mentorship to support me in my leadership development.
3. Seth Gershenson, Stephen B. Holt, and Nicholas W. Papageorge, "Who Believes in Me? The Effect of Student-Teacher Demographic Match on Teacher Expectations," *Economics of Education Review* 52 (June 2016): 209–224.
4. Seth Gershenson et al., "The Long-Run Impacts of Same-Race Teachers," IZA Discussion Papers 10630 (2017), http://ftp.iza.org/dp10630.pdf.
5. Marc V. Levine, *Perspectives on the Current State of the Milwaukee Economy* (Milwaukee: University of Wisconsin-Milwaukee Center for Economic Development, 2013), https://www4.uwm.edu/ced/publications/perspectives.pdf.

Chapter 7

1. Sonja Lyubomirsky, Laura A. King, and Ed Diener, "The Benefits of Frequent Positive Affect: Does Happiness Lead to Success?," *Psychological Bulletin* 131, no. 6 (2005): 803–855.
2. John M. Yeager, Sherri Fisher, and David N. Shearon, *SMART Strengths: Building Character, Resilience, and Relationships in Youth* (New York: Kravis, 2011).
3. Leah Levy, "How Stress Affects the Brain During Learning," *Edudemic,* October 13, 2014, http://www.edudemic.com/stress-affects-brain-learning/.
4. James Campbell Quick, "Crafting an Organizational Culture: Herb's Hand at Southwest Airlines," *Organizational Dynamics* 21, no. 2 (1992): 45.
5. Sarah Henderson, "Laughter and Learning: Humor Boosts Retention," *Edutopia,* March 31, 2015, https://www.edutopia.org/blog/laughter-learning-humor-boosts -retention-sarah-henderson.
6. Bobby Tanzilo, "Some Scoff, But Others Adore MPS' Mock Chicken Leg," October 10, 2013, https://onmilwaukee.com/raisemke/articles/mpsmockchickenleg.html.
7. The One Billion Rising Campaign is an effort to raise awareness about violence against women. Each year, the campaign hosts numerous events around the world. You can learn more about these efforts by visiting their website: https://www.one billionrising.org/.

Chapter 8

1. Alexander Sutherland Neill, *Summerhill School: A New View of Childhood* (New York: St. Martin's Press, 1992).
2. Neill, *Summerhill School*, 4.

Chapter 9

1. Trauma-sensitive schools recognize that when students are impacted by trauma, it can affect how they work, learn, and behave in school. These schools use tools and practices to recognize the signs of trauma and to help students move through it. You can learn more and find resources by visiting https://traumasensitiveschools.org/.
2. The use of the talking piece is a tradition of many Native American tribes. The talking piece is often a stick made from carved wood, but it may also be a stone, shell, or any object of importance to the one leading the circle or gathering. The talking piece is traditionally passed from one person to another in the circle, and the person holding the talking stick is the only one to speak.
3. Luís Valdez and Domingo Martinez Paredes, "In Lak'Ech: You Are My Other Me," Voices in Urban Education, Brown University, Annenberg Institute of School Reform, http://vue.annenberginstitute.org/perspectives/lak'ech-you-are-my-other.
4. A detailed description of how this worked is included in appendix B.

Chapter 10

1. "Terminology," United Nations Peacekeeping, https://peacekeeping.un.org/en /terminology.
2. *Measuring Peacebuilding Cost-Effectiveness*, Institute for Economics and Peace (Sydney: IEP, 2017), http://visionofhumanity.org/app/uploads/2017/03/Measuring-Peace building_WEB.pdf.
3. *Suicide Risk and Prevention for Lesbian, Gay, Bisexual, and Transgender Youth*, Suicide Prevention Resource Center (Newton, MA: Education Development Center, Inc., 2008), http://www.sprc.org/library/SPRC_LGBT_Youth.pdf.
4. A copy of the Alliance 2014–2015 daily schedule is included in appendix B.
5. Alexandra Rockey Fleming and Bob Meadow, "A School to Feel Safe: Bullied at Their Old Schools, Junior High Kids of Every Stripe Find a Welcoming Haven in Milwaukee," *People* 73, no. 9 (March 8, 2010).
6. Numerous examples of pledges like this can be found online.
7. Julia Burdick-Will, "School Violent Crime and Academic Achievement in Chicago," *Sociology of Education* 86, no. 4 (2013): 343 361, doi: 10.1177/0038040713494225.

Chapter 11

1. Robert W. Greenleaf published an article titled "The Servant as Leader" in 1970.
2. Deborah Solomon, "Radical Cheer," *New York Times Magazine*, February 10, 2009, https://www.nytimes.com/2009/02/15/magazine/15wwln_Q4-t.html.
3. William Oncken Jr. and Donald L. Wass, "Management Time: Who's Got the Monkey?" *Harvard Business Review*, November–December, 1999.
4. Paul J. Zak, "The Neuroscience of Trust," *Harvard Business Review*, January– February, 2017, 84–90.
5. Zak, "The Neuroscience of Trust."

Chapter 12

1. Susan Elizabeth Phillips is the international best-selling romance author of *Breathing Room* (London: Piatkus, 2003).

Acknowledgments

To those who have been on this book journey with me . . .

A special thank you to my editor, Nancy Walser, and everyone at the Harvard Education Press for supporting this project and to Carole Learned-Miller for introducing me to Nancy in the first place.

There are many people at the Harvard Graduate School of Education whose inspiration helped to bring this book to life. Thank you to the Ed.L.D. faculty for all of your expertise, encouragement, and support. Thank you to Gretchen Brion-Meisel for sharing your research, feedback, and time with me. And thank you to my peer coaches, my pod, my cohort, my sector change collaborator, my workplace lab team, and the entire Ed.L.D. network. You all inspire me.

A very special thank you goes to my wife, Velvet, for being my first reader—my "that police," as I often called you. You sweetly found all my redundant words, run-on sentences, and unnecessary uses of "that" and "so." I appreciated how you questioned me when something wasn't clear, highlighted the pieces you loved, and reminded me to write every day. Your wisdom and encouragement have been a true blessing throughout this process. Know that I love you and that I am grateful.

To my children, Felicia and Jeremy, you deserve so much more than this acknowledgment could ever offer. You weren't just my cheerleaders in the vision for Alliance; you immersed yourselves in the mission with me—becoming students at Alliance and sharing your high school experience with me in not-so-typical parent-child ways. I want you to know that having you with me in the journey made my every day more joyful, and I can't thank you enough. I am proud to say that you are my children and that you are Alliance graduates, as well.

And thank you to my large and extended Alliance family—the staff, students, families, and community members who built this vision and made this book possible.

To the teachers and staff: Thank you for making the school different by caring with every bit of yourselves. Your talent and your love have not gone unnoticed.

To the students, past and present: You *are* the school. Thank you for bringing your soul to the mission, for choosing to be your authentic selves every day, and for taking care of each other in such beautiful ways. I wish everyone could know your hearts like I have known them.

To the families: Thank you for trusting us with your precious children. It has been a true pleasure to know you and to know them.

And to the community members and everyone who has supported Alliance in one way or another over the years: You believed. Thank you.

Many young people experience bullying in schools every day, but at Alliance, we found a better way. Thank you to everyone for allowing me to share our story, so that we can change that experience for many more young people. The stories in this book are our stories, and I am so happy that you have been part of my story. This book is possible because of you.

About the Author

Tina M. Owen-Moore has been an educator for twenty years. She started in 1998 as a high school English teacher in Milwaukee, Wisconsin. In 2005, with a grant from the Bill and Melinda Gates Foundation, Tina worked with a group of teachers and students to open the Alliance School, the first school in the nation started with the explicit mission of reducing bullying. She led the in-district charter school from 2005–2016, and has consistently worked to share Alliance's practices so that all schools can be safe and inclusive places for all students.

Tina has received numerous awards and recognition for her work, including being named 2010 *Educator of the Year* by GSAFE Wisconsin, being recognized by the Wisconsin Charter Schools Association with the *Innovator of the Year Award* for her cocreation of the Teacher-Led Network, and receiving an *LGBT Progress Award* from the *Shepherd Express* magazine of Milwaukee. She was also honored with the Marquette University School of Education's *Young Alumna Award* in 2008. The school was awarded the 2011 *Wisconsin Charter School of the Year, Platinum Award*, and in 2015 won recognition as one of the "41 Most Innovative Schools in America" by Noodle.com.

Tina earned her Bachelor of Arts degree from Marquette University and her Master of Arts degree from Alverno College. She is currently enrolled in the Ed.L.D. program at Harvard University, from which she anticipates receiving her doctorate degree in 2019. She is the mother of two adult children, Felicia and Jeremy, and has been a foster and surrogate mother to many others. She currently lives in Chicago, Illinois, with her wife, Velvet, and their two adorable cats, Tiger and Juani.

Index